MANURE

The Adventures of Jim Brown Godwin

MANURE
The Adventures of Jim Brown Godwin

Peggy Godwin
Illustrated by Roger Manley
& James B. Godwin, Jr.

Accomplishing
Innovation Press

Accomplishing
Innovation Press

Accomplishing Innovation Press
1497 Main St. Suite 169
Dunedin, FL 34698A
accomplishinginnovationpress.com
AccomplishingInnovationPress@gmail.com

Cover & Typesetting by Autumn Skye
Edited by Blair Parke

Library of Congress Control Number: 2022947611

Paperback ISBN-13: 979-8-8232-0085-1
Hardcover ISBN-13: 979-8-8232-0086-8
Audiobook ISBN-13: 979-8-8232-0083-7
Ebook ISBN-13: 979-8-8232-0084-4

DEDICATION

To Jim Brown Godwin's grandchildren and especially his great-grandchildren: Peter, Kendyl, Annabelle, Jimmy, and JB; to Peggy Tilley Godwin, his soulmate, who helped make all his dreams come true; and especially to my husband, James Brown Godwin, Jr., who introduced me to this wonderful family.

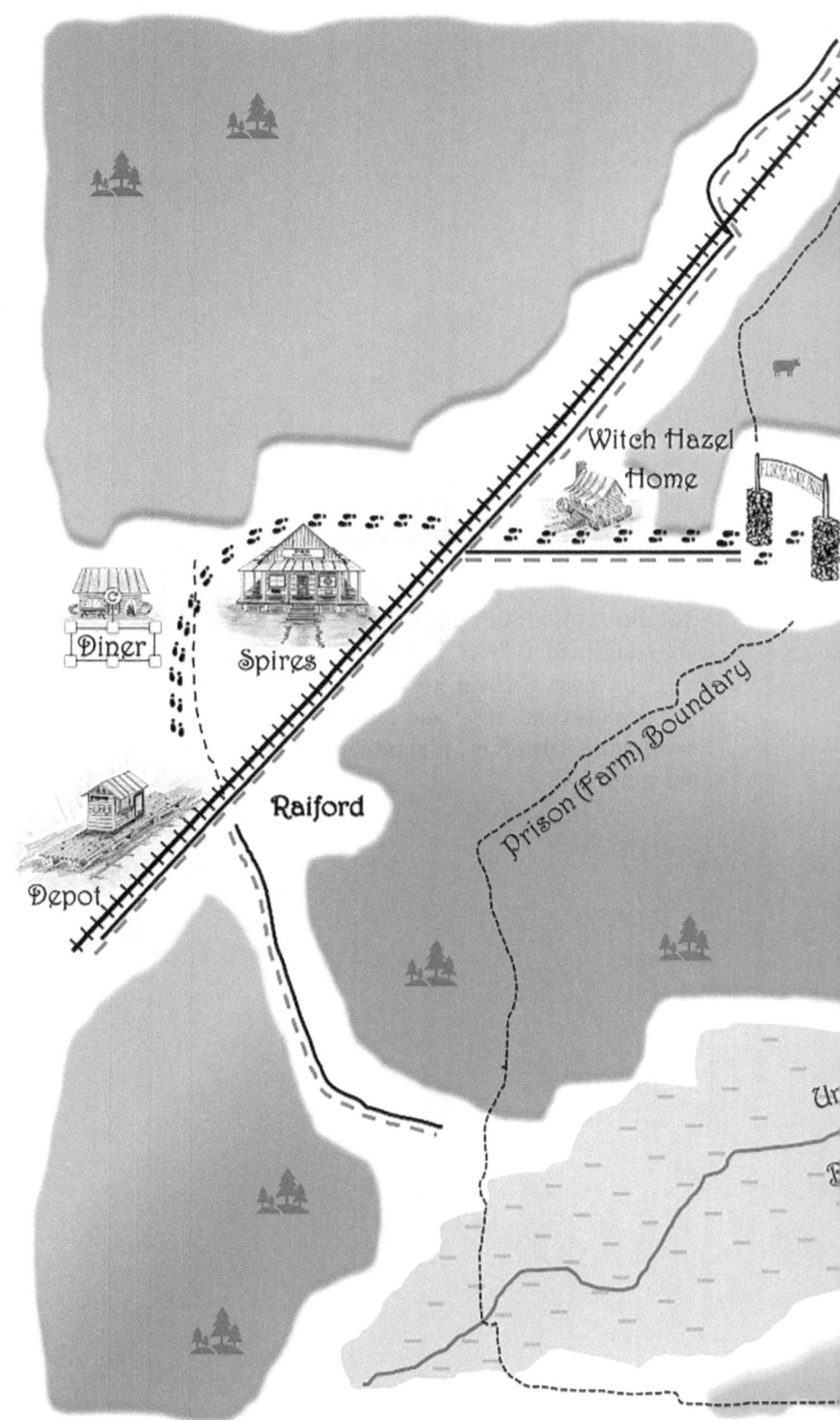

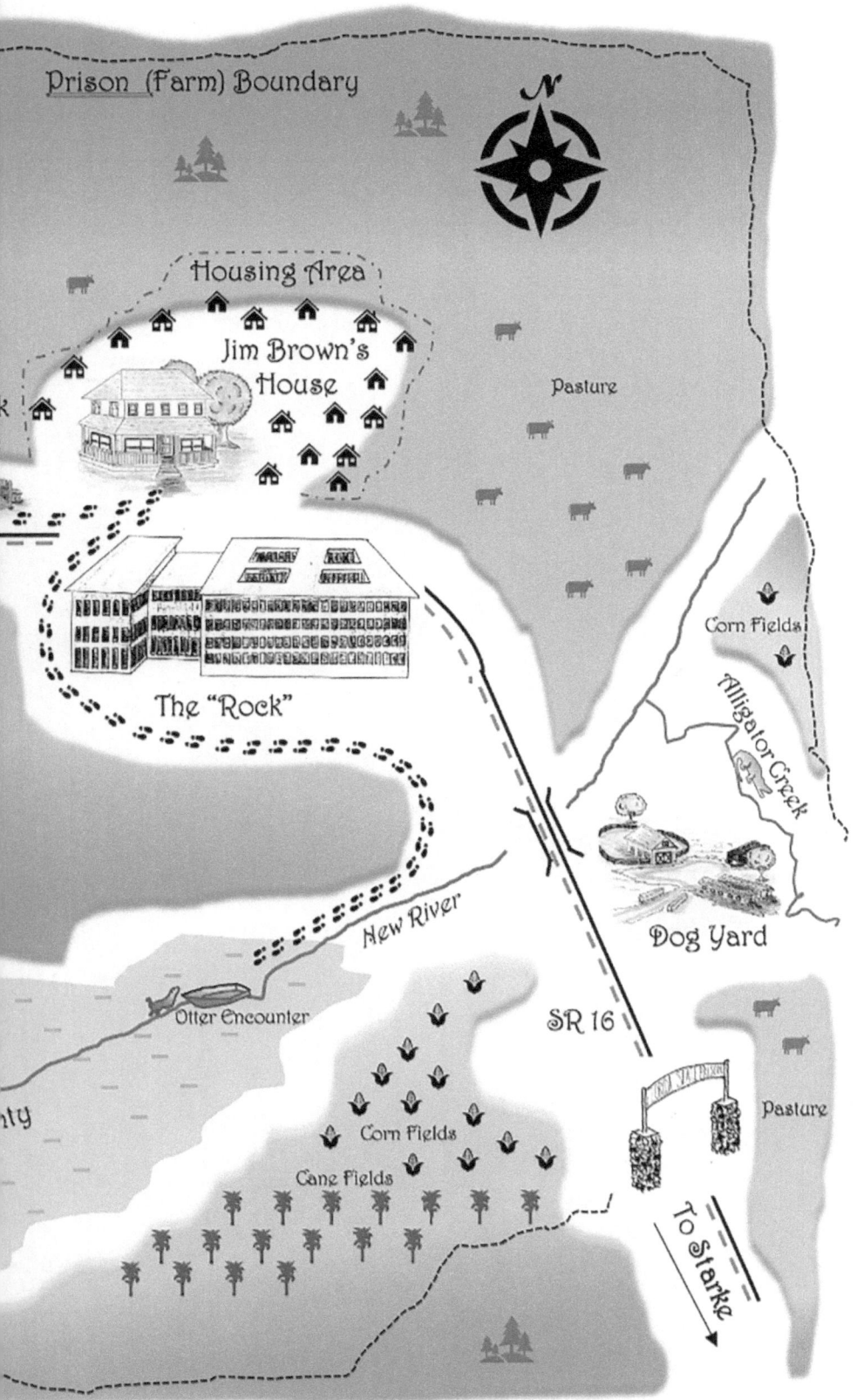

TABLE OF CONTENTS

ACKNOWLEDGEMENTS

MARY HOUTS OF THE HERSHEY MUSEUM, WHO SHARED HER KNOWL- edge of Milton Hershey and the value of interactive activities to help children appreciate their museum experiences; Vineta Raley, who taught so many students to appreciate the written word; the German American Club of Wertheim, Germany, who were truly "Not just neighbors, but true friends"; Myrtle Shaw, my best critic and friend; Carel Chappel, my best friend and supporter; Jim Godwin, Jr., my husband, my inspiration, my champion; Erika Lance, Jen Paquette, Valerie Willis, Beau Lake, Blair Parke, and all the people at 4 Horsemen who made this book possible. Thank you!

A NOTE FROM THE AUTHOR

This is a fictional story inspired by the recollections of James Brown Godwin.

My father, Francis Edward Foley, shared the tale "The Man in the Moon." A version was first published in *The Fordham Monthly*, November 1941.

PROLOGUE

THIS IS NOT THE FIRST STORY TO OFFER LESSONS USING MANURE. MY Russian professor, Dr. George Byrnes, offered this tale attributed to Leo Tolstoi, the famous Russian author, about a young bird caught in an early frost. He chirped in misery until a kind farmer came along, gently picked him up, and placed him in a fresh, warm cow pie. At first, the bird was relieved and enjoyed the warm comfort of the steamy plop of manure, but before long, the smell became quite disagreeable and once again, he began to chirp loudly his discontent. This time, a mangy, lean wolf came prowling down the road. Hearing the distressful cries, he quickly found the bird and gobbled him up. The lessons of this tale are:

1. The one who put you there may not be your enemy.

2. The one who takes you out may not be your friend.

3. Finally, while there, keep your mouth shut. There may be something important to discover.

A second tale is one that was shared by President Ronald Reagan while visiting Fort Leavenworth, Kansas, the school house of the army. It is the story of two brothers; one is an eternal optimist while the other is a pessimist. Their parents sought the help of an imminent psychologist to help bring the boys into balance. Undaunted, the psychologist placed the pessimist in a room filled with every toy a young boy could desire. Then, he quietly stole away, leaving the boy to enjoy the pleasures of this wonderland. He placed the second brother, the optimist, in a room filled with stinking, slimy manure, and closed the door. After an hour, he returned to the first room. Shocked, he found the little boy huddled in misery in the corner of the room. He asked him what was wrong. The little fellow began a litany: 1) This toy was broken, and another needed a battery; 2) This game required a friend to play; and 3) He wasn't interested in geography. Besides, he really was hungry. The doctor sadly shook his head. His treatment had failed. But then, he smiled and picked up his step; for surely his next patient must be in absolute misery by now! Opening the door wide, he stood in astonishment. There, in the steaming piles, the boy was singing and shoveling the manure.

"What are you doing?" he exclaimed.

"Well," replied the boy. "With all this dung, I figured there had to be a pony somewhere!"

It's all a matter of perspective.

Well, now I'm offering you a third story about manure that an amazing man, born and raised in Florida, shared with me. I hope the lessons he learned are lessons you can share. Like the stories above, beware of strangers; it's all in perspective; friends come in all sizes, all ages, and all colors; and finally, know who you are, and stand for what you believe in!

IF

By Rudyard Kipling, 1910
Brother Square-Toes – Rewards and Fairies

If you can keep your head when all about you

    Are losing theirs and blaming it on you;

If you can trust yourself when all men doubt you,

    But make allowance for their doubting too;

If you can wait and not be tired by waiting,

    Or, being lied about, don't deal in lies,

Or, being hated, don't give way to hating,

    And yet don't look too good, nor talk too wise;

If you can dream – and not make dreams your master;

If you can think – and not make thoughts your aim;

If you can meet with Triumph and Disaster

And treat those two imposters just the same;

If you can bear to hear the truth you've spoken

Twisted by knaves to make a trap for fools,

Or watch the things you gave your life to, broken,

And stoop and build 'em up with worn-out tools;

If you can talk with crowds and keep your virtue,

Or walk with kings—and not lose the common touch;

If neither foes nor loving friends can hurt you;

If all men count with you, but none too much;

If you can fill the unforgiving minute

With sixty seconds' worth of distance run—

Yours is the Earth and everything that's in it,

And—which is more—you'll be a Man my son!

Ah, but a man's reach should exceed his grasp.

Or what's a heaven for?

"Andrea del Sarro" called "The Faultless Painter" by Robert Browning

I

SUDDENLY, HIS FACE WAS PLUMMETING TOWARD THE PLATE, AND there was nothing he could do about it! His whole life—all twelve years of it—started to flash before his eyes! Plop! His head hit the warm, soft mound of lumpy, mashed potatoes. *Who would have thought*, he smiled, *that mashed potatoes could make such a heavenly pillow?* He didn't even remember closing his eyes.

For many, it was the last stop on the road to Nowhere—found by those who had lost their way. For others, it was just a place for time to pass. It became a harsh reality they would never forget, no matter how hard they tried. The concrete buildings and barbed wire fences were not the ingredients for fashioning blissful dreams and cherished memories; it was a place to regret and repent. The state legislature talked of reform, but without the money to back their words, Florida State Prison remained a workhouse purposefully overlooked in polite conversation.

1

But for Jim Brown Godwin, it was home—and spell that with a capital "H." Jim Brown lived on the prison grounds, recognizing many of the convicts and knowing all the trustees by name. There wasn't anything unique about this. His father was the assistant superintendent at Raiford, also known as "The Rock" by the inmates or "The State Farm" by the locals. The house and prison came with the job. For Jim Brown, the guards, fences, and occasional sirens were all ordinary, a part of his life—and he liked it that way. The State Farm was his territory, his private kingdom. There were fields to throw a football with his older brother, Bill, and lots to play baseball with his friends. He knew every deer run and the best fishing holes. State Farm was his heaven on earth, but things were about to change—drastically and soon.

The year 1941 was ending on an ominous note. Europe was entering its third year of war, and President Franklin D. Roosevelt providentially signed an order moving Thanksgiving from the third to the fourth Thursday in November. You would think that wouldn't be a big deal, but calendars had been printed years ago with Thanksgiving marked for November 20. Plans had been made, and chaos reigned. Jim Brown and his friends debated which day was appropriate and wondered which day the school would recognize as Thanksgiving. Wow! What if they got both days off!? It was a headache for Jim's father, though, as he had to decide which day the prison would observe. Finally, he marked November 27 on the calendar, rationalizing it would be best to go with the President's ruling; and the other institutions agreed. The meals were planned and family members notified.

As usual, Jim Brown's mom took everything in stride. Taking control, she would turn lemons into lemonade. They would go to Big Mama's, as originally planned, on the twentieth. The day would begin with a Southern breakfast: flakey biscuits slathered in butter, over-easy eggs with extra thick bacon, and creamy grits with more butter. Then the boys would gather around the radio and listen to the broadcast of the Macy's Thanksgiving Day Parade, which had been designated to proceed as originally planned.

On Thanksgiving morning, Bill and Jim Brown tried to bring the parade commentary to life for Harold, their younger brother, but their antics were more frightening for the little fella than wonder-filled. Harold loved it. He giggled non-stop when Bill towered over him, arms extended like a prehistoric monster, and scooped him up as he enacted the arrival of Santa Claus.

Little did they realize, it would be the last Macy's parade broadcasted for years to come.

On cue, they loaded up the car and drove to Big Mama's for their traditional celebration with family and friends—complete with turkey, dressing, and a dessert bar that stretched from the dining room through the living room and out to the backyard, where an ice cream churn waited for the kids to take their stand turning the wooden handle. Laughter and music filled the air. When twilight arrived, the families began to depart. Everyone would be stuffed like turkeys themselves and ready to return to their homes and blissful dreams.

While driving home, Jim Brown's mother took the opportunity to announce that, in keeping with the President's decree, they would celebrate a second Thanksgiving the following Thursday. Bill moaned, and his father groaned, "Eve, have you lost your mind?"

Jim Brown just smiled—dinner at Big Mama's went as tradition held, but to have a turkey dinner at home with all the southern trimmings and leftovers, who could complain? To top the day off, his dad would keep an eye on the turkey, making sure it would be roasted to perfection. Jim Brown would be in charge of the greens, cornbread, and mac n' cheese—he loved to cook. His mother would concentrate on dessert, her specialty. Bill would keep an eye on Harold, who, at three years old, could be a handful, though Bill never left any doubt who was in charge. Yeah, they were stuffed now, but in a week, Jim would be ready to dig in again. Life was GREAT!

As decreed by his mother, the house buzzed as the second Thanksgiving came to life on November 27. She asked the family the traditional question of what should she do with the giblets—should they be fried separately as a tasty treat, or should they be chopped up finely and added to the gravy?

His father replied, "Whatever you want," a very politically correct answer. Jim Brown cocked his head and simply repeated, "Whatever," which said it all. He really didn't care. Since Bill was in the living room with Harold and unable to voice an opinion, the decision was left to his mother. As the boys would have predicted, she began chopping the giblets finely to toss them into the gravy. She knew, even if the boys didn't, giblet gravy was everyone's first choice—and she was right. While the turkey rested on the carving platter, his mother poured the broth from the simmering vegetables and neck bones into the roasting pan. She stirred until all the turkey juices were blended and the roasted tidbits that stuck to the pan were loosened. Then, she added a slurry of cornstarch and cold water and stirred the mixture until it thickened.

Humming, she tossed in the minced giblets and chopped hard-boiled eggs and grabbed a spoon for one last test for seasonings. It was perfect: perfect on the turkey, the dressing, the potatoes, and anything else that made it to their plates. Jim Brown even wondered if it might not help the pumpkin pie, but he never tried; he was a pecan pie man anyway. The family gorged on the feast. However, it would be the last time they would gather around a table overloaded with festive foods and filled with laughter for years to come.

After Jim Brown cleared the dinner table, he joined his brothers and dad in the living room. Loosening the buckle on his belt, he collapsed on the couch. He then looked around and thought, *It just doesn't get any better than this*. His dad was bent over the radio, searching for a station his mom might enjoy—she deserved it for all her hard work. Why, if there were a dance band, he might even twirl her around the living room floor, as she was light on her feet. The boys would always pretend to hide their eyes, but eventually their parents would glide over first to Bill. His dad would graciously offer her hand to his son, and Bill bowed before accepting. Then, Bill would spin his mother once or twice before handing her to Jim Brown, who was becoming quite an expert at the Fox Trot.

But for the moment, Bill was sitting in a wingback chair, legs crossed and reading the newspaper. Jim Brown silently chuckled as he thought how much Bill was beginning to look like their dad. Harold was curled up in a ball, snoring peacefully, at the other end of the couch.

In the kitchen, a trustee was licking the last crumbs from the Thanksgiving plate Eve had prepared. She finished putting away the leftovers and picked up a plate of divinity to take to the boys—Thanksgiving was never complete without her specialty sweet. She smiled at the trustee as she left and knew when she returned in the morning, everything would be spotless. There were indeed a few nice benefits that came with being married to the assistant superintendent of a state prison! Yes, life was perfect, in the moment. Soon, they all were ready to retire to peaceful thoughts and simple dreams.

The following week, decorations for Christmas sprang up everywhere. Unlike the neighbors' red and green garlands, Eve insisted on pink and gold. Mr. Godwin felt it was his concession to her for living in a house filled with men, but Eve would have told him—if he'd asked—that pink was her signature color. It was important to stand out, to show originality, to be unique where they were located. But secretly, she knew it made people smile. Even her friends remarked, "A pink Santa Claus, Eve, really?" or "Where did you ever find your pink poinsettias?" It was her special contribution to the season.

Jim Brown couldn't remember a time when pink didn't reign. If Santa could handle it, it wasn't his problem. Bill, on the other hand, did his best to ignore his mother's idiosyncrasy. It was a good word, and his mother had many—or so he thought. Other than this slight disagreement about the colors, life sparkled. Christmas was in the air.

II

BOOM!

The shock—and it was a shock that shook all Americans to their very core—began with President Franklin Delano Roosevelt speaking these solemn words over the radio:

> Yesterday, December 7, 1941, a date which will live in infamy, the United States of America was suddenly and deliberately attacked by the air forces of the Empire of Japan.

An hour after the radio announcement, Congress was in session, and in less than five minutes, they voted 470 to 1 to declare war against Japan. Jeannette Rankin, a Republican pacifist from Montana, cast the lone dissenting vote.

Jeanette Rankin was a curiosity, even in the Big Sky Country of Montana. She tried to be conventional, but with her feisty spirit and desperate need to question everything, she begged to go to college. She majored in biology and then returned home to teach. Her family hoped she might finally settle down; however, once again, her restless spirit took control. She felt confined by the daily routine. Her creativity compelled her to investigate furniture design, but she abandoned that and moved on to social work, which led her into politics, her true calling. She was driven to make the world a better place.

Her brother, Winston, understood and backed her political campaign financially, as well as personally. He drove her all over the state to drum up support and votes. Some felt she was just a novelty—the first woman to run for Congress from one of only ten states that even allowed women to vote. But, if they thought she would remain a joke, were they in for a big surprise. On April 2, 1917, she reported to Washington, D.C., to be sworn into the 65th Congress. Three days later, she found herself in the midst of a battle she would never forget—the vote on a resolution to enter the First World War!

Though she had never found herself at a loss for words, she was speechless. She was astounded at the lightning speed that Congress moved, especially on matters so monumental.

On the day of the vote, she was still in a quandary. Here in the great hall, where voices were heard, no one was listening. The Speaker called for the vote, and before Jeannette realized it, her name was announced. She remained seated; she remained silent. Her name was called a second time. Never one to shirk her duty, she quietly stood and in a firm voice, ignoring House Rules, she proclaimed, "I want to stand for my country, but I cannot vote for war. I vote no."

She returned to her seat. The final vote was 374 for entry into the war, 50 against. Though she felt hurt and misunderstood, she was comfortable with her decision. Most importantly, she felt she had represented her constituents from Montana. Nationally, she lost the support of many suffragettes who claimed she displayed female fragility. She continued to follow her convictions and gladly served on committees encouraging women's rights and miners' rights—making her unpopular with the mining interests that controlled Montana politics. With her district redrawn, she decided not to run for re-election to the House, but set her aims higher, running for the Senate.

Unsuccessful, Jeannette continued to strive for social causes and peace—nationally as well as throughout the world. Those efforts likewise proved futile. In 1940, the world again found itself teetering on the brink of war. Jeannette again stepped forward and ran for a seat in the House of Representatives; this time, she won.

From the beginning, she worked to keep the United States out of the developing conflicts. She voted against supplies to the British, for fear it would lead to involving our soldiers as well. In May, she proposed a resolution that restricted sending soldiers into conflicts outside the Western

Hemisphere or the insular possessions of the United States, but nothing could stop the oncoming storm of World War II.

After President Roosevelt addressed the Joint Session of Congress, they retired to debate the resolution to go to war. The debate in the House was short and sweet. The Speaker, Sam Rayburn, a Democrat from Texas, painfully remembered Jeannette's debut in 1917. He even stood, applauding her arrival that fateful day, only to be outraged when, three days later, she voted against the declaration of war with Germany. Then, he felt, she had the audacity to use the Great War for her own political ends—women's rights. Surely, she understood the situation was different today; this was a clear-cut, moral response. This time, the price to stay on the sidelines was too costly. He could not risk giving her the floor, refusing to recognize her and continually calling her out of order.

Contrary to her own point of view—that no one would notice her; that finally there was nothing unusual about women serving in the House—she was indeed duly noticed. Her colleagues gathered around her. One by one, they pleaded that she support the declaration for war. It was important to show solidarity, but she blankly stared ahead.

"Jeannette, the Japanese are already at war with us. This is just a formality. Unprovoked, unannounced, they bombed Pearl Harbor. Have you not seen the intelligence reports? They massacred our boys!"

She bit her lip, dropped her eyes, and shook her head. Despite the tragedy, she wondered if war were the only answer. Had Congress exhausted every political option? Was Congress to fail once more and send our boys to war? She wracked her brain, struggling to find a different solution. Then, she slowly raised her head and said one word, "Oil."

"What! Jeannette, don't be so naïve! We halted shipments of oil because our reserves were running low, and we wanted to send the message that the Japanese should not be contemplating expanding their empire into the Dutch East Indies and Philippines while the world was in this chaotic state. You have heard of the effects of supply and demand? They just didn't get the message! We hoped they would remain neutral and concentrate on improving the lots of their own people. Furthermore, haven't you read the reports from China? The Japanese are barbaric!" Sam sneered.

Jeannette frowned.

Another voice added, "My God, open your eyes! They think Hirohito is a God and that they are a superior race!"

Another congressman across the aisle couldn't be still any longer. He boisterously chimed in, "The United Kingdom has already declared war. They're convinced that Malaysia, Hong Kong, and Singapore are at risk!"

In desperation, her colleague continued, "Congresswoman Rankin, what do you want our boys to do when the next assault comes, and you know there will be one? What are you going to say to their parents, their wives, their children? What about the boys who have already sacrificed their lives on your altar of peace?"

In final exasperation, he added in a measured, staccato voice, "Peace comes with a price. You do not seem to appreciate the cost. You stand alone."

With that, her head snapped, and their eyes locked. Until then, she had harbored a small inkling of doubt, but now she had her decision. For there was no doubt in her mind; she did not stand alone. There were others who shared her view; there had to be!

Just then the bell rang to call for the vote. The men returned to their seats crestfallen. *Why didn't she understand? No one wanted war, but if ever a war was justified...*

One after the other, their names were called. Each representative stood and solemnly, in a firm voice, registered his vote. "Yea... Yea... Yea... Yea... Yea..."

The words rang like a bell clapper in her brain.

No... No... No... her conscience silently replied. *We just can't be returning to war!* This time when her name was called, she did not hesitate. She stood erect and confidently, in a loud, clear voice, voted, "Nay."

The House gasped and filled with hisses and boos.

After all the votes were duly recorded, the members began to descend upon her as she made her way to the door. The media joined in, as well as spectators, all screaming threats and obscenities. Congresswoman Rankin tried to state her position.

"As a woman, I can't go to war, and I refuse to send anyone else." Whether she could be heard above the roar was questionable, but it became clear everything was rapidly getting out of control. She dashed to the telephone booth in the House cloak room and called for security to escort her back to her office. She continued to crouch low, seeking refuge. Her thoughts tumbled nonstop, careening about her brain like popcorn popping. She waited and waited for security to come. She was convinced she was right, but she could not comprehend the anger, the hatred, the violence aimed at her. She was voting for their best interests.

And what about the other congressmen—what if they were voting to send themselves to the front line, would they be so quick to say yes? What about their sons to whom the burden would fall? Why did people always dream there was a pot of gold at the end of a rainbow? All she wanted to find was peace. As she pondered these thoughts, the officers finally arrived.

When Jeannette returned to her office, she collapsed. As she composed herself, her eyes spied a telegram propped against a book in the center of her desk. It was from her brother. A smile unconsciously spread across her face. Winston understood; she could always count on his support. She tore open the message, and her face fell. The words were concise:

Montana is 100% against you.

She did stand alone. Those words struck her heart like a dagger.

The next day, when Jeannette's name was called to cast her vote on the resolution to wage war on Germany and Italy, with swollen eyes, she quietly registered, "Present."

That was the best she could do.

III

MEANWHILE, BACK IN STARKE, FLORIDA, THE GODWINS LISTENED
intently to the radio. When Congresswoman Jeannette Rankin registered
her vote, Jim's dad began to rant and rave at the radio. Bill, in his deep
voice, added, "She's got to be the most ignorant or the craziest person in
the world!"

Yeah, thought Jim Brown. *She may be crazy, but boy, you have to admit,
she does have guts! Still, what was she thinking?*

Jim's mom was holding Harold in the rocking chair. She gave a loud gasp, hid her face in Harold's hair, and began to rock faster and faster.

Word of war spread like wildfire, and the streets began to fill with the townsmen pouring out to confirm what they heard and to exchange their views. Barney Sission, who sold popcorn in the movie theater, announced to everyone, "If I'd been in Washington, D.C., I'd have taken that woman by the neck and thrown her out the window!" Then, he confidently added, "Even if I went to jail!" And just about everyone agreed. The *Bradford Times* ran his quote in their next edition to capture the spirit of the town.

That evening, Jim Brown and his father huddled around the radio to listen to the latest news from Pearl Harbor and commentaries on America's entry into the war. If his mother had her wish, she would have switched stations to a talk show or music, but every channel was focused on world events. Sullenly, she settled into her favorite pink chair and tried to concentrate on the needlepoint project she had begun months ago.

Harold had gone to bed early. Tension in the house was thick as pea soup, and the young boy was agreeable when the suggestion was made that he hit the sack. Bill stood brooding in the corner. He studied his mom, dad, and Jim Brown. He knew he would step up to fight, but there was someone he needed to talk to—not tomorrow, but now; not by phone, but face to face. He casually made excuses and slipped upstairs to his bedroom to make his escape through his secret passage. Bill didn't realize his mother was watching his every move and could read his mind. In her heart, she said a prayer that tomorrow would be different and then turned back to her stitching.

Every able-bodied male worth his salt rushed down to the army recruiting office to enlist, which included Bill. Even Owen Tilley, just seventeen, dragged his stepmother with him because he needed her approval to enlist. Some of the townsfolk thought the Godwin boys would sign up together as Jim Brown, like his brother, was athletic and just shy of six feet tall—but Jim Brown was also only eleven years old. Sometimes it can be tough when you are young, yet so big and strong! Everyone had expectations and expected him to pull his weight. Sadly, even his trusted friends sometimes forgot he looked like an adult and was held to those higher values, which cause a whole different set of problems.

There was no way his father, let alone his mother, would have given permission for him to fight. Why, even the army, once informed of his age, would have turned him away! But the townsfolk talked, and the recruiting officer eyed him each time he walked down the street. One of the older men took a swing at him and called him a coward for not enlisting, but Jim Brown caught his arm and gave him a solid punch in the stomach. He left the man doubled over and wheezing to his friends, "See! I told you that boy could fight!"

Wednesday morning, Bill marched into his school's principal's office and asked if there was any way he could graduate early so that he could report for duty with his diploma. The principal was surprised but not shocked. He knew Bill and his brother Jim Brown. With a gentle smile, he replied, "Let me consider this; it is a serious request. Come back this afternoon, and I will have an answer."

That afternoon when Bill returned, the secretary told him to go in. He was caught off guard when he found not just the principal, but all his teachers gathered in the room. "Sit down, Bill," the principal directed and pointed to the one empty chair. "As you can see, I've sought advice from those who are most concerned with your request. The bottom line…"

Bill's eyes bulged as he held his breath.

"We've decided to grant your request, but there are some provisions."

The first to stand was Mrs. Raley, his English teacher. "Bill, you know we are all proud of your decision…"

Here it comes, thought Bill, *the big BUT…*

"But you know what an important step this is. Before you leave Bradford High, we want you prepared for life. I have high hopes for you. As you know, I believe you must not just read, but interpret, not just write, but compose; therefore, I must insist that you take a final exam. I will have the study guide prepared by Friday. You may take the exam whenever you feel ready."

She immediately sat down. There would be no discussion.

The room was silent. Mrs. Raley nudged Coach, his PE instructor, whose thoughts had wandered. "Oh, uh, yeah, uh, it's fine with me. You'll probably get more exercise at basic training than you'd get here. And if anyone has any questions," he paused and looked at Mrs. Raley, "I'll calculate the hours you've spent on the football field, and I'm sure that will cover the semester." Then, he smiled at Bill and sat down.

His history teacher did not need any prompting. "Bill, I know you've given this much thought. Now, rather than reading history, you will be making history. You've been an attentive student. I hope the lessons you've learned in my class will serve you well. I just have one request." He stood up and gave him a small volume, *The Art of War,* by Sun Tzu. "Read as much as you can." With that, he gave Bill a slap on the back and returned to his seat.

One by one, the rest of the teachers rose and spoke. Then, they all stood and applauded. Bill was dumbfounded. He thanked each one for their support and confidence, and he promised to keep in touch. When he left the room, he had a smile on his face as wide as a hippo's behind. He would graduate by Christmas, but his smile began to melt away as he realized he still had the biggest test ahead—he had to tell his parents.

Eve said her prayers daily, hoping this war thing would be over soon. Her thoughts had easily returned to Christmas, which meant it was time to cut down a Christmas tree. Every morning, as her husband left for work, she'd give him a kiss and say, "It's time to get the tree!"

Mr. Godwin knew she was right, and he had already spied a tree one afternoon when he was quail hunting on state property surrounding the prison that would be perfect—not too tall, not too short, and green, not dried. To be on the safe side, he marked a second tree as well, just in case someone beat him to the first. But the week had been busy, and the days flew by. He realized he'd better return with a tree this evening and decided to leave a note for Bill, asking him to come to the prison when he got home.

When Bill returned home from driving the school bus that day, he was glad to see the note hanging on the icebox door. Normally, he would have growled, but this time, he thought it would be the perfect opportunity to break the news to his father. He had a solid plan, and, if he could sell it to his father, his mother would have to agree.

The tree-hunting went as planned. His father realized he and Bill were more quiet than usual, but then again, they were both quiet by nature. As they carried the tree back to the car, Bill broke the awkward silence as he tried to start the conversation through the green branches.

"Gee, Dad, you really found a great tree! Mom will love it!"

"That's what makes a great tree," he agreed.

After a short pause, Bill dove in. He explained that he had gone to the recruiting office that afternoon and would report for a physical next week. For insurance, he included that his teachers were on his side, and he even would earn his diploma by Christmas—though he casually left out there would be the final exams to pass. The nation needed him, and he was ready to answer the call. When Bill finally stopped, he tried to peer through the branches to see his father's reaction.

Not surprised, his dad simply replied, "All right."

Bill was stunned.

After a few moments, his dad stifled a choke with a cough and added. "I'm proud of you." Then, even though Bill couldn't see, he smiled and added, "You know, you still have to tell your mom."

Bill gave an audible groan. He had no idea how his mother would take the news. "Uh, couldn't you…?"

"No," he cut his son off. But, reading his son's mind, his dad responded, "Just tell her straight like you told me, but … wait 'til after dinner."

When they got home, Eve was thrilled to see the tree. Jim Brown and Harold came running to add their cries of approval. They immediately put the tree in a stand and filled it with water. Ideas were voiced where to put the tree, but they soon agreed to place it in front of a window in the living room—where a tree had stood every Christmas as far back as Bill and Jim Brown could remember.

After dinner, Eve brought out a plate of cookies ready to nibble on as they decorated the tree. Mr. Godwin kept staring at Bill, anxiously waiting for the announcement. Bill realized he was on his own and wondered if he should talk to his mother alone on the porch, but then he reckoned he would need to tell Jim Brown and Harold as well. This one was not a hard decision; it would be better to get it over in a single declaration.

As Eve was focused on placing the tinsel on the tree, one strand at a time, and Jim Brown and Harold were eyeing the last cookie on the plate, Bill announced, "I'm going to war." All heads swirled in his direction. His mother almost fell over in a faint. Luckily, his dad was there to catch her.

When she gained her composure, she cried, "You can't! You're too young! I need you here!"

Summoning his most authoritative, adult voice, Bill replied, "I'm ready, and I'm needed there." To soften the blow, he added. "The principal and teachers have it all set that you can see me graduate before Christmas."

Now that caught Jim Brown by surprise! "You mean you can finish school early?" Bill gave a nod. "Well, gee, sign me up!" His mother swooned again, as she had yet to recover from the initial shock. Their parents left the room as their father tried to comfort their mother and support Bill as best he could—which he discovered was more difficult than he had imagined.

To divert attention, and since Jim Brown had been looking for the right moment all evening, he slipped an ornament from the tree and snuck up behind Harold. Gently placing it on his shoulder, he casually remarked, "Hey, Harold, what's that spider doing on your shoulder?"

Harold turned and began to say, "There's no…" when he let out a blood-curdling scream.

As he jumped up, the spider fell. Laughing, Jim Brown caught the ornament and began to chase Harold.

"You know I don't like spiders! Keep away! Keep away!"

The ruckus caught Eve's attention in the dining room, and she immediately returned to intervene. Instantly, sizing up the situation, she calmly said, "Now Harold, it's only a spider Jim Brown made in Sunday School."

Harold eyed him suspiciously. Jim Brown pulled out the silver spider to reassure him that his mother was telling the truth. Then, as his mother was still in control, she suggested, "Why don't you read him the story, Jim Brown?"

Though not quite what he had in mind, he agreed to make peace for his mother's sake. He obediently slipped out to get the Bible.

No one noticed that as he returned to the living room, he slipped two papers inside the Bible. Unperturbed, he sat down.

"Does it got any pictures?" asked Harold, as he approached and began to climb onto Jim Brown's lap.

"Nope," he replied, randomly opening the Bible, displaying large pages with nothing but words. Disappointed, Harold slipped onto the floor and sat down cross-legged—in case he needed to dart away—and looked at his brother, waiting for the story to begin.

"Do you want to hold the spider?"

Harold gave a resounding, "Nope."

"OK, then let's begin." Jim Brown carefully found the pages he inserted and read:

THE CHRISTMAS SPIDER

"Once upon a time, when camels flew over the desert sands and a promise of the Messiah floated on the wind—"

"What's a Messiah?" interrupted Harold.

"He's our Savior, the Baby Jesus," Jim Brown replied, trying to sound confident and knowledgeable. Looking down at Harold, whose eyebrows were scrunched and lips pursed, he realized this undertaking was not going to be short and sweet.

"A baby?" Harold blurted.

"Harold! Stop interrupting!" Jim Brown said, then he looked to Heaven for strength.

Harold's eyes popped. He sat up straight and stuck out his lower lip in a pout. He glared at his brother, leaving no doubt that he was quickly losing interest in the story and the spider.

Jim Brown refocused and changed his tone. "Just listen. You'll catch on." Then, with true confidence, he added, "I promise," and smiled.

Harold relaxed, and Jim Brown resumed. "As I was saying … Mary and Joseph had set out on a long journey from their home in Nazareth to the City of David, Bethlehem. The King had decreed that a census be taken. All his people would be counted in the towns of their families' origin."

"Why?" asked Harold, tilting his head in a quizzical way.

Jim Brown rolled his eyes again. "Because kings do that!"

"Oh," replied Harold, satisfied.

Surprised, Jim Brown gave a nod and happily continued. "When they arrived, it was very late, and all the inns were full. Joseph had travelled slower than other groups making the journey because Mary was soon to give birth. Joseph was very concerned for her welfare. Finally, he found an innkeeper with a soft-hearted wife. Though their inn was indeed full, as all could see, she offered to create comfortable lodgings in the stable. Joseph was doubtful, but Mary gave an encouraging smile. Somehow, she felt secure in this woman's care. Leading the way, the woman dropped her head as she spoke in an apologetic tone, 'It's not much, but…' and her voice quickly transformed to a cheerful cadence, 'it's quiet and warm—and in a jiffy, we'll have it fit for a king!'

"When they arrived, she immediately picked up a worn broom from the corner and, with an unexpected burst of energy, set to work. In her first gusty sweep, she caught a sleeping family of spiders and sent them flying through the air!"

"Oooo!" cried Harold, adding a shiver for emphasis. "Now come the spiders!"

Jim Brown shot a harsh look in Harold's direction.

"Sorry," cowered Harold, and he truly was sorry, as he felt the story was finally getting to the interesting part.

Jim Brown conceded and continued. "The innkeeper's wife was lost in her whirlwind cleaning. Unintentionally, she woke the cows and donkeys, the hens and other barnyard animals, who began to bellow and squawk to protest these unexpected intruders at this time of night. But when the dust settled, the innkeeper's wife stood proudly with a grin on her face. Her rosy cheeks sparkled, and she gave her nose a wrinkle, as a sneeze caught her by surprise. She blushed for a moment and returned to Mary's side, while making a mental list of all that was still needed. Finally, disappearing into the velvet night, she hollered that her husband would return shortly with blankets and provisions."

Jim Brown paused to catch his breath.

"Is that it?" sighed Harold, not disguising his disappointment.

"No," replied Jim Brown, as he turned the page and returned to the story. "In the meantime, the spider family regrouped at the far end of the stable.

"'What's happening?' the little ones cried.

"'I'm not sure,' replied the mother spider, as she stretched her legs and looked for another opening where she might spin a new web. 'It is most unusual. I'm sure something important is about to happen!'

"Only the smallest spider, still dazed but curious, lingered behind in a dark corner to quietly observe. Suddenly, a muffled cry broke the silence. It rapidly grew louder and filled the stable! 'What was that?' cried the spider, as he scurried back to the security of his spider family.

"'Why, it's a baby!' mooed the cow to no one in particular, as she chewed on her hay. Just as the sound had overwhelmed the stable, it quieted down to a whimper, then a soft gurgle, and soon the stable was filled with sweet strains of lullabies."

Harold leaned in and whispered, "Do you know any lullabies, Jim Brown?"

Jim Brown ignored the question.

"All night long, the activity continued. First, the innkeeper arrived, grumbling, carrying the parcel his wife had lovingly prepared. The sight that met his eyes so astonished him, his sour expression immediately melted away, and a surge of energy poured through his protesting body. He assumed the position as head host and began to guide the visitors who were arriving as the news of the blessed infant quickly spread by word, by angels, and by a shining star!

"'Not so close! No more animals! Don't crowd! Shhh! He's sleeping!' he would softly bellow. The gentle smile on his face and the wonder that sparkled in the eyes of those who came created a heavenly air around the earthly scene.

"And come they did, with presents of all kinds—gifts of love, of song, and of prayer. Rumors spread that even kings were on their way."

"With gold, frankincense, and myrrh!" Harold chimed in.

This time, Jim Brown smiled and gave an approving nod. "Right, you are."

Returning to the story, he read, "And the animals also gave gifts: the geese their softest down to line the manger; the cows their warm milk; and even the grumpy donkey tried to sing a lullaby, but all agreed—the donkey included—that it would be better if he gave the gift of silence. Inspired, he set about organizing the dogs and pronounced himself captain of the guard to protect the Holy Child.

"The little spider so wished he had a gift, but every time he inched forward, the animals spat at him and even tried to stomp him! He was not wanted."

Harold couldn't restrain himself and blurted out, "Yeah! I agree! There's no place for a spider!"

Jim Brown frowned.

"But Jim Brown, you know I don't like spiders," he reiterated, as if Jim Brown had missed the admonition the first ten times.

"Just listen to the rest of the story.

"In the early morning light, as everyone quietly slept, the spider cautiously crept onto a rafter, which crossed over the manger. He hoped that he might have just one glimpse of the Blessed Infant.

"On a thin gossamer thread, he lowered himself as close as he dared to go. And that's when it happened!"

"What!" exclaimed Harold, holding his breath.

Jim Brown gave a knowing smile and continued without pausing, "As he hung there, ever so silently, he realized he too was a creature of God. He must have a purpose and talents. There must be a gift that only he could possess to give the Christ Child!"

"What? What?" exclaimed Harold impatiently, as he pulled on Jim Brown's jeans to get his attention.

"At that moment, the Christ Child sneezed, woke up, and smiled at the tiny spider.

"With that, he knew. He went straight to work and began to spin a web of finest lace to protect the baby from dust and hayseed, from fur and feathers, from insects and any other harmful hands that drew too close! When he finished, he proudly looked at his work.

"But his smile soon melted away. He realized his gift wasn't even close to what the baby deserved, and a tear began to fall."

"SEE!" Harold cried with satisfaction.

Jim Brown raised his eyebrow and continued without hesitation.

"But God was watching from above, and He smiled at the diligent worker. He saw what was in his heart. With a wave of His hand, the web began to glow, and the morning dew collected and sparkled on the web like jewels befitting a king, indeed, the Christ Child King sleeping in the manger.

"The lowly spider watched in amazement and felt a wonderous glow from within. His gift was awesome! He even considered that he might dare to think that he, too, was found worthy in God's eyes. Never would his dark corner feel empty again. He was content with himself just as he was—and God smiled in agreement."

Jim Brown closed the Bible and looked at Harold.

"WOW!" Harold sighed, and with a touch of remorse, he bravely asked, "Do you think I could hold the spider?"

"Sure. You can even take him up to bed with you."

Harold shook his head up and down and anxiously reached up to take the spider gently in his hand.

Their mother smiled and thoughtfully added, "You know, one morning, we'll wake up, and there will be a beautiful garland on the tree."

"Will it be pink?" grimaced Harold.

Jim Brown and his father choked in unison, while his mother became speechless.

"What color do you think it should be?" his father asked, trying to regain the higher ground.

"Gold!" Harold replied authoritatively.

Spying the box with the golden garland behind the piano, his father glee-fully responded, "Well, you just might be in luck!"

Harold grinned.

His mother shot her husband an ominous glare and then regained her composure. "You know, the spider is responsible for the garland. It's his present to make our spirits bright and to remind us we all have gifts to share. Maybe, in the morning, we can make some friends to help him spin the garland!" Harold beamed and tore up the stairs.

Jim Brown gave his mom a kiss and followed his brother. Their dad watched, took Eve in his arms, and gave her a hug. Their boys were truly special.

As Jim Brown reached the top of the stairs, he found Harold sitting and scrutinizing—a pretty good word he thought—the spider and won-dered what devious thought he might be concocting—two more good words. Maybe school was making an impression on him.

Harold broke the silence. "Jim Brown, you know, I think critters can be more real than big people."

"Huh?"

"Yeah! They have feelings, and though they might be simple, they are smart. They understand and solve problems. I think I learn more from them than I do from big people."

"You know, you really are smart for a little kid," Jim Brown replied, as he gave a reassuring smile and jostled Harold's hair.

Then, Harold looked down because he was afraid of what he might see in his brother's eyes. A tiny tremor entered his little voice and, in a quiet whisper, he asked, "Jim Brown, Bill really is leaving, isn't he?"

"Yup."

Then he looked up with tears glistening in his eyes and asked, "Is he coming back?"

Jim Brown felt a shock go through his body. "Of course, he is!" he blurted out.

"Is that a critter answer or a big people answer?" Harold challenged.

Having regained his cool, Jim Brown said, "It's the truth! Besides, you know Wanda would kill him if he didn't!"

Harold gave a conspiratorial smile and replied, "I saw him kiss her in the backyard!"

"Oooo! Too much information, little fella! Off to bed!" and they trudged together down the hall. As they got to the bedroom door, Jim Brown hesitated a moment and wondered, *What would a critter say?*

As they were lying in bed in total darkness, a tiny voice broke the silence. "Jim Brown?"

"Yeah?"

"I still don't like snakes… and skeeters… and spiders."

"That's OK, Harold; it's probably a good thing. I don't like them either. Rats are kinda creepy, too," he added to identify with Harold's stream of thoughts.

The tiny voice, barely audible, continued, "But I do like your spider."

"Good," replied Jim Brown with a silent smile and a hope that this deep discussion was now at an end.

"Good," echoed Harold, and then he perked up. "What about girls?"

Jim Brown closed his eyes and started to groan, but he quickly changed it into a mild snore.

Harold patiently waited, positive that Jim Brown was teasing and not truly sleeping. But his eyelids grew heavy and, after a few moments of silence, Harold was breathing deeply in an even, rhythmic pattern. Jim Brown recognized it, and if he weren't asleep, Jim Brown knew he soon would be. In no time, both boys were in deep slumber. Harold dreamed of magical lands with ice cream mountains and chocolate slides, fairies who would grant every wish, and friends that were not people he knew, but people who knew him.

Jim Brown's dreams were becoming radically different. He dreamt of a world without war and corruption, a world with plenty and generosity, a world with doors that were opened to everyone with exciting adventures behind each turn: a rocket travelling into space, a submarine venturing to the bottom of the ocean, jungles yet to be explored. Friends included people he knew, but also mentors he hoped to meet.

Meanwhile, after the last day of school before Christmas break, Bill returned to the principal's office. His mother, dressed in a pink, linen suit and his father in his best coat and tie, with Jim Brown and Harold in tow, were waiting for him. A few teachers, including Mrs. Raley, were there as well. After a few opening remarks, Bill received his diploma. Of course, his mother burst into tears; his father had a handkerchief ready. Several other students also had applied for early graduation to join the army. Some still had requirements to finish, while two had been rejected because the principal felt they were not ready for the army, and the army—no matter how desperate—was not ready for them. Bill was a graduate of one.

That night, they celebrated with Bill's favorite dinner: meatloaf, string beans, mashed potatoes, and a chocolate icebox cake. As the family settled into their evening routines, no one, except Jim Brown, noticed Bill slip away.

IV

CHRISTMAS CAME AND WENT. AS MUCH AS EVERYONE WANTED TO BE
jolly and bright, it was a silent Christmas, filled with love and prayers for
each other and fear and hatred for what was happening abroad. Eve insisted
on a quiet family dinner, and it seemed Bill's seat was inched closer than
usual to his mother's. She kept filling his plate over and over, as if she could
stop time and freeze this moment. Harold, as all youngsters, couldn't wait
to finish dinner and dive into the real meaning of Christmas Eve, opening
presents. To everyone's surprise, except Jim Brown's, Harold pulled out the
first present, a Christmas spider, and gave it to Bill.

New Year's Eve followed. Over the radio, Guy Lombardo and his Royal
Canadians played "Auld Lang Syne," as tradition would have it to welcome
in the New Year—not even a world war could stop the passage of time.

On Monday, January 5, Starke steadied itself for its first blackout
rehearsal. At nine o'clock sharp, the siren would alert everyone to turn off
their lights and close the blinds. The idea was to make the town disappear
from the map to hide it from enemy planes, which were surely on their way.
It all sounded good, except the town commission learned they needed to
inform the Third Interceptor Command before they engaged in any crit-
ical exercises. As permission had not been granted, at the last minute, the
blackout rehearsal was cancelled. The word, however, did not get out in time.

The siren, which blared loudly, woke up babies, confused many adults,
and was ignored by the rest. Men peeked out their windows, looking to the
sky for tornados or meteors or worse. Others locked their doors, convinced

there was a prison break. Everyone flooded the telephone lines, seeking news or explanations. Then, it turned into a complete fiasco.

Lights blinked on and off, dogs barked, and someone claiming to be the air warden called Mr. Johns at the power plant, ordering him to pull the main switch and turn off all the electricity to town. The whole town went black and was in turmoil. Mr. Johns had a miserable time trying to restore power, as there was an unnatural overload. Other towns fared better, or so they reported.

On January 23, a defense mass meeting was scheduled to regroup and answer questions. The citizens of Starke needed to realize they were in jeopardy. They were designated one of four danger zones in the state targeted by "the enemy"—probably due to Camp Blanding being one of the largest army training posts east of the Mississippi, though that did not need to be highlighted. The ex-governor, Fred Cone, was scheduled to kick off the meeting, and all stores were directed to close so no one had any excuse not to be there. Even the BHS band planned a program of patriotic songs, and several church leaders remarked it was everyone's Christian duty to attend. A few looked forward to voicing their disapproval of the recent arrival of rowdy recruits from Camp Blanding and other inconveniences, but their remarks were quickly dismissed, as the meeting focused on the seriousness of their situation and the necessary sacrifices to be shared by all. It was confirmed the company that built the Empire State Building in New York City was indeed in charge of the new constructs at Camp Blanding, though again, rumors of skyscrapers were dispelled.

The program continued into the night, with moments of instruction and moments of hysteria. Rumor-mongering, duty dodgers, hoarders, and whiners were not to be tolerated. Rationing would begin shortly, and registration for the Selective Service was already in full swing if someone had somehow missed the previous announcements. Everyone bit their lips, holding back groans. The message was received loud and clear; the nation was at war. Finally, it was emphasized that in the future, the main electric switch into the county was never, repeat never, to be thrown. The audience applauded. The band played "God Bless America" as the good citizens left in an orderly fashion. It was unusually quiet, as if all the wind had been knocked out of them.

Jim Brown's home life remained routine, almost ordinary—on the outside. The blue star flag hung in the parlor window, signifying Bill was serving his country, as Eve wanted everyone to know that; otherwise, she continued her daily activities pretending nothing had changed—significantly. Everything, she wanted to believe, was "normal," as if Bill were only off to summer camp. Besides, she had convinced herself how long could this war last! Surely, the world will come to its senses; if not, God would put things right. Only Mr. Godwin understood that her faith got her up every morning.

However, the day before he left, Bill pulled Jim Brown aside and said, "Well, Jim Brown, you finally got your wish."

His eyes popped, as he snapped his head around like a dummy on a ventriloquist's knee. He stared bewilderedly into his brother's face. His pain was as visible as the first firework on the Fourth of July or the last strip of bacon on a breakfast platter. Didn't Bill know he was losing his best friend! They had never been apart. They were a team; they were brothers—true blood brothers down to the last drop!

Bill took the lead, as always, and nudged him to the stairs. He wanted to put a few changes in place, and now was the time. Bill continued, not missing a beat. "Sure, you finally get to be the older brother."

What? thought Jim Brown. *That would never happen.* Thoughts flashed through his mind as he tried to sort out what Bill was saying.

Ever since Harold arrived, Jim Brown felt he had become invisible. Bill was the oldest, the brightest, the first, while Jim Brown struggled to meet the bar. When he did bring home a report card with straight As, Harold had a crisis, and his mother's attention turned to the baby. Nope, he was just the middle child.

Bill argued that Jim Brown had it easy. As the oldest, he had the responsibility and had to meet expectations. He was the one their parents experimented on, depended on, and the restrictions they placed on him were tighter than what Jim Brown had. *Yes, Jim Brown, you'll finally see what it's like to be the oldest.*

"I won't be there to deflect Mom's attention. You'll be the one to answer to Dad's demands. But listen," he concluded, "look after Harold. He needs you, and he does rely on you."

Jim Brown smiled in agreement. Harold was weird, but he was a Godwin, and he had spunk. They would be a team, but life would never be the same. Bill sensed that Jim Brown was slipping into a funk, so he pressed on to complete the real purpose of dragging him upstairs. Looking him in the eye, man to man, Bill insisted Jim Brown move out of the room he shared with Harold and into his room. He deserved it, and he would earn it.

Jim Brown was shocked. His emotions swirled as he thought, *I really don't want you to go off to war, but—gee! Finally, a room of my own! That's swell! When did you say you were leaving? Can I help you pack?*

Their mother was upset when she learned what the boys were up to. She wanted to keep Bill's room just the way it was, but it was Bill's way of saying when he came home, he wouldn't be returning there. He had other plans for himself and his sweetheart, Wanda … and Jim Brown knew that, too.

The room was awesome—larger than the room he shared with Harold. There were hardwood floors, deep crown molding, and a double bed. It was on the second floor in the back of the house, away from everyday traffic.

Jim Brown slipped into a chair by Bill's desk, an old kitchen table with the metal top removed and a lamp strategically placed on the right side. He suddenly noticed a strange design on the wall above the desk; it seemed like the skyline of a big city. He smiled. He recognized Bill's artwork for what it was; it reminded him of his own creation next to his bed.

He remembered the day when his mother discovered the flaked off paint and screamed that he had purposefully destroyed the room! She went into a tirade that Tallahassee would never find the money in their budget for paint or for any of the other repairs the house needed. She considered moving the furniture around to cover the insult, then threw up her hands and left, promptly forgetting the moment.

The patch had grown rather large, and he proudly felt it resembled a Tyrannosaurus Rex, a rather good roommate to leave for Harold. He wondered if his mother had discovered Bill's destructive design and wondered what other secrets the room might reveal about his brother. Unconsciously, he compulsively reached over to dislodge a fleck of paint that was just begging to come off. He slipped his finger under the edge, and a large two-inch square dropped behind the table.

His eyes popped, and he looked to his brother, who fortunately seemed lost in personal recollections. Returning his gaze to the wall, he realized the skyline was irretrievably lost. *Would Bill notice? Would he care? After all, it was his room now.* He smiled as he envisioned a Brontosaurus in the making. Silently, he slipped a stack of thick books—a dictionary, a thesaurus, and an atlas, in front of the skyline and slid unnoticed next to Bill on the bed.

Bill casually stood up and walked over to the window. Silently, he gazed across the yard.

Not necessarily talking to anyone, his voice boomed, "That live oak sure is a great climbing tree." He turned his head and squinted his eyes as he searched Jim Brown's face to see if he got the message. Jim Brown, who had been bouncing on the bed, didn't appear to be listening, so Bill pounced and got him in a headlock.

"Hey! What are you doing? I heard you! Sure, I know it's a climbing tree!" Jim Brown sniffed, as he struggled to push his brother off.

Bill sat up, winked, and repeated, "Yes, a *great* climbing tree!"

Then, as if the room filled with magic, Jim Brown knew exactly what his brother was saying. Visions of great escapes and secret missions flooded his mind. A smile slowly began to slip across his face. He looked at Bill and nodded, showing he understood. The tree would be the doorway to untold adventures and freedom. He finally grasped how Bill had mysteriously disappeared all these years. They stood up, and Bill playfully slapped him on the shoulders as they went downstairs to raid the pantry.

That night, they shared the room. Jim Brown slept contentedly with dreams of soaring above the clouds into space.

Bill, on the other hand, was restless. He tossed and turned and stared at the ceiling. He was ready to report for training, but he was anxious about the challenges ahead, and he didn't look forward to saying good-bye to Wanda. They had become "an item" in tenth grade, and he was smitten by the time they were juniors. Wanda was always in charge of the relationship, and going off to war was not in her plan. It was the one time Bill put his foot down. He explained this wasn't a choice. The nation called, and he was ready to answer. He was going to fight for the country, for her, and for their future. His reaction caught Wanda off guard. She burst into tears, and Bill held her in his arms until she stopped. Saying the final good-bye would be the toughest challenge he would ever face, but he knew he would return. Then, thoughts of his return filled his dreams.

The next morning was the worst day in Jim Brown's life, as they all said good-bye to Bill. It wasn't easy for Bill either.

It didn't take long before Bill's absence was keenly felt, beginning the very next morning. As his father was leaving to go to work, he called over his shoulder, "Jim Brown, check the mouse traps before you go to school. Your mother swears she heard one snap last night."

Jim Brown almost choked on the toast he was chewing, but he managed a dutiful, "Yes, sir," before the door banged shut.

His mind flashed back several years, certainly before Harold was born, and his folks were in a heated argument. It seemed that mice had taken up residence in the pantry, and his mother was frantic. With hoots and hollers and the kitchen broom, she had chased two critters out the door that morning. This wasn't going to continue. His father returned that night and set up the traps, which did their jobs effectively. His mother almost "tossed her cookies" when she found the dead creatures, but she managed to get the ash shovel from the fireplace and scooped them into a paper bag before carrying them at an arm's length to the trash bin. That evening, after dinner, she casually mentioned to her husband that they would need more traps.

"Eve, honey, I bought a pack yesterday." He added, "They should do the job, unless a whole swarm move in," ending with a reassuring smile.

She looked him in the eye and declared, "I threw them out."

"What! Why on earth would you do that?" he retorted, totally confused.

This was followed by his mother raising her voice, as she explained that was the only way she could empty the traps! That when they married, she promised to love, honor, and obey, but there was no contract to empty rat traps, and besides ... and then came the flood of tears. Between the sobs, there was something about broken bodies, bulging eyes, and blood and guts. The tears were enough to end the discussion, and his father took her in his arms and whispered comforting words that she was right and he would take care of everything. With that, he turned and said, "I'll pick up a new pack tomorrow, and Bill, see that you check these traps each morning for your mother."

What! How did I get dragged into this! thought Bill, but then his father had used the magical words, "for your mother," who was standing there in a miserable state, streaming with tears, reenforcing the command. "Yes, sir," he obediently replied, but already his mind went to work designing a plan to get out of this chore for, like his mother, Bill had a soft spot for all creatures. Cleaning out the traps first thing in the morning was not the way to begin his day.

Later that evening, as they trudged up the stairs to go to bed, he put his arm around Jim Brown's shoulders and said, "How would you like to earn some money?"

He had Jim Brown's attention. The proposal was that Bill would pay Jim Brown a nickel for every mouse he "disposed of," but Jim Brown would have to pay him a quarter if he missed a mouse and Bill was blamed. Well, that wouldn't happen ... and though he wasn't keen on the chore, he would take the job; besides, he figured the trustees would empty the traps, too, and he could take credit for those, because the bargain was to dispose of the corpses ... he didn't say how. And so, they shook on it.

Well, now the chore was officially passed on to him. He grimaced as he recalled how Bill said his life would change, but it was a small price to keep peace in the house. Anyway, he never did make that much off the proposition, though every penny counted these days.

That night, Jim Brown walked into his new room, his arms filled with the last of his personal belongings. He glanced at the bed and could still see the image of Bill's imprint on the mattress. Carefully, he placed his stuff in a teetering pile on the desk.

It surprised him that he felt this uncomfortable. He'd already spent hours, which would add up to days, even years, sitting at the desk, crouched on the floor, standing by the window. He grabbed his pajamas and went to the bathroom to change and brush his teeth. When he opened the door, he automatically turned to the right but stopped short and corrected his pace to the left, to Bill's room—oops, another correction, to his room.

The desk lamp had a soft glow, giving the room an unfamiliar scape. He switched off the light and walked mechanically over to the bed. After turning down the covers, he sat down, swung his legs up, and fell back onto the pillows.

Suddenly, the room came to life. He stretched out his arms and legs and relaxed into the bed. It couldn't get any better; it was his room.

Just then, the house creaked. Jim Brown smiled as a memory formed perfectly in his mind. He was just a bit older than Harold when he went charging into his parents' room after he woke to similar sounds in the house.

"Dad! Dad! Wake up! Wake up!" he cried as he shook his father's arm.

"What's wrong, son?" his father groggily replied, as he forced his one eye open.

"The house is falling! The house is falling! We have to get out! NOW!"

"G-D, Jim Brown! I'm trying to sleep! It's three in the morning!"

"But, Dad, listen! You can hear them. Bill says there are trolls digging tunnels under the house, and they are going to cave in!"

"Then go tell Bill. This house is old ... it's just settling."

"But, Dad," he whispered in a conspiratorial tone of someone who knows, "they ride on gators!"

"Go to bed ... NOW."

Jim Brown knew that tone in his voice; it meant, "I'm not repeating this." He turned and left, quite confused. He was certain the house was going to collapse; he was trying to save his family, so why didn't his father understand?

In hindsight, Jim Brown realized how ridiculous it had been. He clearly understood his father's impatience, but he also remembered that he never confronted Bill. That was probably a good thing, as he would have laughed until he cried at Jim Brown's expense.

His thoughts then turned inexplicably to other house sounds, and he realized that he might actually have discovered a language people failed to appreciate. The creaking stairs warned of the comings and goings of the family, though he and Bill knew which steps to avoid. Windows rattled with the wind. The doors—now, they had multiple sounds: there was the gentle ding-dong of the doorbell or the continuous buzz of an obnoxious buzzer, the knock of someone arriving—now there was a conundrum. *Were two raps enough, or were four too many?* Jim Brown settled on three raps.

Each door gave a unique squeak. The back door could bang as the boys ran out to play or slam, signifying someone leaving in anger. The screen door quietly shut, sometimes failing to even close. The front door, on the other hand, majestically opened and shut without comment.

Then, there were the seasonal sounds. Summer was announced by the humming and droning of fans. Fall was greeted with the rustle of tree branches knocking on the windows. With winter came the gurgling and clanging of the radiators. Spring was his favorite; it arrived with rain drop symphonies, from light sprinkles to full-blown thunderstorms.

As if on cue, raindrops began to bounce off the roof. Slowly, he then began to doze off as more thoughts raced through his mind. Maybe, during the night, houses might actually speak to one another, like, "Hey, what's your family up to?" or "Gee, you wouldn't believe the mess they make!" Now that was not a comment his house would make. His home was immaculate by the decree of the Queen! Jim Brown recalled one hot, summer morning when he took a break from yard work to get a glass of water. He found his mother in the kitchen leaning over the table, rolling out dough for pie crust. Her forehead was covered with perspiration despite the humming fan, oscillating back and forth, and the windows opened wide, inviting every fly in the county to drop in.

Not ready to return to his chores, Jim Brown took the opportunity to ask his mother why was it so important to keep the house and yard clean; after all, it was their home, their place of rest.

His mother paused and stood up. "Now, where did that come from?" she wondered, and, looking for an excuse to rest, she reached for a glass of water and sat down. "You want me to state the obvious, like, 'A house that's dirty is screaming for attention'?"

"Well, beauty is in the eye of the beholder, and I just thought maybe the leaves might be fine where they were."

"Well, let's examine this more closely. If we don't rake the leaves and they blow into the neighbors' yards, they might be a bit perturbed. Wouldn't you be?" But before he could answer, she continued, "And if you don't clear the leaves, you might miss a snake slithering across the yard and step on it! And if you don't put the rake away, well, it could fall and be covered by leaves, and … well, you can see where this is going … the next thing you know, you'll step on it, and it will fly up and give you a knot on your noggin. Now, the house—now that's a different story." She paused and handed him her glass for a refill, which Jim Brown obliged.

"Let's see. One, 'A place for everything and everything in its place.' You know how miserable it is when you're ready to go play ball with Bill…" At this moment, she stopped and almost choked as Bill's name stuck in her throat. "Well, anyway, if you can't find your mitt because it is covered with your clothes on your unmade bed, well, you'd be frustrated and get mad."

Jim Brown nodded; she had a point.

"Two," she continued, as she was on a roll, "if you leave your toys and games out, pieces can get lost or broken. You have to care and respect the blessings that come your way."

Again, Jim Brown had to agree.

"Three, would you rather eat off a clean plate or a dirty plate? You know mold and germs grow on crumbs, and they can make you sick! And four, you certainly wouldn't want to wear stinky clothes. Why your teachers and friends would think I didn't love you! Five…"

Jim Brown couldn't believe his mother had this many rationales on the tip of her tongue! His yard work began to seem like an escape he would willingly take.

"There's the Good Book."

Oh, no! She can't be bringing in the Bible! Jim Brown shuddered.

"'Honor thy mother and thy father.' You know, God entrusted you to me, and it is my job to keep you safe and protected, which means having a clean house. You wouldn't want me to spend all my time scrubbing and not making pies? What would your friends say? So, I do trust you to do your share." And with that, she paused and looked at him like a fighter waiting in his corner for the second bell to ring.

Jim Brown just smiled and shook his head. "You're right. I'd better get back to the leaves before those snakes take over." In hindsight, Jim Brown thought his mother never would spend her time scrubbing; she'd call the trustee over for that.

His thoughts returned to hearths and homes, the smells of roasting meat and baking cakes, and then, for some unexpected reason, his mind took a spiraling turn from the good and comforts of home to the bad and ugly. Maybe, it was just as well that these walls don't speak. Sometimes the walls are witnesses to secrets that are better kept silent or, blissfully, forgotten.

Without warning, a lightning bolt slashed across the sky, followed by a crash of thunder. The light rain had turned into a full-blown thunderstorm.

A pitter pat of feet came tearing down the hall and, after a short pause, his door creaked open. Harold's tiny voice asked, "You OK, Jim Brown?"

"I'm fine," he replied. "Hey, you want to see what Bill's, I mean, my new bed is like?"

Without giving a response, Harold dove onto the bed and under the covers.

Jim Brown smiled and thought, *Well, maybe I didn't save the family from trolls and a collapsing home those many years ago, but tonight I'm here for Harold.*

Within minutes, they both were fast asleep.

THE WHOLE TOWN BEGAN TO PREPARE FOR WAR. CAMP BLANDING

grew as new recruits arrived for training. Garages were rented to contractors and their families. Lemonade stands and shoeshine boxes were on every corner as the locals looked for the silver lining and opportunities to participate. Everyone was caught up in the frenzy.

Girls were taught to roll compress bandages with gauze provided by the Junior Women's Club, and the boys collected rubber, which created a small mountain on the Bradford Elementary School playground as it waited to be hauled off to recycling centers. The "State Farmers," those whose fathers worked at the prison, including Jim Brown, stacked the highest tower of tires—and they were quite proud of that.

Mothers knitted sweaters, socks, and mittens for the soldiers and spent hours in their victory gardens tending vegetables. Victory gardens were seen not only as patriotic, but also practical, since trucks were reassigned to transport wartime supplies, making it difficult to buy fresh produce at the grocery stores. The PBC—Patriotic Bradford Countians—offered free first-aid classes to anyone who wanted to learn how to wrap a sprained ankle, set a broken bone, or apply a tourniquet to a severed artery. The churches were packed every Sunday, as voices were lifted in prayers for the safety of the soldiers and the country. The men who weren't reporting for military service signed up as air-raid wardens and dim-out monitors.

Everyone was keenly aware history was being made, and they all stood up to play their parts.

The family didn't hear from Bill for several weeks. Then, shortly before Valentine's Day, the phone rang. Eve answered, shrieked, and almost dropped the receiver. Mr. Godwin and Jim Brown rounded opposite corners, almost colliding as they came to her rescue. When they learned it was Bill, there was a mad grab for the receiver, as they all had questions and wanted to hear his voice. Harold seemed to understand, and he quietly slipped his little hand into Jim Brown's.

"Well, Ma," Bill drawled, "I've gained sixty pounds."

"What!" gasped his mother, "You must look like a blimp! What are they doing to you? Aren't they going to feed you when you go into combat?" She paused as she couldn't believe she had said the "C" word. She quickly continued, "You come home right now, and let me feed you properly!" She paused and took a breath, trying to keep her emotions in check.

"Ah, I don't think they'll let me," Bill squeezed in and then started laughing.

"Why are you laughing? This isn't funny. It's not healthy! You just tell them…"

"Really, Ma, it's alright. The sixty pounds is the rucksack they have us carrying all over base. I actually think I've lost a few pounds. They may even have to issue me a new uniform!"

"Oh, honestly, Bill!" and with that, she turned the phone over to his father.

Bill explained that they had sped up boot camp. It was no longer twelve weeks; the powers that be had trimmed it down to six. They would be getting their assignments soon, which was why they were all given some time off to call home and put things in order. His dad understood, listened intently, and then handed the phone to Jim Brown after he said, "Be careful and keep in touch."

Jim Brown couldn't wait to have his turn to talk with Bill. He began firing questions before his mouth got to the receiver.

"Hold on, Sport!" Bill interrupted, "I've only got a few minutes left. There's a line here that's wrapped around the block like a snake!" Then Bill gave him a quick sketch of what life was like. The first thing they did was shave his head. It wasn't so bad because everyone got the same cut, but he was just glad Wanda didn't see him. Then, they took his clothes and issued him uniforms all the way down to his socks and underwear. Finally, everyone was authorized a dog tag with a serial number—no names, no individual identity, just numbers. They crawled through sand and muck, climbed over walls and barriers. They marched and exercised from dawn to dusk and even in the dark. He'd never felt so exhausted and alone, feeling like an insignificant cog in a machine. But, after a while, the machine started to buzz. You made buddies and worked together as a team. You knew they had your back, and you had theirs.

"There's one more thing; I'm learning a new language," Bill added.

"German? Japanese? Italian?" asked Jim Brown, hoping to get a scoop on where his brother might be deployed.

"No, nothing like that. It's military speak. You wouldn't believe all the vocabulary you need. And then, I guess to speed things up, they make up words like AWOL, that's 'absent without leave', or they'll say, 'Report to the SDO ASAP!'—that's 'Go see the staff duty officer as soon as possible,' which means two hours ago. But there are some great words like FUBAR, SNAFU, and Blivet Struck. And you don't just find butter bars and scrambled eggs in the mess hall."

"Blivet Struck?"

"Yeah, that's when you're hit with a five-pound sack filled with ten pounds of manure! And let me tell you—you don't want to do that twice!" and they both started laughing. It felt swell. Bill continued, "The food is good. They serve hobo coffee and SOS—that's 'shit on a shingle'—for breakfast."

"SOS?" choked Jim Brown.

"Hey, you'd ask for a second serving; it's creamed chipped beef on toast."

"If you say so," he responded doubtfully. "Now, what was that Snuffy and Fruitbar?"

"Ah, that's SNAFU and FUBAR—and I'd better leave those until I see you next. Just don't say them around Mom. I don't think she knows; dad might ... listen, I've got to go. Give Harold a hug. I really miss you guys." Then there was a click, silence, and Jim Brown knew Bill was gone. He stood there dumbfounded. He'd forgotten to tell Bill about the rubber drive, that their mother was actually going to teach him how to drive the car, and how he'd changed the room. He didn't get a chance to ask if Bill had learned to drive a tank—it would have been a tight squeeze—or which guns they fired. Bill was a sure-shot with his rifle that still stood in the corner of the closet. He didn't even say good-bye.

"My turn, my turn!" Harold was jumping up and down, reaching for the phone.

"He had to go, Harold," Jim Brown said, as he replaced the receiver on the hook, "but he told me to give you this." And in the next moment, he scooped Harold up and locked him in his arms, squeezing him as hard as he could.

That night, as he lay in bed, he thought about his talk with Bill. He missed him, but other than the haircut, which made him smirk, he knew Bill could handle anything—so far—they'd thrown his way. He grinned as he thought about sharing the military speak with his friends and inventing their own vocabulary ... ALL, "Apply Lessons Learned"—one of his father's favorite sayings ... GOMO, "Game over, Move on"—a JBG original. He continued thinking of snappy phrases and how he might turn them into military speak. Whether you win or lose, don't get lost in the moment—that one might not work; sometimes, words need to be spoken. Tomorrow always comes—TAC—good one. His mind stalled as he settled on the word tomorrow. Tomorrow, tomorrow always comes. His stomach began to churn as his thoughts turned to tomorrow, Valentine's Day. A week at boot camp was a cinch compared to Valentine rituals.

It was a curious time filled with opposites. He didn't want any cards, but he didn't want to be the one without any. He didn't like dropping the cards in the boxes they had decorated in art class, but his stomach flipped as he tried to imagine giving a special card to Peggy Tilley. But there was a catch; he didn't want anyone to know she was special. Hey, he wasn't even sure he wanted *her* to know, but she was since the first day he saw her.

The fateful day, the fateful moment, arrived. He was in the school corridor, holding the card in his hand. There wasn't anything special about it;

it was just one of those, "Roses are red, Violets are blue, Football is Great, and so are YOU!"—or something like that, but it had her name on it. That changed everything.

As he stood there, oblivious to everyone else and wondering how he could secretly slip the card into her hand, she walked right up and gave him a card! She caught him off guard; it wasn't supposed to happen like that! Then, she started to disappear, blending into the wave of students swirling right and left into classrooms.

NO! NO! NO! He dashed after her. She had just joined her girlfriends when he blurted out her name. She turned, and he said, "Here!" as he thrust the card into her hand. For an instant, everything was silent. Then came his worst nightmare; he heard her friends giggle. Out of control, he turned red. His heart raced, and he couldn't remember if he was breathing in or breathing out. He just froze.

Peggy sweetly replied, "Thanks, Jim Brown." She smiled. Once again, he melted back to being normal.

He could hardly remember the rest of the day; it was a blur. At lunch, he snuck away to a quiet corner and opened the envelope she had given him. It was a homemade card—a red heart glued on to a white doily. In her perfect penmanship, she had written,

"Be My Valentine! Love, Peggy."

Could he be so lucky? He tucked her card carefully into his wallet to keep it there forever.

VI

THAT NIGHT, JIM BROWN LAY ON HIS BED, TOSSING AND TURNING. IT wasn't that the mattress was lumpy, though Bill had certainly broken it in after his years of snoring there. He even enjoyed the luxury of stretching out and filling all four corners of the double bed. And by now, he had adjusted to the new room. Even after the first night, Harold had settled into his new domain.

It was thoughts of Peggy, a mixture of dreams and uncertainties, and thoughts of Bill, his brother: the one with the smirky smile, the wizened wink, and the silent body language that spoke volumes. He was gone, and Jim Brown wondered if he'd ever adjust to that.

He needed to sort things out, and the only place he could find answers was fishing. He closed his eyes and slowly waited for the sun to rise.

An hour later, he was walking down the stairs to the kitchen. He saw the light on and knew his dad was up and getting ready for work. Many of the officers thought he slept in his office because he was always there when they arrived and no one ever saw him leave.

As he entered, his dad raised his head and nodded to Jim Brown, acknowledging his presence.

"Fishing," Jim Brown blurted out to the unspoken question, knowing the one word was sufficient. With that, his father ate the last bite of toast and strawberry jam, picked up his hat, and headed to the door.

"Be careful," he called.

"Always!" responded Jim Brown, as the door quietly closed behind his father. He grabbed a quick bite to eat and dashed off a note to his mother. It read, *"Fishing. JB"*—the one word was good enough for her, too. After he tossed some leftover fried chicken into a brown paper bag with some cheese crackers and peanut butter for good measure, he filled a thermos with cold tap water. Then, he strolled over to the back door, picked up his fishing pole, which was leaning in the corner, and took the small bucket on the floor next to it for catching minnows for bait. Soon, he found himself walking in his dad's footprints. He headed to the New River—not far, he knew, from where Ole Mikey stored his flat-bottom boat just beyond the bend. Ole Mikey didn't mind if friends, and even a few acquaintances, borrowed his boat, as long as they returned it as they found it. If not, there would be hell to pay. Ole Mikey had eyes everywhere and friends in strange places.

When Jim Brown arrived at the riverbank, he held his breath and said a prayer, hoping he had arrived early enough and would find the boat tied up as planned. He turned left, walked another hundred yards, and let out a sigh of relief. The boat was hidden well, but it was there. He walked over, gently turned the boat right-side up, and checked for leaks and lazy critters seeking sanctuary. He tossed his pole, the bucket, and sack lunch into the boat and eased it into the water. Big enough to carry two, Jim Brown stretched out and had no trouble filling the open space. Looking up into the sky, he could see wispy clouds and the morning moon. A slight breeze appeared; it was a perfect day for being on the river.

He was glad to be alone. Usually, his friends joined him, and they would share jokes and even go skinny dipping, but Jim Brown often preferred to be alone. He knew if Marty were here, he would be trying to stand up and rock the boat. Even worse, if Deke had joined him, after eating everything in sight, it would be a nonstop, "Are you ready to go back? Are you ready to go home? Do you have anything else to eat?" No, this was the ideal place to sort out his life.

He knew Bill was gone. Training camp didn't sound too inviting, but it was the beginning of a new chapter in Bill's life, his biggest adventure yet. Jim Brown just wished he could be a part of it. On the other hand, there was still so much for him to do here … and there was Harold.

After catching a bucket of minnows, he set the bait and dropped his line. As he sat back, his thoughts and the boat drifted where they would.

Suddenly, he heard splashing and strange sounds. He looked up and focused forty yards ahead, off to the left. He shook his head and strained to make out what the ruckus was about. Sure enough, there was an otter and an alligator in real-life combat, a death struggle, and the otter seemed to be winning! The boat drifted closer, and Jim Brown sized the gator at four, four and a half feet. The otter was a good size, but … he sunk his teeth into the gator's snout, and the gator was not happy. They rolled together, splashing and struggling to break free. Once they broke loose, the gator slowly, with determination, swam away, while the otter kept a steady eye on him just in case he was trying to deceive him and return for a surprise attack.

Jim Brown smiled and called, "Good job, fella!" Simultaneously, he realized the boat had floated significantly closer to the scene. The otter noticed the new intruder, too, and began to swim closer and closer to the boat.

Initially, Jim Brown wasn't concerned, but he was surprised by this impromptu visit. Otters were usually reclusive. Maybe, he thought, after that battle, the otter just wanted to rest, or perhaps he was curious and could smell Jim Brown's lunch, or maybe he was coming to receive a reward for a fight well fought. Closer and closer, the otter paddled. Mesmerizing, his eyes locked on to Jim Brown's. Before he knew it, the otter had climbed aboard. Jim Brown reached for the paddle, just to establish some boundaries, when suddenly the otter lunged and sank his teeth into his upper arm!

"What the heck!" he cried out, but the otter had already released his bite and slithered back into the murky waters, along with his sack lunch.

"Good riddance!" Jim Brown called as he shook the paddle at the escaping rascal. For a moment, the otter turned, as if considering whether this opponent needed another lesson to keep his distance, but then he turned and continued on his way.

Jim Brown scoured the river for the gator. He now held him in great sympathy, but he was nowhere to be seen. He began to paddle in the direction of the launch sight. His revelry was over, his fishing done. He realized his arm hurt, and a circle of blood was beginning to appear on his shirt.

When he arrived home, he found his mother in the kitchen experimenting with a new casserole. It was something he knew his father—a meat-and-potato man—would not care for, though his mom would never know unless Jim Brown dropped a subtle hint. In this case, he strongly suspected Harold would speak loudly for them all. "Yuck!"

"You're home early!" she said, as she continued whipping her egg whites. When she glanced up, she saw the blood on his sleeve and swooned! Jim Brown caught her just in time and placed her in a chair. "My goodness! What happened?"

"Well," began Jim Brown, "there was this gator…"

"A gator!" and a horrified expression covered her face as she reached for his sleeve, expecting to see his arm ripped apart. In a continuous motion, she reached for the phone to call his father.

"No! No! Mom, I'm OK!" he smiled. "This is from the otter!"

"The otter! I am calling your father! NOW!" and she did. His father was at the door in less than ten minutes.

"Son, what happened!"

Jim Brown retold the story while his mother was on the phone with Dr. Foley at the prison hospital.

"Dr. Foley said to bring him right over."

"Now, Eve, you should have called Doc Adams!"

"I know, I know. But this is different. He needs care immediately! And when I told Dr. Foley about the gator and a rabid otter, well, he said to bring him right over. That he had to see this for himself!"

Exasperated, his father sighed. "Now, Eve, no one said anything about a rabid otter. It was probably a mother protecting her den."

"I know a rabid otter when I hear it!"

Shaking his head, as there was nothing left to be said, he loaded a protesting son into his car and drove to the prison infirmary.

When they returned an hour later, Jim Brown had a white bandage on his arm and a sickly green expression on his face. His father explained that even though it was more likely the otter was protecting his territory, they should not take any chances. Jim Brown was prescribed the series of inoculations to prevent rabies. He had received the first three injections today. Then, he would require two tomorrow and the day after. Finally, he would receive one shot each day for eighteen days, twenty-five shots in all.

Jim Brown turned greener as he listened to his father. His mother collapsed into a chair. "Could you write that down for me?" she whispered.

"Doc Foley already has," and he handed her the prescription. "Could have been worse. Doc Foley said they used to cut a large chunk of flesh from around the bite and cauterize the wound—and that didn't always work. The victim would start foaming at the mouth just like a dog." He smiled at Eve, waiting for her reaction.

"I think I would like to lie down now," Jim Brown quietly announced, as he realized his father's attention had turned to his mother. Not thinking anyone would notice, he turned toward the stairs, took hold of the banister to steady himself, and slowly, stair by stair, worked his way to the second floor.

However, as nothing escaped his mother's eye—especially when it came to her boys—she called after him, "I'll be up in a little while with some greens and ham on biscuits!"

Jim Brown hesitated and smiled; food was a cure-all, and she knew their favorites. "That sounds swell, but I'm really not too hungry. My stomach is all in knots."

"It will take a while. And I'm sure you'll be hungry." She then turned to her husband and whispered, "See! I know he can't be well! Do you think he will start foaming at the mouth?"

"Now, Eve, just give him some time." As they walked to the kitchen, in conspiratorial tones, his father whispered, "I just thought you might want to know. The doctor gave him the shots in his abdominal wall—his stomach."

Eve came to an abrupt stop and looked into her husband's eyes, as her own filled with tears. "He'll be fine," he continued, as he put his arm around her waist. The kitchen door swung open. "You know, those greens and ham and biscuits sound mighty good to me…" He smiled. Then, they silently disappeared into the kitchen.

Jim Brown made it to his bedroom and collapsed on the bed. "Will he start foaming?" his mother's words had floated up the stairs. *What would my friends think?* he wondered. *Would the girls scream in terror? Of course, that wasn't terribly important unless it was Peggy Tilley. She wouldn't run away. She might even feel sorry for me.* Then he realized how his buddies would react. "Hey, Jim Brown, you 'otter' not go fishin' with otters; you 'otter' go fishing with us!" Yeah, he was in for it. What would Bill do?

Just then there was a light knock at the door, and Harold peaked in. "What's wrong, Jim Brown? Mom says you're foaming!"

"Oh, no!" he groaned. "Come on in, Harold, and I'll tell you what really happened."

After he finished offering several versions of the gator battle, the otter bite, and the shots, Harold was satisfied and slipped out of the room. About that time, his mother appeared with a tray filled with hot biscuits and ham and greens. Surprised, he found he really was hungry. Then, he remembered that damn otter had taken his lunch! He broke into a smile, as his mother placed the tray in his lap. She responded with a kiss, the ultimate cure-all.

Just as he finished the last forkful of greens, his father stuck his head in. Jim Brown noticed a few tell-tale crumbs on his shirt. "How are you doing?" his father asked, "Want me to take your plate? Do you need a refill? Your mother's made enough to feed an army. You know, I picked up some pain pills if you need them…"

Jim Brown smiled and happily surrendered the empty plate to his father. "No, I'm fine. I think I just need a little more rest."

His dad replied with a silent, understanding nod and quietly closed the door as he left.

VII

THE NEXT DAY, THE WORLD GASPED. THE HEADLINES ANNOUNCED THE
British had lost Singapore to the Japanese. And two weeks later, Florida was
stunned when a German U-boat sank the *Pan Massachusetts*, an oil tanker,
less than twenty miles off her shoreline.

Yes, war had arrived in Jim Brown's backyard.

The Godwins got most of their news from the *Bradford County Telegraph*,
a weekly publication. It was a race to see who would read it first, and usually
it was his father. He was the fastest reader, concentrating on the front page
for local news, page two for news on the war (supplied by official government reports direct from Washington, D.C.), and then he'd skim the other
pages for national news that was sprinkled throughout. If time permitted,
he casually glanced through the classified section.

His mother took the longest to read and was the most destructive, as
she cut out articles of interest. Like his father, there was a routine. First,
she would read the society section, looking for her name, which was frequently mentioned for hosting parties (which she loved), or placing first at
bridge gatherings or canasta parties. Snip, snip. Rev. Harper had his weekly
column, "The Six-inch Sermon," which every good Christian woman read.
That was followed by "Kathleen Norris Says"—a gossipy column about
what proper young ladies should or shouldn't do. There was always something to debate with her friends. Then there was "On the Feminine Side,"
with articles on fashion, recipes, and child-rearing. The recipes were helpful,
particularly with rationing and highlighting new products. Though she had

always been able to stretch a meal, his mother did have a difficult time cutting sugar. No one could beat her chicken salad, though several variations appeared. She agreed dressing attractively and in bright colors was her patriotic duty to raise the national morale, but when they suggested making dresses from potato sacks and swimsuits from shower curtains, well, in her mind, they crossed a line. Likewise, Catherine Conrad Edwards's column on parenting was a bit stodgy. She wondered if she had any children and kept thinking that one day, she would write to the editor and offer to take over that column—wouldn't that make the ladies of Starke sit up straight! Finally, she would settle back and enjoy whatever book was being serialized. Currently, James Cain's *Two Can Sing* was featured.

Bill was a fan of the *Gainesville Sun*. It had better news and a sports section—not to mention comics, and who would miss *Dick Tracy* or *The Phantom*! But he did glance at the high school section to stay alert on the gossip. Unlike his mother, he'd rather not see his name in print, for better or for worse. He was just a rather private person.

That just left Jim Brown and Harold. Harold liked the paper for making pirate hats and covering the floor so he could paint masterpieces—he wasn't up to reading yet, so he didn't have a preference.

Jim Brown, on the other hand, liked the short articles written by Dale Carnegie who contributed biographies of famous men: Lincoln, Edison, Ben Franklin, and General Lee. He wrote stories about how mistakes can lead to opportunities, how being courteous can open doors, and how taking risks can make millions.

This week, Mr. Carnegie wrote about a young man who lived in a small village in Switzerland and worked in an alpine hotel. One winter, just as a group of visitors were due to arrive, the heating went out. The manager didn't know what to do, but this kid stood up and said he could handle the crisis. The manager had nothing to lose. At his direction, the employees immediately began placing logs in the fireplace—soon they were crackling, and a welcoming fire was burning bright. Then he heated bricks and put them under the table to keep the guests' feet warm. He supervised making a hearty stew, just like his mother's, to warm their insides. The evening was such a success that the young man was instantly promoted. Before long, an opportunity came to open a chain of his own hotels, and he jumped at it. His name was Ritz.

Jim Brown could relate to them. He could solve problems. He could take advantage of opportunities, if only they would come his way. He wondered how could he find opportunities in Starke. Yes, those stories could really inspire a fellow.

As the war continued to escalate, to the surprise of all—especially Jim Brown and his friends—the school became a refuge. It was stable—the doors opened on time; the classes went on as expected; and friends were there. Teachers tried to answer questions that adults either wouldn't or couldn't. How could the world be at war? Who are the Germans? Why did the Japanese attack Pearl Harbor?

His teacher, Miss Lester, did her best, providing answers or directing the class to the set of encyclopedias in the classroom. She scheduled study halls in the library to search for historical clues and cultural identities.

One day, when pandemonium reigned, whether out of desperation or inspiration, Miss Lester raised her hands, closed her eyes, and waited until the room calmed down.

She opened her eyes, placed the palms of her hands on her desk, leaned forward, and slowly looked each student in the eye. A smile spread across her face, and she asked, "Aren't you tired of talking about war?" She continued to engage each student; their eyes still locked on her. "What if we talk about peace?"

As if by magic, the tension in the room subsided. The students' heads began to nod in agreement, as new questions formed in their minds. *Where is she going with this? How do you define peace? When is lunch?*

"Have you heard of Utopia?" She paused. The class remained quiet, waiting for clues. No one wanted to give a wrong answer; no one wanted to be first—not yet.

"Utopia," she began in an encouraging tone, "is an imaginary island created by Sir Thomas More, an English lawyer, the Lord High Chancellor to King Henry VIII in 1516. Eventually, he was declared a saint."

"A saint, why?" asked a voice from the back of the room.

"Well," Miss Lester thought, hoping to make her answer complete but concise. "He stood up for God over king, and he got his head chopped off."

"The English thought that was wrong?" cried a chorus of girls.

"Well, at the time…"

"Was he guillotined?" interrupted Daryl Wilson.

"Actually, the French used the guillotine—and that was years later; the English used a sword or axe."

A collective "Oooooooooo" rose from the class.

Realizing they were rapidly going off course, Miss Lester interjected, "If anyone would like to volunteer to write a report for the class on this subject," she paused and looked around.

Frank Foley considered the challenge; he already knew the answer, but he felt it wiser to stay silent and see what else Miss Lester had in store.

"I thought not. Then, let's get back to Sir Thomas More's story." Again, she paused to let them collect their thoughts. Noses scrunched up. Side glances to friends followed by mutual shrugs told her to continue. "It comes from the Greek meaning 'No Where.' It is an ideal vision of what the world could be. You've heard of Plato's Republic and his island of Atlantis? That was another dream of a harmonious society. Even the United States began with experimental communities hoping to find a better life. Our Great Seal includes the words 'Novus Ordo Seclorum' which means…?"

A hand flew up, and someone shouted, "A New Order of the Ages!"

"Yes!" Miss Lester beamed. "I want each of you to design a utopia and build a shadowbox that will display your ideas."

A collective groan went up.

"Oh, come on! You have many examples to pull from. You might want to consider the Native Americans." Suddenly Jim Brown perked up. Not that he was curious about Native Americans, but it was a sign that she was going off script. Miss Lester was very specific about history and felt it sinful not to teach facts, the truths of the past. She was called before the school board to justify her methods, and boy, did they get a lesson.

Indians live in India; the Native Americans were never Indians. Yes, Columbus thought he had reached the Orient, but that mistake was quickly corrected. The New World was inhabited by people who were identified by their own culture and language. There were the Dine—the People; the Sioux—the Enemy; the Ninuog—the Human; and the Lenni Lenape—the Real Men, to name a few. The parents argued she was liberal; the school board suggested progressive; the students loved her.

"Think of them. They built their communities from what Mother Earth provided. The Plains Tribes built portable tepees made from buffalo hides. The Northwestern clans built log houses because trees were plentiful. The Northeastern inhabitants made wigwams, and the Apache made similar dome huts, wickiups, with bendable twigs tied with yucca plants and stuffed with grass. Then you have the Pueblos, who built adobe villages with sand blocks, and the Inuit, who made igloos from ice. Such diversity! How clever! And let's not forget here in Florida, the Calusa—the Fierce People—who built their homes on stilts to keep them dry and covered the roofs with palmetto leaves because they were plentiful. They left the sides open so the winds could blow through," she paused and smiled, as she could see the cogs begin to turn in their minds. "Did you know they were the first to use seashells for tools and decorations?" she queried.

"The early colonists, like the Pilgrims and Puritans, and, later, the Shakers and Mormons, built societies based on religious principles. Think of military forts, the prison farm—communities brought together by their vocations. Even today, entrepreneurs are still trying to build ideal cities for their workers; a happy worker is a loyal, productive worker."

Lillian Morhard raised her hand and asked, "That makes sense, Miss Lester, but I can't think of anyone."

"Really?" Miss Lester grinned and everyone knew Lillian was about to be zinged. "Did anyone have a Hershey bar this week?" Several hands flew up. "Well," she continued, "Mr. Hershey considers all his employees as family, and because he cares about them, he is trying to build a perfect city for their families. He began with individual homes and schools with school busses, a church, a museum, and, what you all would love, an amusement park. Those buildings were the foundation of his town. The factory itself is a part of the town, and Mr. Hershey's home is not an estate miles away. He lives in High Point, a beautiful manor next door to the factory.

"During the Great Depression, Mr. Hershey learned his managers had hired a steam shovel to speed the building of a new hotel. Proudly, the managers announced how much money they were saving because the shovel could do the work of a dozen men. Mr. Hershey asked what happened to the men, and he was told they were let go. Horrified, he ordered the manager to release the steam shovel and rehire the workers. Dumbfounded, the managers followed his orders. Mr. Hershey explained the people were more important. They needed those jobs to provide food and shelter for their families."

The class gave a collective, "WOW!"

"Wish I were his son," someone sighed.

"Sadly, Mr. Hershey doesn't have any children, but he did build an orphanage for boys whose fathers died in coal mining accidents in Pennsylvania." Another "WOW!" filled the classroom. "Right now, Mr. Hershey is trying to create a special, high-calorie chocolate bar for our troops." Heads began to shake in disbelief.

"All right, getting back to your assignment. Consider how your environment affects your culture. With all the diversity, is there a way to blend and yet be individual? How do you define happiness? Consider, could it be to have what you want and to want what you have? You might also weigh in what you don't want: for example, is your utopia a concrete jungle, a police state, a land without life, liberty and the pursuit of happiness?"

The class was silent. Their minds were spinning. The bell rang for lunch.

VIII

AS THE CLASS POURED INTO THE HALL, THE GUYS HUDDLED OUTSIDE the classroom to swap ideas—if anyone had one to share. Denise Edwards barged into the group of guys, "I know exactly what my utopia will be." Without pausing or even looking to see if anyone cared, she confidently continued, "A world of lollipop flowers, milk chocolate streams, and homes made of gingerbread." Then she smiled and looked for agreement; the boys were speechless.

Jim Brown whispered to Wayne Rivers, "Wasn't that the plan of the Wicked Witch?" They both started to snicker.

Deke Roberts broke the silence, "What in the world? Milk chocolate doesn't flow from the ground, and lollipops don't grow like flowers!"

Denise exploded, "Why Deke Roberts, didn't you listen at all? Utopia— No Where! Fantasy! It isn't supposed to be real." She huffed and stood waiting for an apology, which wasn't on the tip of Deke's tongue. "Besides, unbelievers like you would not be welcomed."

She twirled around and started to walk away when Deke called, "But Denise, who is going to take the lollipop paddle and row you in your peanut-brittle boat through the fizzy rapids, under the grape Nehi Falls to the secret lemonade lagoon?" The guys were ready to convulse in laughter and egged him on. "And, and give you his cotton candy jacket to keep you warm as you climb the ice cream Alps?" Deke turned and gave the guys a big smile and an OK sign.

Denise stopped in her tracks and whirled around, her petticoat swirling out to display her pretty legs. "You do understand! I just knew you would!" she said bubbly, as her eyes twinkled in delight. "Maybe I will even make you King of Edwardom!"

Deke blushed, as she took his arm and whispered as they walked away, "Do you think you could help me build my diorama…?" Deke gave an involuntary nod and continued walking arm in arm as if on clouds.

The guys rolled their eyes and said in unison, "Hook, line, and sinker!" They broke into laughter and tears, not knowing if they were crying for joy or in sympathy.

"He does know she's using him, right?" Jim Brown thought out loud.

"Come on, J.B.," answered Frank Foley. "He's been trying to get her attention since fifth grade. Don't burst his bubble!"

"But maybe we should just warn him," murmured Jim Brown.

"Warn him!" chuckled Wayne. "And this coming from the man who did her math homework last week!"

"What! Hey, wait! She just asked me to tutor her!"

"Ri-i-i-ight!" they all replied.

Jim Brown screwed up his face as the memory formed. Then, he slammed the palm of his hand onto his forehead. "Oh, NO! I did do every problem, didn't I?"

As they continued down the corridor to the lunchroom, they considered seriously how they would approach their projects. Wayne described a sports world; after all, what could be more ideal?

Frank proposed a Shangri-La, high in the mountains and dedicated to peace where men would solve world problems. The earth would provide all their necessities. Like the Garden of Eden, nothing could go wrong.

"What about girls?" Jim Brown asked.

"They're a distraction," he shot back.

"Yeah? Well, after a generation, your village and all its advancements will disappear."

"What-t-t-t?" Frank's face dropped as he considered the repercussions. Then, as if a beam of light suddenly broke through the ceiling and landed on his face, he glowed—not necessarily a good sign as his close friends had learned.

Jim Brown rolled his eyes and spoke one dangerous word, as he had a strong suspicion that the answer to that one innocent word would take them on a roller coaster ride, "What?"

"I'll build a beach resort just for procreating," he smugly replied. "I can use the Calusa model ... maybe I'll make it a nudist colony." He grinned.

"Frank, really?" cried Jim Brown, throwing his hands up in desperation. "First you plan a monastic commune where women are not invited, and then you create a nudist colony where I don't think anyone would come—especially girls, even if you did include them. We can't even get them to hold our hands!"

"You are obviously not a man of vision. Marketing is the answer," he smugly replied.

"Well, swell," Jim Brown replied, "And just how are you going to market this idea to Miss Lester?"

Without skipping a beat, he confidently said, "Why, I'll hire her as the head concierge!" With that, he dapperly turned on his heels and strolled, whistling down the corridor. Jim Brown stood dumbfounded. Sometimes, he didn't know if Frank was serious or just joking, and this was one of them.

Jim Brown's thoughts returned to his own project. He was bursting with ideas for a utopia on the moon and couldn't wait until he got home that afternoon to put his ideas into action.

When the school bus pulled up to the State Farm, Jim Brown jumped off and bounded up to his house. He had reached the attic before the back door slammed shut. Without hesitation, he pushed through stacks of books and old clothes. He was startled by an old cobb web, which entangled itself around his face. He checked to make sure the owner wasn't attached, and then proceeded to the back, right-hand corner where Bill had dumped his life-defining treasures, waiting to be reclaimed when he returned.

Jim Brown didn't think Bill would mind this intrusion. As a matter of fact, if he were home, he would probably insist and even, accidentally, take over the project; it was right up his alley. He hoped Bill might inspire him from the other side of the world, mind-melding, as brothers can do, or by pulling some long-forgotten memory pressed into the folds of his brain, waiting for a moment like this to come to life.

As if his thoughts had travelled across space and time, his eyes lost no time spotting his quarry—Bill's telescope! He worked his way through the trunks and boxes to capture his prey and carry it down to the back porch, where he would set it up facing east.

He couldn't wait until twilight. Everything was falling into place. The sky was clear, the moon was approaching its full stage, and he was sure the lenses would be clean; Bill took great care of his possessions. His thoughts drifted over what he might find. If the moon were made of cheese, as storytellers said, it sure would make things easy—mac 'n cheese, cheese pizza, grilled cheese sandwiches, cherry cheesecake—his city would be well-fed!

He couldn't remember what they had for dinner, but he wolfed it down and dashed outside. Everything was perfect! He put his eye on the viewing lens, focused, and saw the moon. It was unbelievable! He forgot all about the diorama and, in the moment, was mesmerized by the moon itself. The surface reminded him of his mother's pie crust, with gentle lumps puffing up over the surface and craters, probably made from meteor impacts. He wondered how he could survey the surface, whether a compass would work on the moon.

"Jim Brown!" called Harold, breaking his moon trance.

"Not now, Harold; I'm doing homework!" he replied.

There was no response. *That's unusual*, he thought but went no further. He returned his focus to the school assignment.

The moon's craters and plains definitely did not resemble cheese, a slight, though not unexpected, setback. He then wondered about the far side of the moon, the dark side, the never-seen mystery. Bill had explained, using a basketball and a baseball, how the moon rotated ever so slowly as it went around the Earth, so the same side was always turned in our direction. It was aggravating not to see if there were frozen seas or boiling volcanos, but it also meant he was free to fill in the blanks with his imagination. Forget Denise's chocolate streams and ice cream Alps; his diorama would be filled with exotic animals!

There could be dinosaurs thrown from Earth when a meteor crashed, sending eggs and rocks flying through space and landing on the moon. They survived and evolved over the centuries like Darwin proposed. They could be blue to accommodate the lack of light and oxygen, and they would have fur to protect them from the cold. This was actually fun, as each problem challenged his intellect and imagination. Jim Brown leaned back from the telescope. He was not quite sure how this amazing, uncharted moonscape could be tamed into a utopia. He peered again into the lens to study whatever was available.

Though bright and accessible, the moon was not giving up her secrets. Maybe, he considered, it was so hot, creatures lived beneath the surface in caves and subterranean vaults filled with precious stones hanging from stalactites and imbedded in towering stalagmites. Fresh water streams lazily flowed through the terraces while light and fresh air came from portals, opening to the surface.

While this all seemed to have a certain credence, he suddenly remembered what Doc Adams had once told him. "The heart of the Hippocratic Oath was 'To do no harm.'" So, he wondered, how would his society blend with the "Lunarians" who already called the moon home? He wouldn't want to destroy or impede a developing community in the name of science. He knew how sad Miss Lester felt when she explained that so much was lost or stolen from the Native American cultures by invading Europeans. She would not like that. What if, after all these years, the Lunarians had been watching us, and, perhaps, they were more advanced? He decided to simplify his plan. He would build his utopia on the moon's surface a new society, not to assimilate or conquer but rather to observe and discover from afar.

He began to consider the immediate needs of his new colony. He envisioned his society under a transparent dome to create and maintain a healthy atmosphere. The water would be recycled, as there did not appear to be rivers or oceans on the moon. They were in space, and the key to survival would be to waste not and want not.

His first proposal was to replace schools with lessons that would be streamed into your mind while you slept, but then he realized there would be no debating, no free thinking, no creativity! He quickly flipped to Plan B: Miss Lester would head the department of education. She'd jump at the idea, and it would save her from being Frank's concierge ... she would be perfect, and that was what a utopia was all about.

Once again, his project was back on track! Then, just as unexpectedly, the project derailed, and his heart sank. He remembered a conversation with his friend Frank. Frank explained that alcohol was nothing but the waste product of yeast. Yeast ate sugar, which then was converted to alcohol until their whole environment became polluted and killed the yeast—ending the production. Jim Brown never got over the thought that booze was nothing more than yeast poop, but now he had to consider how this construct might repeat in his city in a bottle. His dream turned into a nightmare. Not only could they destroy themselves, but there would be no wind to fly kites, no rivers to spawn fish. It would take decades for trees to grow, if they could, which meant there would be no new oxygen, no apples, no climbing.

He returned to his initial plan, creating his ideal city underground. However, the sun might never touch their faces, and stars would remain mysteries. And, of course, if there was life, he would be back interfering with the Lunarian culture! It was not looking good. Miss Lester did mention fantasy, so perhaps he didn't have to solve all the problems.

He then began to rub his chin and brushed against a new whisker. Unconsciously, he pulled at the stub as he pondered, like Mr. Hershey, what else his utopia required: a library, a gymnasium, a multi-purpose community hall for village meetings, concerts, dances and movies. Then he added onto his mental list, much to his surprise, a church. Just like the Pilgrims, church attendance would be mandatory; God would be prominent in his utopia. Though he had not quite figured out "this God thing," he knew he did believe, and if a community were to exist in space, surely, they would need a God to guide them and to trust in. No one would ever dare disagree. He certainly would not want to try. The universe would be a lonely place without God. Once again, he sighed; his lunar utopia was becoming quite complicated.

Out of nowhere, a new idea began to come into focus. The cogs in his brain began to whirl as ideas churned out, one after the other. No one would believe it! He had his answer; it was obvious. The answer was Starke!

Starke was his utopia! It provided everything he wanted. Miss Lester could still teach; Kingsley Lake was just down the road with deer trails and fishing holes; his friends were here. Together they could design an amusement park—maybe one based on the moon with rocket rides, moon rock candy, and moon cave mazes.

His mind came to a halt when a vision of Peggy Tilley appeared—and wherever she was, there was Heaven—but that was a detail he would keep to himself. Yes, Peggy Tilley, not transported to the moon looking down on the Earth, but Peggy Tilley, here in Starke, holding his hand and gazing at the moon as it ought to be. God had already created utopia right before his eyes!

For a moment, he let his mind drift and imagined holding Peggy's hand, slipping his arm around her trim waist, and pulling her close for that first kiss! Then ... Harold appeared at the door. As if on cue, he heard him shout his name. Try as he might, he could not recapture Peggy's image. He surrendered and dutifully turned his attention to his little brother. "What's up?"

Harold smiled. "You done yet? Can I look?"

"Sure." Jim Brown lifted him up and helped him adjust the lens.

"Wow! Where'd you get this?"

It was Jim Brown's turn to smile. "It's Bill's. Come on, Harold. I have to put this away for now. Besides, I think it's time I get you ready for bed."

"Really?"

"Really." Mission accomplished. Project designed. As he lugged the telescope back upstairs with Harold in tow, he dreamed that, someday, he could invite Peggy to see the moon through the telescope ... or, as he brought himself back to reality, the gang might really have fun with it, too.

He carefully tucked Harold into bed and then returned to his room. In the back of his closet, he secured the telescope in the corner and then picked up an empty shoebox Bill had left behind. "Thanks, Bill," he whispered. With paste, crayons, popsicle sticks, and paper, he went to work on his diorama. He found an old mirror that was perfect for a lake, and he fashioned an alligator out of clay to lazily rest on the bank. Utopia was completed in no time.

As he lay down to go to sleep, the moonbeams magically streamed through his window. He could focus on the moon's craters and mountains. It seemed so desolate—so lonely. He actually felt in his heart that God was not there. It dawned on him that God made the moon to protect the Earth, to pull the tides and put love in our hearts. God thought of everything. The moon was the Earth's guardian.

Drifting off to sleep, he felt confident that his diorama would be the best. It met all the criteria, and it had a twist that would shock everyone. His artwork, he preferred to think of it as his construction, was perfect, or at least up to his standards. Yup, his decision was right. Utopia was right before his eyes. "Want what you have and have what you want"; that was what Miss Lester said. Some might disagree with him, but he was smart enough to see beyond their limited visions. Starke was a great place to dream and to make dreams come true. Still, maybe someday, he could visit the moon ... and that was the last thought he had until the sun rose.

IX

THE FIRST WEEK IN MARCH, JIM

Brown saw Hannah Nelson wandering aimlessly in the dirt parking lot outside the school. She was a tiny thing, a few years younger than he, and strangely, in these familiar surroundings, she looked very lost.

"Hey, Hannah," he called.

"Something wrong?"

She looked up. Her large, soulful brown eyes, glistening with tears, locked on him. She walked over. When she was just inches away, her tiny voice whispered, "My brother ... Brendan!" Then her small arms wrapped around his waist, as she buried her head in his stomach and began to cry uncontrollably.

Jim Brown was shocked. His hands flew up, and he went to step back, but then he knew. He knew Brendan. He knew Brendan had joined the army right out of high school two years ago.

And he knew, without words, that Brendan was not coming home. He slowly lowered his arms and placed them around Hannah's frail, little body, letting her cry her heart out.

He wanted to say something, but again, there were no words. He couldn't say everything would be all right because he understood nothing would ever be the same. He tried to think what his folks would say, but his mind went blank. Then he wondered what comfort Pastor Adkins would offer, and he realized his faith wasn't strong enough to mend her heart. So, he just stood there and held her until her small frame stopped sobbing. Hannah looked up, her eyes still shining with tears, and said, "Thanks, Jim Brown." She turned, lifted her little chin, and courageously walked toward the school doors. Soon, she was lost in the mob of students rushing to class.

Jim Brown couldn't move. He felt as if his feet were cemented to the ground. Then, he heard the tardy bell ring and made a mad dash to class. As he walked into the room, he saw Miss Rose, a substitute teacher; like her name, she was pretty, but covered with thorns. She was a stickler for rules; she never asked questions. She always carried a stack of tardy slips in her pocket, ready for such occasions. Even before he slid into his desk, the slip was pressed into his hand.

For the next few minutes, he couldn't concentrate. He couldn't hear what Miss Rose was saying. He only thought of Hannah and thought it could have been Bill. What if it had been Bill? He could never hear of another soldier's death without making a personal connection. He looked at the tardy slip and smiled; this one was worth it.

Tuesday was St. Patrick's Day, a day that totally transformed Frank Foley into a leprechaun. He arrived at school in a top hat and green vest, carrying his grandfather's shillelagh, a sturdy walking stick—good for beating misbehaving ne'er-do-wells or for support—which was promptly confiscated until the end of the school day. Of course, on this day—and only this day—he signed his papers with an "O." He explained that when his relatives came over on the "Coffin Bridge," there were so many that the registrar "dropped the O's" in the last names in the ocean for alphabetical convenience—small price, at least to some, for citizenship.

Miss Lester unintentionally turned the class over to Frank, as he shared Irish-American history and their contributions. He proudly pointed out that there were more Irish slaves than any other racial group in the seventeenth century. Because the Irish were allies with Spain, the Brits sold many Irishmen into slavery after they sank the Spanish Armada to avoid a Catholic revolt. Eight Irishmen signed the Declaration of Independence, and four signed the Constitution. His ancestors fought valiantly in the Civil War, most notably, the Immovable Fighting 69th of Pennsylvania, who stopped Pickett's Charge at Gettysburg. Matthew Brady, known for his photographs documenting the war, was also Irish. Irishmen gave their lives laying railroad tracks, digging canals, and working in coal mines. Of course, they could be credited with building many a still and drinking the whiskey, too; so much so that the weekend roundups of the drunken workers were placed in "paddy wagons"—so named for those devoted to St. Patrick. Being a clever group, the lads soon learned if you can't beat 'em, join 'em, and they became the foundation of the police force in many major cities. Signs were posted everywhere, "Irishmen and dogs need not apply!" But they showed up and earned their place in America.

"So, we celebrate this day with pride and invite you all to join us. Stand up. Serve. Be American!" Frank concluded. The class burst into applause, and Frank gave a ceremonious bow.

Miss Lester was actually amazed to hear what Frank said and made note to double-check some points. But all in all, Frank was beaming, and Miss Lester took pride in his stance.

Jim Brown, on the other hand, though proud to think there was some Irish blood in his veins, didn't like wearing green but hated getting pinched. He got around the first problem because he could point to his eyes, which were green. Problem solved. Word got around that it was not a good idea to even think, let alone try, to pinch him. Frank learned that the hard way.

As everyone celebrated the day in their own way, few knew that across the state, a top-secret mission was being deployed to the Pacific, to parts unknown. Nothing more would be heard for a month.

On the twenty-fourth of March, Jim Brown saw Hannah with her friends on the Pratt Street playground. He had thought of Brendan that morning; it would have been his twenty-first birthday. He knew what he had to do. With resolve, he marched over to the playground, straight to Hannah, and gave her a bear hug. Without a word, he turned and marched quickly away before anyone could see the tears stream down his cheeks. But he heard Hannah's sweet voice call, "Thanks, Jim Brown." He knew that she knew that he remembered. He smiled to himself and lifted his hand to give an awkward, backward wave.

Later that week, his mother and Mrs. Morhard drove with their kids to Jacksonville; it was an annual event that Jim Brown circled on his calendar, and, originally, he wasn't included.

The purpose of the trip was to buy Easter suits, and Bill's hand-me-downs had always been good enough, until the year came when he caught up to Bill. That Easter, his shirt cuffs hung out from under the jacket sleeves by six inches, and the pants stopped two inches above his ankles.

"Never again!" swore his mother, and he joined the annual trek. Bill had always played down the outing, and Jim Brown wasn't sure if he was trying to protect his feelings or if he was just trying to keep this special trek all to himself! But, from his first experience, Jim Brown was hooked. The drive was long, and the roads were bumpy, but his mother loved to drive and shifted with ease from first to fourth gear before they'd left their driveway. With the windows down and the air blowing against their faces, the car ride felt terrific! It never rained on Jacksonville Day, always sunny and bright.

While talking to Mrs. Morhard, his mother occasionally became distracted and the speedometer tipped over the speed limit. On the times a policeman appeared, they could always trust their mother's smile and innocence to talk her way out of the ticket. Jim Brown and Bill knew there would be a black-and-white soda at Woolworth's counter at the end of the day to bribe them not to mention the incident to their father.

Compared to Starke and Raiford, the two towns bordering the prison, Jacksonville was a metropolis. You could see the latest and greatest of anything, and, sometimes, you might even bump into a celebrity walking down the street! Of course, they did have to try on suits, as their mother exclaimed, "My, how you boys have grown!" She actually made the excursion fun. Jim Brown never got the hang of coming out and modeling the clothes, though his mother did have an eye for style. Once the suits were selected, again, her charm came on. Certainly, she should get a discount; didn't the salesman agree? Usually, he did. Afterward, their mother and Mrs. Morhard would go to the women's section while Jim Brown and Bill would be left to their own devices, promising to meet up in an hour for lunch and then more shopping.

They would make a beeline to the escalator, moving stairs. The first step was always a challenge. After a few false starts, Jim Brown would count to three, close his eyes, take a giant step, and grab for the moving, rubber rail to steady himself as his left foot dragged to catch up with the rest of his body. Then, he would gaze over the department store and sometimes find his mother disappearing into the racks of clothes. After a few trips, the escalator lost some of its novelty. The boys would race up to the second floor two steps at a time. Then, they took on the challenge to go up the down escalator, much to the frustration of the department store manager. Sternly, he explained the dangers and inconvenience to shoppers. Once, he even dared to throw them out of the store, but their mother appeared carrying several shopping bags, so the manager thought twice about evicting the boys.

This was the first time they went to Jacksonville without Bill, and he was left with Harold in tow. It was tough, but he also hoped his mother would take the time to shop for his birthday present, something other than clothes. He did casually mention a shotgun to his father. His mother understood the importance of this birthday wish, but there was a built-in hesitance and a lack of knowledge. He had no idea what she might buy, but his father would know.

After selecting just the right suits, Harold and Jim Brown made a dash to the escalator and onto the toy department: home of basketballs, baseballs, footballs, kick balls, fishing rods and reels, camping gear, board games—a magical, awesome world of fun. Harold picked up a toy truck, while a horse-racing game caught Jim Brown's eye. It was a rectangular metal box with a flywheel and six different colored horses lined up for a race. After carefully winding the wheel with string provided, the player steadied the box and, in a fluid motion, pulled on the string. The box whirled to life as tiny metal beads bounced off the wheel and propelled the horses forward in their lanes. Eventually, one horse crossed the finish line.

Along the racetrack were circles in various colors matching the horses, where bets could be placed with chips, which were also provided. *This had potential,* thought Jim Brown. Why, even Harold might catch on. Time flew by, and Jim Brown found himself dragging a screaming Harold to find their mother.

She found them.

X

ON APRIL 3, THE FAMILY CELEBRATED JIM BROWN'S TWELFTH BIRTHDAY.

Though wages were meager, the employees of the prison had some privileges the town folk didn't. Once a week, freshly picked vegetables and fruit were delivered, as well as bottles of milk from the dairy. Then, once a month, a slab of pork or occasionally beef would appear. Cane syrup, which was also made at the Farm, was seasonally available. Other institutions would send their produce in exchange; for example, Belle Glade would send sugar. It wasn't quite as white and refined as store-bought, but when mixed 50/50 with white sugar, it would make the smoothest fudge. His birthday feast would have all the trimmings.

However, being patriotic, his mother decided to try a recipe for a flourless, sugarless cake the women's club had recommended. Jim Brown screwed up his face as his mother placed the brown blob with candles in front of him. He tried to smile, which actually was effortless because he began to think that the cake resembled a cow pie, and he wondered who would be the first to take a courageous bite. Before they'd finished singing "Happy Birthday," Harold had blown out the candles.

His mother then appeared, with her arms loaded with presents: the usual clothes from relatives, a book from Big Mama, and a board game from Mama were among the gifts. His mother did take the hint about the horse-racing box, but his heart began to sink. Then, his mother pushed a small box in front of him and said, "It's from Bill." She choked back tears and continued, "He gave it to me before he left. He said to tell you it comes with the room

64

and your new responsibilities." With great expectations, he opened the box … and saw a razor. He closed his eyes and the box simultaneously.

His mother smiled and added, "If you have any questions, you know your father has answers."

"Now, Eve, honey," his dad interrupted, as he had been not been a part of the conversation 'til now. "You know the boy can figure this out on his own." Turning to Jim Brown, he added, "The important thing to remember is to have a sharp blade."

As if on cue, his mom smiled and quietly pulled a box of new Gillette double-sided blades and shaving cream from her apron pocket. Then, she bent over and whispered in his ear, "Be careful. Your dad still nicks himself on occasion … if you do, that's what this is for," and she slipped a white, styptic pencil into his hand and kissed the top of his head.

In the midst of this unexpected moment, he didn't notice his father standing in front of him. Their eyes locked. "Son," he began, "turning twelve is a big thing. Societies around the world mark twelve as the beginning of manhood. Why, up north, I'd be giving you your first pair of long pants, and if I were the King of Saudi Arabia, which I'm not, I would be giving you a special curved dagger to wear at your waist."

Jim Brown smiled at that thought of his father wearing flowing, white robes and a "ghutra" secured with an "egal," the cord which wrapped around the ghutra to protect his head from the sun. Anyway, he was quite content with the pocket knife his dad had given him several Christmases earlier.

"Some cultures have tests and physical endurance—which I can tell you sound pretty painful—but you're lucky to be a Godwin here in Starke, because here…" and from out of nowhere, he pulled out a shotgun tied with a red ribbon.

"Mine?" Jim Brown cried out, reaching for the gun.

"Not so fast!" and the gun vanished as quickly as it had appeared. "As I was saying, this gift is a rite of passage and, therefore, comes with responsibility. So, before you accept this shotgun…" and here, his voice became ice-cold, "you must agree to these rules—they must never be broken; otherwise, the gun will disappear. You will have broken a trust between you and me. It would be a disappointment that would take years to mend."

Jim Brown was momentarily shocked. He knew about guns—even Bill had taught him how to fire his—but his father had said he could disappoint him! That's something he could never do! He leaned in and gave his father his full attention.

"One, NEVER, and I mean never, point this gun at a person. Guns maim and kill. This is a hunting gun, and I never want you to have the burden that you accidentally shot another human being.

"Two, NEVER take the safety off until you're about to shoot … and immediately put it back on when you're finished.

"Three, this is a hunting gun. What you shoot, you eat.

"Four, NEVER shoot without purpose. There may be times when you have to kill a creature—if it were rabid or attacking someone—but never shoot a living creature without purpose.

"Five, NEVER put down a loaded gun.

"Six, ALWAYS carry your gun with the muzzle down.

"Seven, if you are climbing over a fence or a fallen tree, if there is a round in the chamber, ALWAYS remove the shell first.

"Eight, ALWAYS unload your shotgun after hunting or target-practicing.

"Nine, despite rule eight, ALWAYS double-check the chamber to make sure that the gun is unloaded before you clean it, and ALWAYS keep your gun clean.

"Now, here are rules you should already know by heart, specifically for dove-hunting.

"Ten, ALWAYS visually know where you are aiming.

"Eleven, DON'T shoot at anything at eye level.

"Twelve, ALWAYS separate from each other when you reach your designated spot in a dove field, or blind and be aware where everyone else is. And finally…

"DO NOT leave your assigned area without making sure others around you know you're moving or leaving."

His dad ended with, "These are not the only rules, but they will prepare you for hunting season, which will be here before you know it." Then he grinned, patted Jim Brown on the back, and finally presented the gun. Eve could see the glistening of a tear in his eye, and she knew he was thinking of Bill and a similar day not many years ago. And, he probably recalled the very day his father had given him his first shotgun; it was one of those things you never forgot.

Yes, thought Jim Brown as he took the gun, *this is the BEST birthday!* The weight was perfect, the length just right, the wood smooth as satin. He began to raise the gun, when he felt a tight grip on his shoulder.

He gave an inaudible ouch, as he automatically turned and was captured by his father's steely eyes and firm voice. "Understand, James Brown, these rules are concrete. You never break them. They are not words you know; they are words you live by."

Jim Brown was stunned. His father never called him by his given name unless he was in trouble or the matter was serious. And he understood the weight of the moment. He locked eyes with his father and, as if giving an oath—which he was—he simply replied, "Yes, sir." That was all he needed to say.

After a brief pause, his dad added, "That shotgun has a pretty powerful recoil. We should probably be together the first few times you take her out."

Jim Brown smiled and said, "I'd like that."

Suddenly, not to be forgotten, Harold yelled out, "Can I hold it?"

Everyone, except Harold, cried back, "No!" And everyone laughed, except Harold.

"Oh," said his father, as if in an after-thought, though Jim Brown knew everything his father said was well calculated. "Here's some light bed reading," and he slipped him a small pamphlet.

Jim Brown smiled and recognized it immediately. He had received a similar publication when his dad had given him his first fishing pole—and that was before he could even read! He knew exactly where it was, in the drawer in the nightstand on the right side of his bed. This pamphlet was "The Official Florida State List of Rules and Regulations for Hunting Seasons."

"By the way," his father paused and waited until he had Jim Brown's total attention, "never loan your gun. Also, under no circumstance will I ever pay any fines that you and your friends may stack up. Never."

"Yes, sir. Understood."

That evening, the family walked to the prison for the annual Easter program, performed by the inmates. This year it was titled "The Shadow of the Cross." One hundred inmates participated in the orchestra and choir, and even more were involved designing the costumes, the stage settings and lighting, and, of course, setting up the refreshments. Even suits for the inmates were made in the prison for this occasion. For a moment, one might forget they were inside prison gates.

There were always risks and complications, but Mr. Godwin knew it was worth the effort for both the prisoners and their family members who attended, as well as the community citizens who ventured to come.

There were so many misconceptions of the penitentiary, and this production gave Mr. Godwin and the prisoners a chance to shine. He was proud of the production. Jim Brown wasn't so happy to be spending his birthday there, but after he settled in, he realized that the choir had talent and was surprised to hear how low the bass singers' voices went. The whole auditorium seemed to vibrate. A contingent from Camp Blanding sat together, all dressed in their starched uniforms.

Harold began to fidget, not a good sign, so he quietly scooped him up before his folks or those around him noticed. Harold appreciated his brother's attention. His lap was softer than the metal chairs, and he searched his pockets, hoping he might find a piece of candy. Jim Brown gave him a squeeze; the moment reminded him of Bill. His mind drifted, and he wondered, as always, where Bill was … *maybe he was celebrating Easter with strangers. Maybe someone gave him a piece of Easter candy. Maybe* … the scraping of chairs and the rustle of dresses and crinolines brought Jim Brown back to reality. Harold had fallen asleep, so he carefully picked him up and followed his parents out. His father and mother stopped to talk with a few friends and local dignitaries while Jim Brown continued on his way home with Harold.

Easter followed that Sunday, April 5. The church was crowded; everyone dressed in their best—mothers wearing fresh corsages and fathers a bit uncomfortable in their suits and ties. Little girls modeled their dresses over layers of ruffled petticoats, while the boys made a beeline to the Easter egg hunt. War or not, the ladies of the church were determined to keep with tradition for the children's sake. Pleased as punch, their smiles were as wide as the children's once the hunt began. Jim Brown lost interest in the carnage, as the older kids dashed after the eggs and candies, pushing aside younger children and occasionally pilfering from their baskets. This was one of those times that even if he wore a sign that said, "Just turned twelve," people would smirk, judging that, once again, an older child was looking for a way to obtain candy meant for the youngsters under false pretenses. Resigned to the inevitable, he wandered over to the table where the ladies had set out cookies and lemonade for all.

And there was Peggy Tilley; he stopped in stride when she looked up. He stood straight and tall in his new clothes, and for once, he was thankful his mother insisted on the navy blue blazer instead of the light blue seersucker suit (which reminded him of something his grandfather would wear) that the salesman had pushed. The way Peggy sighed, he knew, at least he hoped, she thought he was the most handsome fellow around. Before he could say anything, he was surrounded by a swarm of parents and laughing children who emptied the trays in minutes. The moment was lost; however, the day was a success.

Monday, the festive mood continued as they celebrated "Army Day," with parades and barbecue. Also, a big surprise arrived—a birthday card from Bill. Not actually a card, as there were no card shops where Bill was, but a plain piece of white paper with a hand-drawn picture of a hula girl—at least, with a little imagination, Jim Brown thought it was a hula girl—with the message, *"Wish I were there! Thinking of you! Happy Birthday! Bill."*

Jim Brown sighed and thought how much he did miss his big brother. He wondered, *Where exactly are you? What are you doing? Are you safe? Have you shot anyone? Have they shot at you? Who's got your back?* His mind swirled with these unanswered questions.

Quietly, he whispered, "Sure wish you were here, too," and dropped his head. Then, he noticed in the corner of the letter a well-drawn football with the letters BHS—Bradford High School. His face broke into a grin. It was their secret code, and Bill remembered. If everything were all right, Bill would draw a football. Times might be difficult, but he was safe. Bill came up with the symbols. He and Jim Brown were a team and played football patterns like clockwork, nothing to it. If he drew a baseball, Jim Brown would understand that conditions were dangerous. Baseball was a different matter; Jim Brown had the upper hand. One day while they were practicing, Bill tried to pitch a fastball. "Throw harder!" Jim Brown called. Bill wound up and fired the ball in. Jim Brown tossed the ball back and called, "Harder!" Once again, he threw. "Harder!" Jim Brown cried with irritation.

You want it harder, thought Bill, *well, here it comes!* Bill gave it everything he had, and the ball flew with speed and accuracy. The smug smile quickly faded when he realized his brother had caught the ball bare-handed and was casually tossing it up and down. Then, Jim Brown gave a steely-eyed look to his brother, took aim, and threw the ball back with an effortless grace. Bill caught it and swore a blue streak. His hand stung, as if he'd been attacked by a swarm of bees.

"Harder!" called Jim Brown with a wicked grin. Yes, a baseball stung. But the most ominous sign would be a tornado, their school mascot. It meant disregard everything in the letter and say a heartfelt prayer—his unit would be entering combat.

Suddenly, he remembered the razor stored away on the top shelf in the bathroom medicine cabinet. *Thanks, big brother. I know you've got my back, but REALLY?* Well, maybe he would give it a try, if not tonight, someday soon … maybe.

XI

FOUR DAYS LATER, ON APRIL 10, ALL AMERICANS—PARTICULARLY
Floridians—received another jolt.

A warm, west wind drifted over the Jacksonville Beach as spring vacationers and lovers strolled along the shoreline, playing tag with the waves and counting the twinkling stars; it was a quarter past ten. Music floated from the boardwalk amusement park where children laughed, as they enjoyed nighttime rides and saltwater taffy. Life was good. Suddenly, a loud blast broke the evening calm, and flames shot into the sky over the ocean.

Only a few days before, the USS *Gulfamerica* had left Port Arthur, Texas, loaded with 90,000 barrels of oil. It was one of the first merchant ships to be fitted with deck guns and seven armed guards, but Captain Anderson was fairly confident the trip to New York would be uneventful. He would take precautions, keep watch, run drills, and maintain radio silence, but there was no need for a convoy, or so he thought.

The German U-boats, submarines, however, were prowling off the coast, looking for tankers, just like the USS *Gulfamerica,* carrying wartime supplies. In daylight, they would remain submerged on the continental shelf, unseen, invisible, but at night, they would resurface. Coastal lighthouses, beach homes, and street lamps innocently provided the stage lighting for the U-boats to stalk their prey.

On this warm, clear night, the German submarine, U-123, sited the USS *Gulfamerica* four miles off the coast of Jacksonville. As the men on board the *USS Gulfamerica* settled into their nightly routines, the U-boat

moved right to left, dancing a deadly waltz as she glided into position to strike. Some of the men on board the USS *Gulfamerica* were taking a break on deck, pointing and laughing at the lights from the boardwalk. Little did they realize those very lights sealed their doom.

From the beach, people watched in horror as the battled played out. Two torpedoes hit the starboard side, immediately setting the oil on fire. The captain didn't even have time to return a single shot; he ordered his men to abandon ship. The ocean waves turned angry as they crashed against the ship's hulls. Fifty shades of black morphed into horrifying images against a wall of towering flames. The people on shore felt they were looking at an illusion of the gates of hell; the sailors in the water knew this was no illusion. Ominously, the U-boat continued to stalk her prey. The crowd on shore watched as her black silhouette came into view. She calmly, brazenly, glided between the shore and the tanker, and proceeded to strafe the tanker with machine guns, killing sailors and knocking out the radio antenna. The people froze in terror, helpless.

The sailors continued to scramble into lifeboats and life rafts. The burning oil and their bulky lifejackets, constructed from cork covered with canvas, made swimming difficult. The dark shadows from the USS *Gulfamerica,* highlighted by the bursting oil barrels, danced a silent reel on the horizon. Smoke, in clawing fingers, reached toward the sky, while billowing, black clouds covered the wounded ship like a death shroud.

For a moment, everyone remained stunned, paralyzed, and mesmerized as scenes of life and death played out. Their lives were like a snow globe that some unseen hand was shaking up and down, back and forth, from side to side. Words from news reports filled the radio air waves—struggle, torpedoes, firewalls, pain, cries, blood, burned flesh—as broadcasters covered the story. The next day, cold, black-and-white letters would splash across the *Jacksonville Times Union*:

USS Gulfamerica Attacked Off Florida Coast: Spectators Watched In Horror

It wouldn't be some far-away country; it would be their hometown. The newspaper would quote their neighbors; it would print a photograph of their beloved seashore. But that was tomorrow. The enemy was here, now. Spontaneously, as if on cue, everyone sprang into action, and rescue efforts began.

The navy base was alerted. Mothers huddled their children and shuffled them away from shore. Men launched whatever they could find that would float, while volunteers assembled supplies. Makeshift clinics sprouted up along the beach to tend to sailors, should they make it to shore. Lights continued to flood the beach as men rushed back and forth in organized chaos. The U-boat slipped silently away; its job was done.

Two lifeboats, one with ten sailors, including the captain, and one with three, were rescued. Another three sailors were pulled from a life raft and two more from the ocean. For six hours, the men bobbed in the waves amid the burning debris and refuse. Nineteen men lost their lives that night. Later, newspapers reported three more ships and two freighters were sunk off Cape Canaveral, presumably by the same wolf pack of German submarines.

Jim Brown was confused. He didn't understand why we were fighting the Germans, nor why they would fight us. He asked his father, who paused and repeated what was reported on the radio and in the newspapers—war was declared, and we are defending American values. That night, he sat down and wrote the one person he knew would give him a straight answer—Bill.

Every afternoon, Jim Brown would meet the postman convinced Bill's letter was there, starting the day after he wrote his note. It wasn't that he thought his letter had magically crossed the continent and Pacific Ocean and found his brother, but he did believe that he and Bill were connected. Perhaps, somehow, maybe because his question was so important, his thoughts flew through the night, and Bill had already sent his reply. But the days passed, and Jim Brown's burning question began to fade.

Then, unexpectedly, one night at the dinner table, his mother casually said, "Jim Brown, you got a letter today." There on the table was a letter with Bill's unmistakable handwriting. He grabbed the letter and tore it open. It read:

Hey, J.B.—Hope you're keeping everyone straight at home. Sorry it's taken so long to get back to you, but writing paper and time are difficult to come by these days; and I'm not sure when a mail-drop will be by, but I wanted to answer your question—or at least try. I'm not sure either how we got into this mess, but I imagine the Germans, like the Japs, are fighting for the same reason we are, defending our nations. The real causes will only be known when the fighting is over, and the victors sorted everything out. But I'll tell you this; these Japs are throwing everything they have at us. I've heard they'll shoot prisoners of war for any reason. Word is out they don't like red hair! I just don't understand.

I have learned that fear is a great teacher—that's something they don't teach you during training. Oh, I think they alluded to it. "Don't worry; when you get into battle, you'll know what to do." I thought they meant survival instinct, like keep your head down when bullets are flying—but there's something more. It's easier to face your fears than to freeze or run away. Fear motivates and cements the unit, though I don't think anyone would actually say that. I sure hope I make it through because

I would love to know what the heck they're fighting for, where all this hatred came from, and that there is a reason, a purpose, so much blood is being shed.

At times, this really feels like a black hole in space. We're cut from time—there is no past; there is no future, just an eternal present. I'll tell you this; I've met some great guys, and we all have each other's backs. I know you don't want to hear this, but I would give my life for any of them. So, say a prayer for us—that's something else I've learned, and don't waste a minute. Study hard—I know you think I was smart, and maybe I am, but I wish I had paid more attention. Play hard; you'd be surprised at what the body can endure—sleepless nights, days without food, marching miles with bullets flying, and worse. Give everyone a hug and a kiss—don't worry about Wanda. I'll take care of that when I get home, but if you see her, tell her I'm fine. Bill.

Jim Brown noted a tornado in the bottom corner. He took in a deep breath and held it for a moment. That night, he would say a prayer—at least give it his best effort.

"So, what did he say?" His mother's words broke his train of thought.

"Oh, nothing—just guy stuff." He knew his mother would not take the news well. Buying time, he finished the last bite of the nameless casserole on his plate.

"Nothing?" she repeated expectantly.

Jim Brown heard a choke in her voice and looked into her eyes. He realized tears were forming. "Oh, ah, he did say to say 'Hi,' and give you a hug." Dutifully, he got up and gave her a bear hug before cleaning off the table.

For six days, the tanker in Jacksonville burned. The navy retrieved one of the guns from the bow, but the ship and her cargo were lost. All 445 feet groaned and roared as the oil barrels continued to burst. Jim Brown and his friends begged their parents to take them to the beach, but his mother declined, saying, "Surely, it must be sunk by now!" But in her heart, she couldn't view the tragedy. She pictured the ship burning, the bow rising above the ocean before plummeting to the depths. She knew Bill was on a ship; it could happen to Bill. It could happen to her son. She took to her bed for three days; the blinds were drawn, and she refused to talk to anyone.

His father knew it was time to call in the big gun, Pat Brown. Jim Brown knew that Pat Brown was his mother's best friend since forever. He grimaced as he recalled the family story—if he had been a girl, his name would have been Patricia; however, when he arrived, his mother settled on James, after his father, and Brown, after her inseparable best friend. She arrived before his father had time to hang up the receiver. Without a word, she went straight to the refrigerator, grabbed a cold cucumber and a knife from the kitchen drawer, and glided silently up the stairs like a ghostly apparition. They heard a tap on the door, a jiggle on the knob, the door creak open, and then silently close. Jim Brown and Harold looked at each other, eyes opened wide, speechless. Their father remained unruffled, reading—or perhaps hiding behind—the newspaper. The boys sat quietly, waiting for something, though they weren't sure what.

The kitchen clock ticked on. After an hour, their father glanced over the paper. The boys looked up anxiously, and he gave a nod. Jim Brown smiled, as he thought how many words could be spoken in silence. He jumped up with Harold at his heels and scrambled up the stairs, taking them two at a time. Harold diligently stomped on each step until Jim Brown whirled around with his finger over his lips. Harold got the message and changed his pace to an exaggerated tip-toe.

They reached their mother's room together. Jim Brown bent over and peeked through the keyhole while Harold squirmed to look through every crack or crevice available. What did they see?

Their mom was still in bed, but she was sitting up, leaning back against every available pillow. She had on her favorite bed jacket, a pale blue brocade, and two slices of cucumber stared back from where her eyes should have been. Mrs. Brown sat in a chair by the nightstand, whispering words Jim Brown could not decipher. She was expertly painting his mother's fingernails.

With this information, the boys silently returned to the kitchen. Their father placed the paper on the table and again, in silence, waited for their report. Jim Brown gave a brief account as his father listened intently. Harold nodded his head, suggesting he was there and saw it all, too. Then, there was silence.

His father looked up and asked, "What color was the polish?"

Jim Brown thought a moment and said, "Red."

"What shade?"

What shade! "Ah, well, it was a bright color, like maybe, ah, red candied apples?" he offered.

His dad smiled and repeated, "Red candied apples, you say?" followed with an appreciative nod. Without another word, he stood up, folded the paper under his arm, and left the kitchen. They thought they heard the screen door open and shut. The boys looked at each other and shrugged, uncertain what anything meant. But if their dad was off to work, it was a good sign—or at least they took it that way. The back door slammed shut as they ran outside to play.

Suddenly, Jim Brown realized how great it was to be outside in the fresh air. He hadn't noticed that he had hardly taken a breath while his family scene unfolded. Without a second thought, he took several deep breaths and felt as if he were coming back to life. Harold, on the other hand, was already running in circles, flapping his arms like wings and calling to the birds. It was a perfect opportunity to swoop down, grab Harold, and toss him high into the sky, only to catch him, twirl around, and blast him off again like a rocket into the clouds—much to Harold's delight.

That evening, when they came in from play, Jim Brown noticed a large bouquet of flowers on the dining room table. He immediately recognized they were an "Any-Times Bouquet," one of those his father brought home for all the times he could have, should have, or just plain forgot to have for his mother. But he also realized this one had a different look about it; it was something special, like he wanted to be there for her but didn't know what to say. *Gee, Dad, you really know how to make Mom feel better. Way to go!* And, he was right.

On the morning of the fourth day since she had retired to her room, their mom, dressed in a starched, shirtwaist dress and floral apron, appeared in the kitchen, scrambling eggs. Life, momentarily, pretended to be normal, again.

On April 16, the USS *Gulfamerica* slowly sank beneath the waves. Tar balls and oil continued to wash up on the shoreline for months and even years after. It was a wake-up call for the East Coast.

Civilian patrols were set in place to enforce lights out. The navy stepped up convoy maneuvers, while the Coast Guard's neutrality patrol transformed overnight to meet wartime demands. If it was a fight the Germans wanted, it was a fight they'd get.

XII

ON APRIL 18, HEADLINES REPORTED A RAID BY SIXTEEN BOMBERS OVER Japan. Jimmy Doolittle, the famous civilian pilot now serving in the newly formed Army Air Corps, led the squadron. The planes took off on a secret mission from the USS *Hornet*, a newly commissioned aircraft carrier. They flew just two hundred feet above the Pacific Ocean, battling winds and rough seas to avoid detection. Their targets were Tokyo and other Japanese cities with military factories and ammunition plants. The Japanese were finally having a taste of their own medicine. Perhaps now they would understand they would not be so safe and secure on their islands across the ocean; the Yanks were coming.

A month later, more details were reported. The USS *Hornet* had been discovered by a passing Japanese boat, forcing the pilots to leave before scheduled. With their fuel supply already stretched to the limit, it seemed a doomed mission. After dropping their payloads, the planes were to head to China and join the Flying Tigers, a group of American volunteers lead by General Claire Lee Chennault. Though the Tigers were only three squadrons strong, they had earned the respect of the world for distracting the Japanese military while the Americans recouped and grew in strength.

One plane landed safely on Russian soil. The crew were immediately captured and held as prisoners because Russia had yet to declare war. The rest crashed into the China Sea or on Chinese territory. Most were rescued by the Chinese who had been at war with the Japanese for some time.

They were grateful to see these foreigners and graciously gave any support they could.

The Japanese captured eight flyers and executed three without trial. Then, they returned to China to embark on a killing spree. Approximately 250,000 Chinese lost their lives for harboring the pilots and their crew. It continued to be a long and ugly war.

As Jim Brown read the reports, he wondered if the pilots were trained across the state at Eglin. The requirements and tests for pilots were simplified to attract the much-needed volunteers; many of the new recruits went there for training. Sure enough, his father learned that Doolittle and his men had trained there under the supervision of navy officers. The air strips were shortened to three-hundred feet to simulate the deck on the USS *Hornet*. Twenty-four B-25 Mitchells were reassigned from the 17th Bombardment Group and had been modified for this one mission. Additional fuel tanks were installed to increase their flying range; and machine guns were replaced with wooden dowels to make them lighter while maintaining the appearance of a fully armed bomber. Training was intensified, including low-altitude approaches to bombing targets, rapid bombing practice, and evasive action. The pilots must have understood their mission, the dangers, and the importance, but once again, even the keenest imagination could not predict what was in store. The bottom line, Florida was taking a lead role in this war. Even if Bill didn't know, Florida had his back, literally.

Things only got worse when the Japanese took over the Philippines. The newspapers and radios were filled with reports from battles in the Coral Sea and a place called Midway. The tidy universe run by grown-ups had turned upside down.

Women were reporting to the recruiting stations and assembly plants. Children gave up their penny candy treats for war stamps and wrote to soldier pen pals they hoped someday to meet. Smiles and laughter were less frequent. Adults stared vacantly and shook their heads while walking down the streets, lost in thoughts of world events. Outside the barber shop, men's voices would drop to whispers when children walked by—as if ignorance might somehow protect them. And mothers just prayed that the war would end, soon. Everyone, young and old, was feeling the effects of war.

Because so many men were serving in the armed forces, there was a shortage of prison guards. Trusted inmates were appointed tower guards to fill the vacancies. It was a gamble; but most trustees knew it might help cut their prison time with exemplary behavior, and if they did try to escape and were caught, the sweatbox was a reality.

Sweatboxes were a series of concrete cubicles in the prison yard just large enough to hold one man. In the summer time, they were hot as ovens, and in the rainy season, they were cold, damp, and miserable. Flies and yellow-jackets always added to the misery, and, sometimes, a sadistic guard would toss in a spoonful of sugar to attract fire ants. The box became a real hell hole to anyone who found himself ordered inside.

Unfortunately, one morning, things did go awry; a trustee made a break. Whether the train whistle was too strong a call or perhaps his buddy pressured him with threats of physical pain or promises of riches, once they escaped, the trustee lowered a rope to his pal and pulled him up. Quickly, they grabbed the guns and were over the wall and on their way to freedom. If they could make their way through the sugar cane without stepping on a rattlesnake and cross the New River to throw off the dogs, cut through the brush and palmetto to the railroad tracks at Lawtey … they had a chance.

The prison called Jim Brown's father, who was at home eating break-fast, to let him know of the escape. He immediately ordered a hunting party formed and said he'd be right over. After he hung up the phone, he paused and looked at Jim Brown, who was finishing his scrambled eggs and canned salmon, a specialty of his father's.

"Do you want to come?" he asked.

Jim Brown, who had overheard the call, didn't pause at all. He stuffed the last, rather large forkful of eggs into his mouth and followed his father out the door. On the drive over, the car was silent. Jim Brown realized that his mother had no idea where they were going; it was probably just as well. She was still in bed and more than likely they'd be home before she got up.

Then Jim Brown looked at his father and wondered what he was thinking. Obviously, he knew the missing inmates. He knew them all by name, and he probably knew where they were going. Even Jim Brown had a good idea. They wouldn't stop at the homes nearby unless they saw some clothes left hanging on the clotheslines, as they'd want to get rid of their prison stripes as soon as possible. They would head toward the New River to cover their tracks and then dash to a gentle curve in the railroad tracks, where the trains slowed down just enough to give them time to jump on board.

Jim Brown wondered why his father had asked him to come along, and he wondered whether Bill had ever gone on a manhunt. A manhunt, the very word sent a shiver down his spine, but that's what it was. They would be hunting down men. He smiled, and his chest puffed out as he thought maybe his dad felt he was man enough for the job. He did get the shotgun for his birthday. Then, he frowned, maybe it was that he helped care for the dogs, and surely, they'd be called out.

The dog pens weren't far from their house, and Jim Brown loved to go and exercise the bloodhounds. They weren't yappy and high-strung like Superintendent Chapman's bird dogs. The hounds just slept in their pens unless someone opened the door with food or a leash. Then, slowly, they would stand and stretch their legs. Their beady eyes would twinkle as they peered out from under their wrinkly brows, and their noses would sniff the air for a scent of identification. Then, they would saunter over, giving droopy smiles and nudging, as if asking, "What's up?" But once you gave them a scent, they became alive, alert, and on a one-track course. Their noses were glued to the ground, and they were off! Their concentration never broke until they had cornered their prey. They were trusted and loyal, and Jim Brown loved them.

When they arrived, all the guards were assembled and the dogs loaded in their cages. Mr. Godwin walked over to a rather large quarter horse that a trustee was holding for him, put his foot in the stirrup, and with effort, hoisted himself onto the saddle.

Jim Brown scurried over to the dog wagon. The dog master recognized him, and gave him a hand as he hopped on board. No orders were necessary; each man knew what was expected. They mounted their horses with Godwin in the lead.

When they were within a mile of the railroad tracks, the guards let the dogs out and gave them the scent. In no time, the convicts were caught. Jim Brown helped round up the dogs and caught a glimpse of one of the prisoners, recognizing him as one of the trustees who worked in the yard and occasionally took Harold on walks. Guess he wouldn't be seeing him for a while. He'd be off to the sweatbox; there'd be time to regret his escape … and time to plan the next.

Just then, they heard the train roll by. The whistle vibrated in the hearts of the convicts and guards. The guards smiled at one another, nodding their heads in silent agreement; they'd caught the men just in time.

The convicts closed their eyes, pursed their lips, and sadly shook their heads. So close.

XIII

OCCASIONALLY, INCONSOLABLE WAILS OF GRIEF ROSE FROM HOMES when telegrams arrived, saying their son or father was not coming home. The blue star flags would then change to gold stars. But tears of joy would fill the lanes when blue, V-mail letters arrived with news from the front … though most letters were censored with dark ink streaks, slashing out all sensitive information, which the government deemed was just about everything.

"Look here! Look here!" cried Mrs. Carlson one morning, waving a blue envelope in her hand, "a letter from Earle!"

Everyone within earshot stopped what they were doing and came running to catch the latest news reported by their hometown hero. A tall, slender scarecrow dressed in blue denim overalls, a plaid flannel shirt, and rubber boots that came up to the knees tramped over. A wide brim straw hat covered her face from the sun, and a few women gasped when they recognized Mrs. Raley.

Mrs. Raley was everyone's high school English teacher. With the arch of an eyebrow, she could silence a room of teenagers or reduce a parent to a quivering bowl of Jell-O. She was a wizard who could bring Shakespeare to life and encourage students with no hope to college. She always wore stylish skirts with matching vests and a scarf tied in a loose knot around her neck. She walked effortlessly in high-heeled shoes; her silk stockings never had runs, and the seams were always in line. She'd never be without a touch of rouge on her round cheeks and the exact shade of matching lipstick applied expertly to her thin lips.

On Sundays, a smart pillbox hat perched on her permed hair, as she always sat ramrod straight in the third row, listening to the preacher. Did Mrs. Raley, with her impossibly high standards, really work in a victory garden? Would her hands get in the dirt; would her fingers pull weeds? Who would have thought—did this icon of Bradford High even need to eat food? The ladies parted like the Red Sea as Mrs. Raley made her way to the front. She gave each woman a smile of recognition as she came to hear the news. Unfazed, Mrs. Carlson ripped open the envelope, took a deep breath, and started.

"It says, 'Dear Mom.'" She sighed and closed her eyes, holding the letter tight to her chest. Then she cleared her throat and began again. She cocked her head like a red robin as she searched the letter for news, but everything was inked out. She shuffled through the pages and continued, "Oh, here we are. 'The weather is...'" She paused and quickly picked up again, "'We eat food...'" Her eyebrows frowned as she tried to make sense of the words and then continued, "'Thanks for the package; Frank and Sparky ate all the candy, but I did get a cookie or two. They were great. Everyone says, 'Hi!' If you see Eugenie, tell her I miss her. Love, Earle.'" With a sigh, she clutched the letter again to her heart and tried valiantly to smile at the neighbors who were hanging onto every word. But tears glistened in her eyes, and she dropped her head to hide her true emotions. Several neighbors reached over to hug her and whisper how nice it was to have a letter, how lucky the boys were to receive her care package.

Suddenly, a voice, slow and deliberate—with a slight Midwestern accent that stood out in Starke—said, "'We eat food'! Let me see those papers!" It was Mrs. Raley. She took the pages without ceremony from Mrs. Carlson and held them up, one by one to the sun, to see if she could decipher anything Earle had written beneath the dark slashes. She remembered him quite well, second row over, fourth seat from the back, a daydreamer whom she corralled and taught to write—even poetry!

Everyone stood in shock. Mrs. Griffis, generally a calm and soft-spoken woman, snatched the papers back from Mrs. Raley and returned them to a grateful Mrs. Carlson. The ladies returned to their morning chores; only Mrs. Raley remained in the road, shaking her head in disbelief.

Just then, Jim Brown and his buddies came whizzing around the corner on their bikes. Like everything else, war had changed their games. They were no longer cowboys or pirates or firemen; they were soldiers, sailors, and, today, pilots flying in formation. The bikes were no longer horses; they became jeeps and tanks, destroyers and battleships. Today, they were bombers with fighter escorts. The basic goal and rules never changed—good against evil; attack and retreat; plot, execute, and go home at day's end. But to the mothers and businessmen nearby, it all looked the same. Only Mrs. Raley smiled as she picked up the nuances and appreciated their use of imagination.

The afternoon shift began to arrive at the community victory garden. Everyone had small vegetable gardens in their backyards, but this was a gathering place for fresh air, support, gossip … and children were welcomed. In the late afternoon, when mothers were exhausted and children filled with energy, it was just the place to meet. You didn't have to know how to grow anything; there were plenty of authorities ready to give directions and point out the unacceptable patches. There were few rules, though everyone agreed to limit zucchini plants.

Soldiers brought them back from Italy after "the War to end all Wars." They were an immediate hit—and they grew abundantly, too abundantly. The zucchini had arrived with Italian recipes that included tomatoes and one with eggplant, onions, and sausages, but the Southern cooks immediately took them to heart and added their own unique touches. They sliced the green cylinders into coins, simply seasoned with salt and pepper, simmered, and smothered the veggies in butter. True to Southern style, they were a touch overcooked, but they liked them that way. Then, sautéed onions were added for flavor. Bacon made anything better. Someone suggested adding a cheese-and-cracker-crumb topping, which also made its way onto various other casseroles.

When all else fails, Southern cooks turn to their second favorite, non-secret ingredient, sugar, which brought the zucchini into the line of desserts.

It started as a sweet, quick bread and then made its way into the cake section in family recipe boxes. They even included a chocolate variety, which frequently graced their tables. Children became convinced that vegetables should be taken from the entree course and permanently placed on the dessert tray. If something as disgusting as zucchini could be transformed into cake perhaps there was hope for broccoli, cauliflower, and beets.

Secret baskets of zucchinis were left on doorsteps, and food banks always had a healthy supply. Starke was one of the strawberry capitals of Florida, but the zucchini, wanted or not, was making a move on the title. That would not be tolerated, for the zucchini had to be reined in.

On the other hand, tomatoes were always welcomed. Though they did require added attention, since they needed to be protected from critters and pecking birds, there was always a demand. Mrs. Shoffner insisted on planting flowers in her plot ... because she liked them, and she swore they would bring bees that were needed to pollenate the vegetable plants. No one would argue, and the flowers were lovely.

The children were helpful, to a point. When they tired or became too rambunctious, the mothers would bring out snacks. They would eagerly retreat to enjoy the treats, and then break into groups to play games of pick-up jacks, hopscotch, marbles, hide and seek, kick the can, freeze, Simon says ... until it was time to go home and prepare dinner.

Those who worked the gardens were welcomed to enjoy the harvests, but most of the vegetables went to the churches' food pantries for distribution. Truth be told, the clergy helped by sending wayward teens and repentant husbands for penance when help was desperately needed, though no one knew exactly who had been designated or when they might appear ... it was just assumed everyone working in the garden had time and goodness of heart.

Father Vince Germano was glad to comply. Though his parish was small, many folks came to St. Edward's Catholic Church for help ... and his door was always open. He was new to Starke and still an outsider, but he already loved the people and was determined to find his place—which was a challenge, but his whole life had been filled with challenges.

XIV

VINCE GERMANO WAS BORN AND RAISED IN NEW YORK CITY, THE
Bronx to be precise. Life had not been easy, and he and his best friend, Joe
Green, had made a pact that they would get out of the broken-down tene-
ments and gang-dominated streets and make something of their lives. Joe
went to West Point, and Vince remembered the first letter he wrote after
surviving Beast Barracks.

> *"There is nothing that West Point or even life can throw at
> me now. I can handle anything after all I've been through. I
> know, well, I hope, no, I truly believe I can take on the world."*

And Joe would get his chance, thought Vince.

> *"But Vince, even after all this, I really don't think I could
> take on the seminary like you ... I've enclosed the Cadet
> Prayer. Maybe it will help."*

Vince smiled and folded up the letter. Joe had been right; seminary
school was not easy. Many young men had signed up because they were
pleasing their mothers or running away from something. They didn't belong,
and truth be told, initially, Vince might have been one of those, but along
the way, he found his calling. He found God. He was not climbing mountains to transcend the evil in the world. Like David, he was running straight

toward the Goliaths. At 5' 8," he already had scars brought from the neighborhood, but now he was armed with weapons to fight and salves to heal. Like Joe, he too was dressed in armor, but of a different kind, invisible but just as effective.

He heard that Carl Jung, a psychologist, carved over his doorway, "Vocatus atque non vocatus, Deus est."—that is, "Called or not called, God is." The quote said it all; God did exist. We did not create Him out of need; He created us out of love. It was in man's need that he found God's love. If he was lost, God guided him. If he was lonely, God was at his side. If there was ugliness, God's eyes found beauty. And in sadness, and there was sadness everywhere these days, only God could bring understanding and give comfort. No matter how awful circumstances were, Vince knew God would give him wisdom—in time. It would not be easy, but easy was not the road he sought.

Many times, Vince thought of applying to the military ordinariate to become a Marine after he was ordained. He would join Joe and his pals, and keep them out of trouble, with both sword and the Word. But the papers were still in his nightstand, and he was here in Starke.

Joe, on the other hand, was now stationed across the country in the DTC, the Desert Training Center, also called CAMA, the California-Arizona Maneuver Area. It was a remote post, commanded by MG George S. Patton, Jr., designed to condition soldiers to fight in "inhospitable arenas." There would be no women to distract them, no electricity to provide comforts. Temperatures would fluctuate from below freezing at night to soaring temperatures above one-hundred degrees in the day. They would live in tents with bare cots and cook their rations on "Patton Stoves," tin cans filled with sand and rocks soaked in oil. The troops called it "The Place God Forgot." Soon, they would find themselves in combat in the desert of North Africa where God was waiting for them. How well they took their training to heart would determine life or death. Visions of Beast Barracks swirled through his mind.

Once again, the army provided all the necessities they needed to survive … minus one or two. But survive he would; win he would; defeat was not an option. The men generally divided into four groups: those who embraced sacrifice; those who adjusted their expectations and adapted to the circumstances; those who accepted the challenge and thought outside the box — they were sub-divided into two groups: the Loose Cannons and the Brilliant;

and finally, the Dreamers, those who did not connect to reality—they were the ones that scared Joe the most. Joe was a dreamer, when he jumped into the sack each night and thought of Betsy, his pregnant wife. He dreamt of her and their family-to-be. He would hold Vince to his promise to be there and baptize his first born, and he even dared to dream of being there.

But the Dreamers were different. They dreamt with their eyes wide open and saw themselves marching down Fifth Avenue in a ticker-tape parade, kissing every girl in sight; they did not consider the battles that must be fought and won before they got there. They day-dreamed during instructions and misplaced maps and strategic battle plans. These very actions might cost them their lives and, worse, the lives of the men in their companies. Joe hoped Vince had a special line to God, and that his prayers to guard and guide him as he set out to protect and defend the world might be answered.

"Grant us peace, dear Lord, in our hearts, our families, our communities, our nation, and throughout the world," Vince prayed each morning. In that moment, a warm calm descended. He felt total acceptance, which gave him a strength to meet any challenge the day presented. "Thy Will be done."

Father Germano enjoyed working in the garden when time permitted, though he was one of those who needed direction. There were barely enough trees in the city to meet the needs of the dogs; gardens were boxes that sat on stoops or pots precariously balanced on fire escapes.

For Father Germano, the victory garden was an opportunity to exercise, to enjoy the sunshine and fresh air, and a chance to sow agape, unconditional love, into others. It also gave him time to reflect and compose some of his best sermons.

Today, he was wrestling with the concept of loneliness. With the prison just down the road, punishment was solitary confinement, a giant leap from, "Go to your room," or "Sit in the corner." And there were those, particularly women, who feared being alone and even felt a profound sadness at the very thought of being alone. Yet, Christ sought to be alone—forty days in the desert, an hour in the Garden of Gethsemane. Solitude was a blessing, an opportunity to reflect on who you are and to listen with your heart to hear what God sees. How could the two definitions be reconciled?

Author Henry David Thoreau sought constructive solitude: appreciate the moment, appreciate nature, appreciate self. Learn from the past; plan for the future; live in the moment. Vince reasoned we might miss our sons and fathers, family members, and friends who bring warmth and community, but through God and prayer, we are always connected. He smiled when he realized that God had given him yet another conundrum from which to wrestle a truth.

Just then a twig snapped, and Father Germano turned his head. Hillary Davis had just stood up to stretch, two plots over from him. She suddenly saw the priest and gave a shy smile. *It's strange,* he thought, *how one could be surrounded by people and still be unaware and alone.* He returned a friendly wave to Hillary and then went back to pulling weeds—or at least what he hoped were weeds.

His mind quietly drifted back to his train of thoughts. Punishment, as in solitude, could be a blessing, but what else helps a person grow? Even more precisely, what could he assign his penitents for reconciliation after they made good confessions? He prided himself that he tried to think outside the box. Yes, there would be the expected three "Hail Mary's" and the mandatory "Act of Contrition," but he always wanted to add something special, something that might be a meaningful experience that would lead to permanent change in the person. His favorite was to do a good deed, which always was met with, "Huh?" He learned to have a few suggestions ready: help an elderly neighbor; spend special time with your younger siblings—which was challenged with, "How much time are we talking about?"; sit with someone at lunch who needs companionship; give your mother a compliment.

Then, there were the special cases. If someone confessed to stealing, he always suggested they try to return or pay for the item, but then he directed them to go to the library and read the biography of St. Francis, who not only loved animals and created the first nativity creche, but also embraced poverty and gave all he had to the poor. The librarian knew something was up because there was always a waiting list for the tattered book, but she never knew why.

The most difficult cases were those who denied God. Though he had experienced doubt, he could not understand how anyone could choose to turn his back from the Creator of love. One day, out of the blue, he shared the story about two young Ugandan boys, Daudi Okelo and Jildo Irwa, who did not have all the opportunities the boys in Starke had. Missionaries came to their village and introduced them to God. Their hearts were set on fire, and they wanted to share this knowledge and love with all their neighbors, and, like the original apostles James and John, they set out with nothing.

Unlike James and John, they travelled on old elephant paths and crossed lion-hunting grounds until they entered a village and stayed until the seed of faith was sowed. News of the boys circulated quickly, and people looked forward to their visits—but not all people. Some of the elders were extremely angry with their "Good News." All people, men and women, were equal. This God was a God of love; He did not demand sacrifice. He did not respect the village doctors and traditions. They were losing their authority, and that could not be tolerated.

Arriving in a new village, the elders met them and demanded the boys give up their faith. Daudi, the older, stepped forward and said that would be impossible. The Chief's righthand man immediately sent a spear flying straight through his heart, killing him. Okelo stood there stunned. The Chief then turned to him and said, "This is where your God leads you. Go back to your village and tell them. Do not return."

Okelo stood firm and replied, "I followed Daudi, and his words are inscribed on my heart. Our God has built a mansion for us, and I will not turn back." With that, a second spear was thrown, and Okelo fell next to Daudi, dead as well.

The elders smiled, pleased with what they had done, but the skies darkened, and God's favor left the village. Again, the Word travelled quickly, and the seeds of faith the elders thought they had destroyed sprung up more rapidly. Even many of the elders who had witnessed the murders repented.

"Try to imagine that faith," Father Germano would say, and then sit quietly. "Blessed are those who believe and do not demand proof," he added, though he silently thought, *Proof is all around you! Just open your eyes!*

Suddenly, Father Germano sprang up, this time startling Mrs. Davis. He realized that as he was lost in thought, time had passed, and he was due back at the church to hear confessions!

"If only wings came with the job," he muttered to himself. Quickly, he gathered his tools and darted for the gate, almost colliding with Mrs. Davis who had been daydreaming—and had also lost track of time. She, too, was late for her next appointment.

Coming to a screeching halt, he played the gentleman, letting Mrs. Davis pass through the gate first. He noticed her arms were full and wondered if he should offer to help her carry her load, but before the words could escape his lips, she was gone. With a sigh of relief, he trudged over to his car. He realized that his arms were already full. What would he have done if he had posed the question and she accepted? Just then, her car sped by, leaving him in a cloud of dust. Coughing, he hoped there was a clean cassock in his office.

Father Germano got into his car, said a prayer for his car to start, and turned the key. With a sputter, the motor began to hum, and he headed onto State Road 301. He glanced at the speedometer—his weak spot. He had already received two warnings, the first while he was rushing to administer last rites to a dying parishioner, which was understandable; the second, less forgivable. He was tired and hungry, and home was still ten miles down the road.

A mysterious smile, followed by a curious chuckle, brought him back to reality. He was recalling last week's penitents, in particular, Bobby Haskel from the First Baptist Church. He was only twelve years old. Father Germano recognized him from his Saturday job, bagging groceries at the local grocery story. He had wondered what drew him to the confessional; after all, a Baptist on Catholic property, as he had learned, was never a good sign.

While he was deciding which voice to use, soft and consoling or booming, God-like, which he actually learned by mimicking a Baptist preacher, Bobby Haskel stepped into the confessional.

Father Germano studied him through the screen. Bobby looked around at the unfamiliar surroundings and decided to kneel down on the cushion provided, and boldly announced, "I'm here to confess."

Father Germano wondered if this was a dare or perhaps curiosity but decided, for the time being, to go along. "I'm here to give absolution," he responded.

"What?"

"I'm here to forgive your sins."

"You can do that?" he fired back.

"Sure. John 20:23 (GNT): 'If you forgive people's sins, they are forgiven; if you do not forgive them, they are not forgiven.'"

Bobby was taken aback and thought the next time he saw Paster Walker, he'd have to ask him if he had those powers, too.

Feeling time had lapsed, Father Germano prodded, "So, have you been in any fights? Did you cheat in school? Did you steal an apple from Norman's?" Still no answer. "Have you talked back to your folks? Been joy riding?"

"Gee, I don't have a license!" Bobby blurted out.

"Well, that would be worse. What about sex?"

"Does kissing Mary Lou behind the football bleachers count?"

"What was your intent?"

"Wait a minute! You mean you want me to spill my guts about EVERYTHING?" At that point, both his voice and his resolve cracked.

"That's the idea."

After another awkward pause, Bobby stammered, "Well, maybe I'm not ready for this."

"Listen, Bobby, the door is always open. Maybe you could say the 23rd Psalm as you walk home. You know, 'The Lord is my Shepherd...'"

"You know that?"

"Before I left the seminary, I had to memorize all 150 psalms."

"Wow!" Then, without another word, Bobby got up and left. It wasn't until he had walked two blocks and finished reciting the psalm, as best he could, that he realized the priest had called him by name. He needed to talk to Frank Foley to straighten things out and make sure he wasn't going to hell for this dumb, practical joke that backfired—kaboom, and what's absolution!

Father Germano was left wondering if Bobby got what he wanted out of the experience and why he chose to see him in the first place. Once again, he was just left wondering what purpose God had in store for him at St. Edward's.

XV

MAY ARRIVED, WITH MOTHER'S DAY MARKED ON THE CALENDAR FOR the tenth. The boys, including Jim Brown's father, had set plans in motion weeks earlier. Originally, when the boys were small, Mr. Godwin took over the kitchen and prepared a hearty breakfast of deer sausage, over-easy eggs—which didn't always go over easy and ended up hard-fried—with cinnamon rolls—a treat from the prison—and fresh, hot coffee. As the years passed, Bill and Jim Brown grew, and breakfast became pancakes and sausage served in bed.

But now that Harold had arrived and Bill was serving in the Marines, the menu had changed to accommodate the manpower. Jim Brown had become an expert at making biscuits. Because he made them by hand, literally, his mother noted that the secret to his recipe was the size of his super, extra-large hands, which he used to measure the dry ingredients. She may have been right because no one could come close to his buttery, flakey, melt-in-your-mouth delicacies—even Jim Brown had hit-and-miss batches. With help, Harold could fill the cereal bowls and peel bananas, a bit smushed by the time they reached his mother but recognizable. With effort, the tray made it up the stairs. Any sloshes were covered by the beautiful bouquet of flowers his father produced out of nowhere and the kisses the boys supplied.

Jim Brown closely watched his mother as she smiled when presents appeared. He knew what she was thinking, but this time, he was wrong. She truly was pleased and glad to have her boys, she did appreciate all they had done. Yes, she did miss Bill—every second of every hour of every day, but today, she would enjoy what God provided. She gave a special wink to Jim Brown to let him know. After breakfast, everyone scrambled into their Sunday best, and it was on to church. His mother always stood out, dressed in style, surrounded by her family and a smile that said it all.

Pastor Walker gave a suitable service, and everyone returned home to make their mothers queens for the day!

Harold was the center of attraction, as he did his best to entertain his mom. Jim Brown stood on the sidelines, cleaning up the mess and later distracting Harold to give his mother quiet time to relax, to read, and to respond to the telephone line, which was quite busy. His father took over for dinner. Once again, Jim Brown was left to clean up by himself. Suddenly, he remembered Bill's words, "You're going to miss me when I'm gone." He smiled and unconsciously shook his head. Bill was right; maybe being the oldest wasn't all it was cracked up to be. At that moment, his mother slipped into the kitchen and gave him a kiss on the cheek and a hug. There were rewards—which Bill forgot to mention. He had measured up, and his Mother's Day was complete.

On the last day of school, Friday, the twenty-nineth of May, Jim Brown sprinted down the school hallway and out to the bus line. Waving his report card high above his head, he bounded up the stairs and stopped cold in front of the bus driver. There sat Walter Frakes.

Bill was, or had been, the bus driver. Because the prison bordered both Bradford and Union County lines, the parents at the prison farm had been given the choice, which schools their children would attend. They unanimously chose the Bradford school system because it had the better reputation; that is where Bill and Walter came in. The parents had to supply transportation, and graduating seniors readily filled the driver's seat. Walter had taken over when Bill reported to boot camp.

He gave Jim Brown a smile of recognition as he swatted a fly and added, "Let the good times roll!" followed by a casual salute and a tip of his baseball cap.

"Sure," replied Jim Brown, as his smile faded to a grimace. He knew Bill was gone. He even took pride knowing that he was fighting in the Pacific. Why, in patriotic moments when he and his friends prowled down by Alligator Creek, searching for enemy soldiers, scouting patrol lanes, and planning their attacks, they couldn't wait to join Bill and other soldiers! But for one brief moment, he could picture his brother—his large frame filling the driver's seat, his arms stretched over the steering wheel, and his voice greeting him with a familiar, "Get to the back!"

He so wanted to share his report card with Bill! Bill was a wizard at arithmetic while Jim Brown preferred history, but he knew he had to get through the course, and Bill was just the mentor he needed. He could explain the mathematical procedures when necessary, but generally he just made learning fun. For example, when Jim Brown had to memorize multiplication tables, Bill took him out to the yard with a basket of baseballs. It started off great.

Bill tossed an easy, soft fly ball and yelled, "Two times two!"

With equal grace, Jim Brown replied, "Four!" as he caught and then returned the ball.

Bill followed with, "Five times five!"

Again, the ball sailed into Jim Brown's glove and he shouted, "Twenty-five!" He thought, *This is a piece of cake!*

But suddenly, without warning, Bill reeled off, "Eight times six! Nine times seven! Six times four!" and fired three fast balls one right after the other!

Jim Brown caught the balls, but Bill explained they didn't count because Jim Brown didn't give the products—forty-eight, sixty-three, and twenty-four—before each catch.

Jim Brown was furious. *How could anyone?* Bill just grinned; rules were rules. Jim Brown promised himself that Bill would never catch him unprepared again—no matter what!

That month, every night he went to sleep droning, "Six, twelve, eighteen, twenty-four, thirty, thirty-six, forty-two, forty-eight, fifty-four, sixty. Seven, fourteen, twenty-one twenty-eight, thirty-five, forty-two, forty-nine, fifty-four—no, fifty-three—no, no, no—fifty-six, sixty-three, seventy. Eight, sixteen, twenty-four..." The multiplication tables from one to five never gave him problems. Pretty soon, six through eleven weren't bad. He practiced all the way through fifteen times fifteen—that's two-hundred twenty-five.

Now at the end of the year, he not only had passed the course with flying colors but had earned the mathematics award, and Bill, who made it possible, wasn't there to share the moment. He just wanted Bill home. Slowly, he trudged down the aisle to the back of the bus and collapsed on the rear bench, lost in thought.

He began to realize how different summer vacation would be without Bill. *Not just that Bill wouldn't be there to bring him home with a perfect line drive or catch his spiral touchdown pass, but he wouldn't be there for the important stuff, like who could discuss seriously whether there was life on other planets as they gazed at the evening stars? Who else knew the statistics and could expertly argue who would win the national pennant? Who could fill the silence shared when fishing? Who would help him escape or complete his chores?* He'd miss his laugh and their quiet talks about girls ... now girls, they were still a mystery to Jim Brown, but Bill had figured them out ... or so he thought.

He recalled one evening, shortly before Bill left, sitting together on the back porch. Bill gazed at the stars and repeated the one question that burned in Jim Brown's heart, "How do you recognize love? Well, the first time you look into a girl's eyes and you realize she sees something in you beyond what you thought possible, you know something is different."

"Isn't that what moms do?" Jim Brown asked in earnest.

Bill immediately rolled of his eyes, his usual response when asked to explain the obvious. "Of course, moms do. They have to because they brought you into the world, and it is their responsibility to see that you succeed. But they push you, like when Mom asks if you've finished your homework before you go out to play or insists that you eat all your vegetables to make you big and strong. But when someone special looks at you, she doesn't need words. She just pulls you into the future, and you can't wait to get there! And the best part is, even if you mess up, you know she'll still be there." Bill paused and then continued, "You can't begin to dream of what life would be like with her, but you know life without her would be a nightmare. And finally," and here, he paused again and sighed, "the unmistakable sign: just holding her hand makes your whole-body shiver!"

Yes, Bill knew. But then Jim Brown stole a glimpse of his brother, whose thoughts had obviously gone to a private realm, a bit of skepticism arose as he silently disputed, *But Wanda? Really!*

Meanwhile, back on the bus, the kids continued to pour on board, laughing and screaming. The school year was over, and summer vacation had begun. Freedom—pure and simple. Walter casually reached for his earplugs before closing the door.

The bus bounced down the dusty, dirt road back to the State Farm.

As he scowled, Jim Brown's mind slowly relaxed, and his afternoon plans emerged. He actually managed a smile. That Friday had been circled and starred on Jim Brown's calendar for months. Back in April, he had talked with his mother about having the State Farmers over for a camp-out to celebrate the beginning of summer vacation. She dropped her pruning shears and rolled her eyes.

"Who? What?" she replied, raising her eyebrows in irritation.

"You know, Mom, the guys. We can set up tents and build a camp fire, roast hot dogs; you know, that kind of stuff. You won't have to do a thing!"

"Oh, I don't know about that. How many did you say?"

"Maybe four or five."

She crossed her arms, dropped her head, and knit her eyebrows together—not a good sign. She exhaled loudly and said, "It's so far off—four or five? We really need to run this by your father."

Jim Brown could feel the "Big No" coming. "But Mom," he cried in exasperation.

"What if it rains? There might be a prison break. What about snakes and rabid dogs?" Rabies always seemed to be on her mind since the otter incident. "Did you say build a fire? I just don't know if you are big enough!" With that, she tilted her head back to look him in the eye and realized her head kept going back further and further as she searched for his face.

"Big enough?" his voice cracked.

His mother began to smile and started to laugh. "Well, you've got me there."

Jim Brown realized there was a crack, an opportunity, a chance. "If you only think of the what if's, mights and maybes—I'll never grow up! It'll be all right. We'll be safe. I promise!" he pleaded.

"Well, maybe you can set up in the backyard."

The backyard! All his plans were shattered. "The backyard!" he protested, "Why I was thinking…"

"The backyard, Jim Brown. Take it or leave it."

"But what about Harold! He'll ruin everything!"

"Now, Harold is too small. I'll keep him in the house that night, I promise."

And with that, they reached a tentative agreement.

Just then, Mrs. Shoffner came screeching into the driveway in her car and honked her horn twice. Relieved, his mother stood up and walked over to the car as the dust settled.

"Eve! Eve! I just had to tell you! I was at the antique store in Waldo, and they have a table just like yours!" Her eyes popped, and a bead of sweat trickled down her face.

"Slow down, Caroline!" Eve leaned against the car. "Which table?" she asked, as her eyes sparkled with wonder.

"You know," she blurted before Eve could ask any more questions, "The busted one in the backyard—the one the help does your laundry on. It could be a treasure! I'm sure it's an Eastlake Victorian," she added.

"Really? That piece of junk!"

"Yes! Definitely. I'd love to stay and chat, but I'm already late, and you know Daryl expects dinner on the table on time. I'll see you at church!" She thrust her hand through the window and gave a wave as she gunned the motor and pulled out before she could be drawn into a longer conversation—which was a certain possibility.

Eve barely had time to push herself off the car door, but already she was digesting the news Caroline brought. An Antique! A Treasure! Immediately, she began to scheme ways for her husband to take the table into the prison and repair the broken leg. She wondered how many other women would recognize "the treasure," but she could trust Caroline to point that out. She smiled as she walked backed to the house. She totally forgot about the camp-out plans.

Jim Brown didn't. He was already inside calling his friends, setting the date on the calendar. And now the day had arrived. Before he knew it, the bus pulled to a stop. Jim Brown dashed down the aisle and waited for Walter to open the door. Like a streak of lightning, he disappeared up the road to put his plans into motion.

XVI

BY 4:30 P.M., THE GUYS BEGAN TO ARRIVE WITH BACKPACKS, TENTS, and sleeping bags. Buck Leo was the first to be dropped off. It was difficult to tell as he was concealed under layers of survival gear and mosquito netting. In his hand, he tightly gripped a book on tying knots.

"This is just overnight?" Jim Brown's mother whispered. "Good thing you're not hiking into the woods. I wouldn't give him a hundred feet!" Then she gave him a playful nudge to go help. Jim Brown stifled a laugh.

On the other end of the spectrum, Deke Roberts arrived with a sleeping bag and a blanket loosely wrapped around a few poles tucked under his arm.

Jim Brown shrugged and said, "You can tent with me."

"Yes!" Deke exclaimed as he dropped the poles and tossed his sleeping bag into the nearest tent. It was Wayne Rivers' tent. Jim Brown gave another shrug and felt they could sort things out later. Besides, he didn't plan to do much sleeping anyway.

Frank Foley was the last to arrive, but he wasn't late. He arrived precisely at 5 p.m. on the dot.

The afternoon went well. Well, all right, there were a few hiccups, like Harold smashing his nose against the window and sticking out his tongue—several times. And when the guys made a beeline for the pantry, his mother wasn't thrilled with all the racket and dirt tracks. She even had the nerve to question their idea of "roughing it." Wayne suggested they could cut back on the house trips if they didn't brush their teeth, which was met with a rousing cheer.

Four fairly reliable tents were pitched, and by dusk, they had dug a trench and collected enough branches to build what would pass as a respectable campfire. They tossed a football around and congratulated each other on surviving yet another year.

Once darkness descended, the campfire crackled, the stars twinkled above, and the atmosphere changed. Out came bags of contraband—chips, jawbreakers, beef jerky, and licorice sticks. Challenges of truth or dare and a few rounds of paper, stone, and scissors put everyone in relaxed and bonded moods. They were birds of a feather, peas in a pod, guys celebrating the end of school and the freedom of summer vacation.

They were a motley crew. Buck Leo was tall and skinny, with wavy light brown hair and perfect teeth, which sparkled when he smiled. What he lacked in ability, he made up for with stuff—and he had it all. Since he was an only child, his parents doted on him and bought him everything before he even knew he wanted it.

Then there was Deke Roberts, also tall, but a muscular, star athlete. His true gifts were his looks—blonde hair and twinkling blue eyes, which conned adults and mesmerized young girls.

Frank Foley was the only Catholic in the bunch, whatever that meant. He went to church every Sunday and could say the "Our Father" in Latin faster than Jim Brown could say it in English, which was frequently put to the test. He was average height, stocky, and had a mellow voice that could carry a tune better than anyone. He also had an IQ that ran off the chart. Frank attributed everything to being Irish. His one drawback was that he wore glasses, which kept him from playing most sports, but he could draw up the most devious plays for football and cheered the loudest. He kept the stats during baseball season and was a true team player.

Wayne Rivers wasn't the brightest bulb in the bunch, but he was honest, loyal, and trustworthy. When he committed to something, it was a hundred percent—which also gave him a stubborn streak. A bit on the slender side, somehow, he always managed to carry his weight and then some. He was the first to have a girlfriend, which gave him a mark of distinction.

Marty Russell, who wasn't a State Farmer—his dad was the town butcher—had found his place in the group, but he called to say he couldn't make it. Jim Brown wondered why, but he knew better than to ask. Marty's life was, what some might call, complicated.

So, the five campers huddled around the glowing campfire embers and waited for someone to scare the living daylights out of them with a ghost story!

XVII

"IT WAS A DARK AND STORMY NIGHT," BEGAN WAYNE.

"No!" screamed everyone in unison, as they tossed empty candy wrappers his way.

When they settled back down, they noticed an eerie silence had filled the air. A breeze came out of nowhere and mystically stirred up the campfire embers. Flames soared, dancing skyward.

Taking advantage of the moment, Deke Roberts reached over, and in one, smooth motion, he grabbed a flashlight from Buck Leo's stash. He pressed the switch forward and positioned the light just under his chin, creating a chilling countenance. He continued in an equally ghoulish voice, "It's called … 'The Parallel Universe'…" He dramatically paused and frowned. No one was on board. "You know, there really is such a thing," he spoke with authority. He locked eyes with them and continued, "You all dream, don't you?" They nodded in unison. "Well, dreams are real—made of pure, creative energy. Justice triumphs over evil. You hit the grand slam or catch the fly ball and throw to first for the double play. Or…" Again, he paused dramatically and mischievously raised his eyebrow as he smirked at Frank, "You kiss a girl right on the lips!"

As if a balloon popped, several guys leaned backed, disengaged; Frank groaned. "Nightmare!" he said, and they all uncomfortably grinned at each other.

Jim Brown was shocked. He had been trying to decide if he should share "The Alligator Man of Apalachicola" or "The Tale of the Black Moccasin King" when Deke stole the stage. He knew they were all waiting on him because, hey, he was the best storyteller, but then he wondered where this was leading and how Deke was going to get himself out of this mess. Anyway, the darker it was, the easier it would be to capture their minds, peel away their defenses, and release their inner most fears. He focused back on Deke and allowed himself to be transported to this strange land in Deke's imagination.

Deke feigned being offended and threw his hands out to his side, as if begging for their trust. "Really, dreams are real, and you've got the power to control what happens, or so I thought."

Again, the boys' curiosity got the best of them, and they leaned in. It was Deke's turn to smile. He stretched back and continued.

"Let me tell you. Last week, I went for a walk in the field, just to get away. It had been one of those kinds of days." They all nodded—no words needed.

"There, in a circle of pines, just over to the left," he directed with his hands, "I saw a large, silver cone, three stories high and about forty feet in diameter. There were no doors or windows that I could make out from where I was, so, ever so slowly, I moved in closer."

Deke had dropped his voice and, raising it again, he shouted, "Suddenly, an opening appeared where I knew there wasn't one a minute before! I slipped behind the nearest tree and crouched down. I watched. I waited, but nothing happened. I rubbed my eyes; the black slit was still there. I wondered if I should get you guys."

They all smiled and nodded; that would be the smart thing to do, but then Deke wasn't known for being the brightest light in the attic.

"NO," he bellowed with confidence. "I wouldn't get you all. If there were danger, we all could be killed; no one would be left to save the world, and everyone would be mad at me. But, if there were a treasure, well, I'd have to share it with you all." He paused as everyone snickered, thinking maybe he wasn't so dumb after all.

"I stood up, stretched, and stepped into the open. Nothing happened. I thought, what the heck, I have to go all the way now. After all, it might be an unexploded bomb or a new weapon secretly developed by the soldiers from Camp Blanding ... or ... it might be an object fallen from space even ... a real spaceship! I couldn't walk away, could I?"

"You couldn't walk away. You didn't walk away. What was it?" Wayne cried in desperation.

"Of course not," gloated Deke. "I marched right up, but as I got closer, I did have a few doubts. But nothing happened, except ... maybe a twig or two snapped, which made me gulp, even though my mouth was as dry as a cotton ball. The trees didn't rustle; the birds didn't chirp. It was more silent than a cemetery.

"You know, silence has a sound. The sound of all your thoughts colliding in your brain at once, or that strange phenomenon that magnifies sounds you might otherwise miss, like the proverbial pin dropping or fly buzzing. No, silence is noisy and can really be distracting when you're trying to concentrate. So, I decided to stop thinking."

"How did you know you stopped?" interrupted Frank. Deke glared.

"No, really, good question," smirked Frank.

Ignoring him, Deke continued, "The opening seemed to call—what's the purpose of an opening but to enter, to see what is on the other side? The choice was made by the silence. Like a robot, I walked straight to my destiny.

"The silence never broke. Even though I felt as if someone was watching my every step, I've never felt more alone in my life. For better, or for worse, I walked to the opening and peaked in. Nothing stops State Farm Boys." Now, they all were holding their breath.

"It was difficult to make anything out. The corridor was dark, except for a stream of light that ran along the floorboards. I took a deep breath and slowly let it out. It obviously wasn't a bomb I could trigger, no signs of danger, but then it wasn't Granny's parlor with lemonade and cookies. I followed the light."

The boys shook their heads, as if to say he shouldn't have gone, and Deke shrugged his shoulders.

"Suddenly, one of the walls began to move. Maybe I had stepped on a hidden switch…"

"Or maybe it was your body temperature or the vibrations your movements made. Yeah, it was you," Buck solemnly declared.

"Maybe they were watching after all. Yeah, maybe they threw the switch," Deke returned.

"They?" the campers collectively cried.

"There had to be someone, but I still couldn't see anyone. I grabbed my pocket knife, just in case; I wasn't going to be caught unprepared. Never in a million years would you believe what happened next. A door slid open revealing a brightly lit room, filled with every candy you could imagine. I thought I'd hit the jackpot. I didn't know who I was dealing with, but I sure liked their taste.

"Then, out of the corner of my eye, I realized the wall across the hall retracted. Inside were miniature copies of all the landmarks around the world—the Sphinx and pyramids, the Eiffel Tower and the Arc de Triomphe, the Brandenburg Gate and castles—every wonder of the world, and even some I didn't recognize.

"I forgot that I was inside a creepy, steel cone and walked over, wondering how it could get any better. Then, like a warning, I felt a chill go up my spine. I realized that though everything was familiar, it just didn't belong. Like a smile on Miss Rose's face or your brother letting you have the last brownie, something was wrong. That's when I turned the corner and stopped in my tracks.

"Another door slid open, disclosing a white, bright, sterile room. The walls were lined with shelves, and each shelf was filled with rows of jars labeled with strange markings. But there was no mistaking; each jar contained a body part! On the far side stood three creatures dressed in white lab coats, concentrating on a picture. They didn't see me … yet.

"One selected a slack sack from a pile on the table in a corner. He took off his coat and slipped the sack over his head. The others began to whistle and beep, as if laughing, and then began talking in a strange language. The one with the sack over his head raised his arm, and the others became silent. He ceremoniously lifted a jar containing grey matter from the shelf, unscrewed the lid, and poured the contents onto the top of his head. I was mesmerized and didn't move a muscle.

"A minute later, from high screechy tones to a low booming bass, the character repeated, 'Hello, hello, hello,' like someone testing a mic at town hall. He settled on mid-range and clearly spoke, 'Hello, my name is Tom, Tom Ferguson.' The other two clapped. Their voices dropped as they continued to critique 'Tom.' Suddenly, the leader whirled around, and our eyes locked. I realized that the sack he so casually pulled over his head was a human face, and the jar must have been brains. Shocked back to reality, I realized I needed to get out … FAST.

"The creatures began to squabble—I didn't need anyone to translate what they had in mind. I had intruded, seen the unspeakable, and now there was only one thing to do … add me to their collection!

"I bolted down the hall, praying the slit was still there. One turn, and I could see I had a chance. Without hesitating, I made a dash toward the opening; it was closing fast. Though I couldn't hear them, I knew the three were literally hot on my trail. I could feel their breath.

"I know you all think I didn't have a chance. I know I'm not the fastest sprinter, but there are miracles or maybe that stuff we studied in biology, adrenaline, really might work! That's all I can figure, because I made it just in time to dive through the mysterious opening.

"I didn't slow down; I knew they would follow. I wondered if they could breathe our air—maybe I could get a break. But then I remembered, of course they could, because I could breathe inside the cone. Maybe they would dissolve in the sunlight—and I hoped I was right.

"I took the risk—yeah, I know Coach says, 'Never, NEVER look back; it breaks your stride.' But I had to know if they were there! And then I wished I'd followed Coach's advice. They were there—levitating, flying over the ground, getting closer by the second. My heart was pounding so hard, I thought it would break through my chest. My throat burned, so I could barely breathe! I thought my body was going to give out and save the creatures the trouble of catching me. I ran with all my might.

"The tree shadows looked like gnarly witches' fingers, reaching out to stop me, and then I tripped on an exposed root. I was just about to surrender when it happened. I saw the form of a boy, curled under a bush by a towering pine, one-hundred feet ahead. I bounced up and charged on. As I got closer, I realized the kid was me! I must be dreaming. I must be asleep, and it's all a dream!

"'Wake up!' I called. 'Wake up, you fool!' But what do you think I did? Do you think I batted an eye?"

"No," a voice came from somewhere. "As you said, you're a fool." Several stuffed chuckles followed.

Deke ignored them. "No. And the creatures continued coming, closer and closer. They were coming! With all hope gone, I hurled myself toward the body. There was nothing left to do." Deke paused and dramatically looked toward the sky.

"And!" Wayne broke the silence.

Deke continue to be silent. "And what?" he finally grinned.

"And what happened?" Wayne replied agitatedly.

"Oh, you want to know what happened next," Deke replied in a droll tone, feeling vindicated from the earlier slight. "Well, as I jumped, I felt a sensation of being pulled, and I collapsed. I don't know how long I was out, but when I opened my eyes, it felt as if no time had passed. I looked around for the creatures, the cone, but there wasn't a sign of anything. I didn't know where I was, but I realized my arms and legs were still attached and my brain was still working."

"How did you know?" called Buck.

"Because for the first time, I knew what it was to feel alive. Breathing never felt so good. The air never smelled so sweet. The creatures were gone. They weren't hoovering over me or gnawing on my leg. The silver cone was gone. My adrenaline was no longer pumping. I realized it was just me in the field. I sat for a moment and tried to piece together what had happened in the last hour—it was so real, but it didn't make any sense. I did think I sure wished Jim Brown and Frank had been with me."

"Didn't you want me there?" asked Buck.

"You wouldn't have been any help," said Deke, rolling his eyes.

"Oh, you wanted us to save you?" smiled Jim Brown.

"Well, in a way. I figured if they saw Jim Brown, they couldn't resist getting his body parts, and Frank's brain, need I say more? Besides, I can run faster than Frank."

"Hey, you said there were three aliens; maybe you should have added Buck to your list," Wayne added.

"Just leave me out of your dreams." The guys all laughed.

"It didn't end there," Deke interrupted.

"What?" several chimed.

"No. I was still confused and upset. I just wanted to get back to civilization, to people I knew and understood—to reality. I remembered I had a nickel in my pocket—I felt for it, and it was still there—so I took off for the five and dime; a cream soda would really hit the spot. My throat was parched and getting dryer with every step I took.

"On the way, I gathered my thoughts and wondered, *What if it all were true? Where were they from? Why did they collect a room full of candy? And what about the body parts?*"

Deke meant the questions to be rhetorical, but Frank decided it was his turn to speak. "Easy. First, let's examine your sore throat. Were you snoring? Now, where were they from? Had to be from another planet. You yourself said they travelled in a silver cone. There's nothing here on earth like that, and no one levitates. The candy is the easiest to answer. A Hershey's bar in every pocket, and the world would be at peace. They have good taste."

Jim Brown had to jump in. "Or maybe they were going to use the candy to lure kids to capture them and dissect their bodies! And what about those models? Were they selected to appreciate what our culture and intellect had achieved, or are they targets for the next wave?"

"Guys, do you want to hear the rest, or not?" Deke exploded, feeling a bit frustrated. "You're missing the point!" he huffed. "As I said, I was going to get a cream soda. When I arrived, I'd just about given up sorting through the experience—no one would believe me anyway," he added with a sigh, looking at his so-called friends. "Maybe it was just a crazy dream. And that's when I heard him, clear as day. The man sitting at the counter said to Mr. Sterling, 'Hello, my name is Tom, Tom Ferguson.' I stopped dead in my tracks, whirled around, and lit out of there as fast as I could."

"Didn't you look so you could describe him to the police?" someone broke in.

"Nope. Didn't care. I knew that voice. If something happened, Mr. Sterling could describe him."

"If he's alive," Wayne solemnly said.

"Well, I didn't think of that! But hey, I escaped from them once that day, you don't think I'd stick around a second time!"

"Hey, Deke, you sure you got away the first time? Are you sure you're really sitting here? Can we trust you? You said you couldn't remember what happened after you jumped? Maybe…" Jim Brown surmised.

"Yeah," the gang chimed in. "How do we know if you are really the same fellow we thought you were?"

"Swell. You fellas know it's me!" cried Deke in his defense.

"That's, 'It is I,'" corrected Frank.

"No, that must be Deke," said Wayne in support. "He never has his I's and me's correct." And the gang cracked up.

"Whatever!" moaned Deke in resignation, "But I'm telling you, they're here! And we'd better be ready. We'll have to pull together when they come."

"What about the Germans and Japs? I'm not sure I believe in aliens, but those guys are for real," Wayne said, changing the mood.

It was the elephant in the room. Something in the back of all their minds, but something no one had answers for. They also were concerned for Jim Brown, as he was the only one who had a brother in the fight. They all knew it had made a big change in his life this year, but he never shared those deep thoughts, not even with them.

Frank coughed, and all eyes gratefully, expectantly turned to him.

"I have a story," he said hesitantly. "It's not scary," he began and gave a nod to Deke, who greedily accepted Frank's validation. "But, it's true."

XVIII

THE BOYS GASPED IN ANTICIPATION. TRUTH, INDEED, COULD BE stranger than fiction.

"WHAT?" interrupted Deke, "You don't think mine was true?" he cried, while sarcastically grabbing his wounded heart.

Frank paused only long enough to slip Deke a look that said, "Let it go," while the others ignored him completely. Their attention had eagerly glued on to Frank, and he now controlled their minds.

His voice dropped in a conspiratorial tone. "I learned this from my grandpa, who knows every tale and every legend from the days when druids roamed Ireland and human sacrifices were offered to Crum Cruach."

"Crum who?" asked Buck.

"Shhh!" replied the circle. Frank continued.

"The moon is a man dwelling in the sky; a man who watches the actions of men on Earth."

Like dominoes falling, one after the other, they looked up to the sky and waited for the shimmering orb to appear from behind the clouds. As if on cue, there it was. Then, they turned back to Frank for more.

"He was hurled there by an angry spirit for boasting that men were the perfection of creation. In a terrible rage, the spirit threw him into space and condemned him to watch the lives of these 'perfect' creatures until," and here, he dramatically paused, "he found one."

"Well, here I am," beamed Deke, which was followed by the usual groan, given in unison.

"Wait," interrupted Wayne, "I don't get it."

"It's just a myth," Jim Brown responded, a bit disappointed.

"You might say that," Frank casually responded, "but last night, I saw him. I heard him." As Frank calculated, once again he had control. "His face was contorted and great, steaming clouds gushed from his mouth. Lightning flashed from his eyes. Now you all had to have seen that." He paused and looked to see if everyone was nodding in agreement. They were. "And then, that sound! I'll never forget it—a cynical, despairing, cruel laugh."

"Why?"

Frank wasn't sure who asked, but he had the answer.

"Just think about it. Like the Titanic—the ship that couldn't sink—and there on her maiden voyage, she hits an iceberg and plummets to the bottom of the ocean. Tell all those freezing passengers, clinging to the rails as she pitched and broke apart, the men and women and children bobbing in the icy waves, about the perfect design that was perfectly built and perfectly sailed by perfect men to the perfect disaster." Each listener gave a shiver.

"And then there's the War to end all Wars—the World War. Prejudice, intrigue, greed and secret treaties—the world goes to war. We sign the Treaty of Versailles and say that justice has triumphed and democracy is saved, but at what price? Only Marshal Foch declared that in twenty years we'd be back at war. He missed it by two months and four days. How would you feel if you had to watch all that after swearing men were perfect?"

Frank, carried by his convictions like a preacher from the pulpit, dropped his voice and continued, "Yesterday, in the paper, there was an article about a bomb that was dropped on an English cemetery. There, a disemboweled grave had hurled up a skeleton, yellowed and molded by years of burial. Its skull was crushed like a shattered eggshell, and the empty eye sockets stared into the sky. Moonlight reflected from the eye sockets, creating spotlights illuminating the tilted head stone so the man in the moon could read the simple epitaph:

Nigel Philpott, Pvt. HM 102nd Pioneers

He died in the preservation of democracy.

"I think that's what I heard, the Man in the Moon and Nigel, crying, together."

"But you do think we should be fighting this war, don't ya, Frank?" asked Jim Brown, the pain and confusion obvious, as his unspoken thoughts of Bill were clear to all.

"Of course!" replied Frank without hesitation. "We were attacked. That's justification right there. Can't stop others from making bad decisions. The President immediately declared to the world we were at war. We all heard him on the radio." He looked around again and saw everyone nodding in agreement. "Right away, I told my mom as soon as I could, I'd be off to defend our nation." Frank jumped up and crossed his heart. "We stand for liberty, justice, and equality." To give added confirmation, he gave a salute and quoted the New Testament, "'There is no greater Love than a man lay down his life for a friend,' John 15:13." (GNT)

"Though I do prefer, 'Have the salt of friendship among yourselves and live in peace with one another,'" Buck added with a smile.

Jim Brown couldn't quite place the quote, and Wayne saw it in his eyes. "Mark, chapter 9, verse something or other. It was one of the verses we had to memorize for Sunday school," he added sheepishly. "But do you think the Germans will invade? I mean, do you think they'll bring the war here? Do you think we'll be speaking German?" Wayne's eyes bulged, and his voice was flustered.

"No and no." It was Jim Brown whose voice reflected confidence in its strong, deep tone. Everyone unconsciously leaned back and gave a collective sigh, as if the whole world was put right again. They believed in Jim Brown, though Jim Brown himself was beginning to reconsider.

"I'm not that keen on killing, or being killed for that matter, but I will stand and defend when duty calls," Frank added stoically.

This time, Jim Brown smiled and nodded in agreement. Then and there, they all made a pact to have each other's back, wherever life took them. It was great to have friends.

Wayne was the first to break the silence. "But is it true?"

"What?" someone cried out while the rest just moaned.

"Really! I mean the Man in the Moon and the skeleton?" retorted Wayne defensively, crossing his arms over his chest, staring defiantly over the fire.

"Well, I do agree with Frank," Wayne continued, "but I don't see how we got ourselves into this mess. Maybe we kids should rule the world! Maybe we have better answers..." he proudly suggested, raising an all-knowing eyebrow.

"Be careful, Mr. Perfect. I think the Man in the Moon is tired of watching the world and is looking for a replacement, someone just like you; someone he can suck up and put in his place!" With that, Frank made a loud, slurping sound and menacingly reached out his arms toward Wayne.

"Hey, maybe Wayne has a point," Buck maliciously chimed in. "Like what if there were Men on the Moon or Martians and aliens? What if they're behind all this? What if they could look like us and talk like us just to get us riled up so we killed each other, and then they would come and take over the Earth? Maybe they're watching us right now."

Now this was a discussion Jim Brown could really sink his teeth into.

About that time, his father drove in from a late meeting in Tallahassee. The headlights crossed the yard like beams radiating from the eyes of some outer space creature, catching the boys by surprise. His dad got out and gave a friendly wave, yelling, "Don't let the bed bugs bite!" and walked up to the house.

"I wish he hadn't said that!" groused Wayne, as he began to swat at imaginary insects and to scratch imaginary bites. Deke, seizing the moment, leaned back and casually stretched while snatching a blade of grass. Then, with stealth, he began to tickle the back of Wayne's neck. Wayne swatted viciously at his head. Realizing it was Deke, he glared and shook his head, "You jerk!"

Just then a bat swooped down, capturing a mouthful of insects that had been drawn to the fire.

"See," Deke grinned. "You don't have to worry. The bats have arrived!"

Wayne groaned and pulled a blanket over his head.

The boys retreated and returned with pillows as an old-fashioned pillow fight broke out. Soon the yard was cover with feathers, and in the morning light, the ground looked as if it were covered in snow.

The campout was a success.

XIX

FATHER'S DAY ARRIVED ON JUNE 21 THAT YEAR. AS EXPECTED, THE
boys were downstairs in their Sunday best, waiting for their mother to
appear. Their dad had disappeared and then reappeared with a freshly cut
gardenia. Then, patiently, he took his position next to the boys. Suddenly,
they all stretched their necks in unison. The ties he had finished with perfect Windsor knots—which, his wife insisted, were necessary to be in style—
pinched. As if on cue, their mother sailed down the stairs in a shirtwaist
dress and matching scarf, making last-minute adjustments. Their dad met
her and presented the homespun corsage. Jim Brown noted it was more
beautiful than a store-bought flower, and it had a delightful perfume not
to be found in a bottle. The family got in their car and joined the flood of
people going to church.

The Baptist church, as well as every other church in town, was packed.
The family took their usual seats and waited for the organist to begin.
Keeping with tradition, she began the prelude to "God of Our Fathers"
as the pastor took the podium. He was known for his fire-and-brimstone
speeches that would shake the rafters while keeping the congregation attentive and sitting ramrod straight in the pews. Today, he was more calm and
serene. He opened by having all the fathers stand and be recognized, and
then he mentioned by name those who could not join them this day, those
at war. A few sniffles could be heard as tears flowed.

At this point, he traditionally would have begun a litany of all the biblical fathers, beginning with Adam, not the best example, but he always

emphasized that he lived 930 years, enough time to repent and make corrections. Then, he would continue listing the rest of the Old Testament patriarchs, including some by name and others by deeds. Jim Brown always remembered dozing off somewhere between Jacob and his twelve sons and Jesse the father of David. But when the pastor arrived at the New Testament, the accounts picked up. He would begin with Zechariah, the father of John the Baptist, and Joseph, the appointed father of Jesus, and then there were Jairus, the chief of a synagogue, whose daughter was healed, and, of course, the father and his prodigal son. Jim Brown gave a side glance to his father and noted that he, too, was also settling in for a long sermon. But this Father's Day, the pastor took a different path to everyone's surprise.

He announced that General Douglas MacArthur had been selected "Father of the Year." Serving in the Pacific, standing for God and country, who deserved the honor more? Then, he read a prayer that General MacArthur wrote to his son:

Build me a son, O Lord, who will be strong enough to know when he is weak,

And brave enough to face himself when he is afraid;

One who will be proud and unbending in honest defeat,

And humble and gentle in victory.

Build me a son whose wishes will not take the place of deeds;

A son who will know Thee — and that is to know himself as the foundation stone.

Lead him, I pray, not in the path of ease,

But under stress and spur of difficulties and challenges.

Here let him learn compassion for those who fail.

Build me a son whose heart will be clear, whose goal will be high,

A son who will master himself before he seeks to master other men,

Who will reach into the future, yet never forget the past.

After all these things are his, add, I pray, enough of a sense of humor,

So that he may always be serious, yet never take himself too seriously.

Give him humility, so that he may always remember the simplicity of true greatness,

The open mind of true wisdom, and the weakness of true strength.

Then, I, his father, will dare to whisper, "I have not lived in vain."

Everyone was silent as the words and their many layered meanings sunk in. Not to be forgotten, not to disappoint, the pastor immediately dove into an abbreviated version of the fathers of the Bible.

Jim Brown became lost in his own thoughts. *Where was Bill? Would he ever be a father?* Could he even imagine Bill with a son! Unexpectedly, a small chuckle escaped as he pictured Bill with a crying infant in a stinking diaper, covered with vomit. He quickly disguised it with a cough, but it did not fool his mother who gave a disapproving glance. The choir then broke the silence as they led the congregation in another song, followed by prayer. He turned to his parents, who were caught up in a religious moment, and then he noticed Harold who had amazingly managed to strike a prayerful pose as well.

After church, it was straight home for a Father's Day feast with bacon and eggs, grits and gravy, and warm biscuits with homemade strawberry jam. Life—even in war—could have its wonderful moments. Father's Day differed from Mother's Day. Fathers didn't require the same dutiful attention; fathers just wanted time. Usually, they slipped out the back door. Their destinations were no surprise—either Kinsley Lake to fish, or the hunting camp to run the dogs and train the pups for the season ahead. Either destination gave the fathers the opportunity to relax and dip into what whiskey or homemade moonshine was available. At sunset, they would return home—no worse for wear—to sit down to a home-cooked meal and the glory of their children—which ran from quiet calm to outrageous tackling and takedowns.

The days passed, and everyone focused on the next holiday—the Fourth of July. Buntings appeared while fireworks—legal and contraband—were brought out from their hiding places. As Starke began to celebrate, news broke—four German saboteurs had been captured. What caught everyone by surprise was how easily they had managed to sneak onto their guarded shores. It was reported in the newspapers that on June 16, a U-boat had dropped the men off close to Ponte Verde. They easily swam ashore with explosives, money, documents, and clothes, where they blended in with the locals and tourists enjoying a summer day at the beach. Jim Brown tried to remember if he was there that day. Wayne's mom had driven the gang to the beach for another end-of-school ritual. It just sent shivers up his spine wondering if one of the men had tossed a ball to him or just watched them play.

The following day, the story continued on the front page of the newspaper. The saboteurs had buried the explosives and cash like pirates and casually rode a bus into Jacksonville, where they separated and registered at two hotels, the Mayflower and the Seminole. No one noticed anything unusual. They bought more clothes and prepared for the next leg of their journey; some went to Cincinnati, the rest to Chicago. Each man had three thousand dollars, a handkerchief covered with invisible ink with the names and addresses of safe houses along the way, and a specific mission to destroy a designated railroad line or communications system. Fortunately, or unfortunately if you were one of the German spies, a fellow compatriot exposed their plot to the FBI.

The war that once seemed far away was now just hours down the road. Camp Blanding continued to train soldiers but also accepted a new assignment to secure German prisoners of war. As long as Bill was serving, Jim

Brown thought, he wished he could be stationed closer to home. The Pacific was on the other side of the world. He was truly needed at home now.

On his bedroom wall, Jim Brown had taped a large poster of the world. Over the central part of North Florida was a silver star, which marked Starke; then, tiny pins identified battles that were reported on the radio. A special, red-tipped pin marked where Jim Brown thought his brother might be. Tonight, he added another pin close to Jacksonville.

He fired imaginary bullets at phantom enemies in the shadows that danced across the walls and ceiling, but it offered little comfort and made no sense at all. In his heart, he knew Bill was facing real enemies, real bullets, and real dangers in a real hell on earth. In his heart, he wondered if his friends truly understood how he felt; he wasn't even sure himself. He didn't want to upset his folks with all his questions, so he kept them and his feelings bottled up inside.

That Fourth of July, the county splurged and pulled out all the stoppers with a firework show that everyone would remember. Families gathered around Kingsley Lake to enjoy the spectacle, complete with politicians, music, and food—watermelon, corn on the cob, barbecued chicken, hot dogs, and sheet cakes covered with thick boiled icing. Someone had saved up their rations—or someone turned his head—to make that happen.

As the fireworks exploded, Jim Brown's thoughts returned to Bill, but not fond memories of past Independence Day celebrations. Instead, he realized that the explosions Bill heard would not bring cascading showers of twinkling stars; rather they signaled incoming death. He thought about all the sacrifices Bill was making.

Suddenly, he felt someone staring at him and casually glanced around. His eyes locked with Wanda, Bill's girlfriend. Her stare was more like a glare, and Jim Brown tried to smile. He never did get along with her, and sometimes he wondered what Bill ever saw in her, but she was being faithful to Bill while he was gone—at least so far—and so he made the effort to be nice. Fortunately, she broke off and turned with what Jim Brown would later recall as a huff, and they both settled back watching the Roman candles screech and the cherry bombs pop, filling the sky with twinkling star explosions, followed by ooohs and aaahs.

In the coming weeks, his folks were preoccupied with their lives—his dad with the prison and his mom with the house and her social circles. Jim Brown was left alone to do pretty much what he wanted and very little of what he did not. He chose friends and sports, followed by chores and Harold. The summer days passed uneventful, like train cars at a railroad crossing—one, followed by another, then another and another. He had forgotten about the tree and its escape route, until one summer morning.

Jim Brown had wanted to go fishing, but his mother insisted he watch Harold. He stole a glance down the road, hoping to see Grinner, his only chance to escape. His mother had a soft spot for him and felt it her Christian duty to look after him, which meant Jim Brown would pick up her share of the Christian load.

He had met Grinner when he was almost four years old. His mother gave birth to him in prison, and he was allowed to remain with her in the West Wing. He always wondered what that must be like. She was now a trustee and bussed to work in the prison officers' homes. Grinner came along, but as he got older, he was constantly under foot. She asked Mrs. Godwin if he might pull some weeds in her garden or perhaps be a gofer for the other trustees working in the yard, outside and away from trouble.

One morning, Jim Brown's mother called, "Jim Brown! Little Sambo's going to help you pull weeds!"

Huh? Jim Brown looked up and thought he saw a black woman grimace. Next to her stood a stocky, little fellow, just over three feet tall, dressed in denim overalls and a ten-gallon Stetson hat that just about covered all other features. She bent over, and Jim Brown could read her lips.

"Go on, honey. I'll be alright. Listen to Mr. Jim Brown, and do as he says. I'll be back before you know it." She gave him a gentle push, and he began to walk over, glancing back over his shoulder with each hesitating step.

What was his mother thinking? Jim Brown shook his head and went back to pulling weeds. The little shadow was by his side. He studied Jim Brown's every move and then copied him step by step. He even gave his best effort to stand up in sync with Jim Brown, stretching out his arms and twisting his back from side to side before they moved from one section to the next. Silence reigned, not as a barrier but more like a comforting blanket. It suited Jim Brown; it suited the little fellow, too.

As noon approached, Jim Brown, hot and sweaty, got up and went to the kitchen. He grabbed a towel, soaked it in cold water, and wiped the dirt from his hands and face.

Outside, under an oak, the little fellow took off his hat and sat on his haunches, forlorn and looking around—maybe for some distraction, maybe for his mother. Jim Brown realized no one was coming, and the kid was probably as hungry as he was. He grabbed some bread and bologna and made two sandwiches. Then, he went outside and sat down beside him. As pathetic as he was, this little fellow deserved more. He handed him a sandwich.

At first, Grinner was startled; he didn't even hear Jim Brown approach. He quickly took the sandwich before this big fellow could change his mind and hungrily took a bite.

"Got any mayonnaise?" he quietly whispered. "I like mayonnaise," he continued, dropping his head. His eyes glistened with tears; he had learned to hold them back. After all, no one saw, no one listened, and no one cared. He'd grown accustomed to talking with his shadow. His mother said God always hears, even words spoken in silence. He didn't understand that, but he believed everything his mother said, and he listened to every word she spoke. Then, he cocked his head toward a blade of grass—the only living thing that seemed to answer with a sway in the wind—when a voice broke his trance.

"Me, too," replied Jim Brown, as his tongue reached to catch a crumb dropping from his mouth.

Shocked that a human voice responded, the fellow sat up. Looking straight ahead, as he dared not look Jim Brown in the eye, he boldly pressed on, "I likes mustard … and pickles, too."

"Dill or sweet?" asked Jim Brown.

"Sweet … and crunchy!" he smiled, quite satisfied with himself and his answer.

Jim Brown got up and disappeared. Again, the little fellow hunched over, as if it had all been a dream. He felt lost again, not lost in thought or lost like where am I (after all, he was positively certain of that!), but the deep-down, forgotten lost, as if he were alone in the universe and had nowhere to go.

Moments later, Jim Brown returned with two more bologna sandwiches, slathered with mayonnaise and mustard and pickles. The fellow couldn't believe his eyes as he gratefully took the sandwich. Jim Brown couldn't believe how quickly he wolfed it down—and he hoped it wouldn't make him sick! Then, he found the little guy grinning from ear to ear. His dark features so highlighted his bright white teeth that his face seemed to disappear like a Cheshire Cat, leaving only the smile.

Jim Brown laughed and said, "I don't know your name, but I'm calling you Grinner."

"Suits me fine," said the little guy, and that's the way it was.

In the weeks that followed, Grinner would just show up unannounced and dive into whatever Jim Brown was working on. They never talked, but they knew each other pretty well. Jim Brown's chores were completed in less than half the time, so one day when Grinner arrived, Jim Brown dropped what he was doing, and said, "Let's go fishing!" Leaning against the fence were two fishing poles: one new and tall; the other used and short. That was the one Grinner grabbed as he eagerly shook his head in agreement. Just as in the garden, Grinner studied every move Jim Brown made. It wasn't long before they would return regularly with a mess of fish. Jim Brown would let Grinner take as many as he wanted, but he only took two—never the largest; just two nice ones, one for his mom and one for him, Jim Brown assumed.

One day while picking up pinecones in the yard, things became silent, not quiet, but ghostly silent. Jim Brown turned on his heels and took in the scene in a single glance. Grinner's mouth was open, his eyes popped, and at his feet was a pigmy rattler getting ready to strike! In a single motion, he took the pick and stabbed the snake behind his eyes. It twisted and turned and angrily hissed. Jim Brown then took the hoe and cut off its head. Grinner raced over and grabbed his leg. He wrapped his arms around and squeezed so tight, Jim Brown was sure his blood was going to be cut off.

"Is it dead?" he whispered, as he tried to find the courage to open his eyes and see for himself.

"Yes. It's dead," Jim Brown replied calmly, though his heart was racing now that the crisis was over.

"We gonna bury it?" asked Grinner, looking for guidance.

Jim Brown took the pick and stabbed both sections of the snake and said, "No, this one's going straight to hell!" And he flung it into a pile of burning leaves not too far away.

"Straight to hell," replied Grinner, feeling totally relieved and at peace. From then on, Grinner had his back. Jim Brown was someone to believe in, someone to trust. Jim Brown was a friend.

Grinner wasn't around for long. He was already over the age that the women were allowed to keep their children. Jim Brown thought he probably didn't have family to go to and would be put into the foster care system.

Grinner never said, but still every once in a while, he would return, looking for his mother and looking for Jim Brown.

Bill used to tease him about "his little ward," but Jim Brown just shrugged him off. Today was a day he really wished he would show up, and he wished Bill would drive up the road as well, but that wasn't happening. Life wasn't something you planned; life just happened.

So here he was. As usual, Harold was rambunctious and not in the mood to listen, and Jim Brown was irritated and not in the mood to be ignored. Harold picked up a bow and arrow and aimed it at Jim Brown. He threatened to shoot it if Jim Brown didn't immediately put down the bamboo fishing pole he was working on and come play with him. Jim Brown never looked up but kept warning him not to point the arrow at him.

Harold became more impatient and kept the arrow pointed squarely at his brother. Jim Brown finally looked up and gave him a cold stare like their father's. "For the last time, Harold…"

But it was too late. Whether his fingers really slipped and Jim Brown got in the way, as he later wailed to their mother, or he deliberately shot the arrow as Jim Brown tried to protest, the arrow came flying and stuck into Jim Brown's calf. Perhaps it was the shock or the pain, Jim Brown couldn't remember; he pulled the arrow out and went flying after Harold, who was high-tailing it up to the big house. It only took a few steps to catch him. Jim Brown grabbed his brother around the waist, hoisted him up, and began to beat him with the arrow, screaming, "I told you to put that arrow down! I'm gonna break that bow in two... You'll never shoot that bow again, you little son of a..."

Harold's screams, yelps, and hollers sailed through the open windows and brought their mother running into the yard. He broke away and bawled in her arms. "Jim Brown's gonna kill me! I didn't do nuthin'! It was an ax-dent!" The tears continued to flow.

Jim Brown waited patiently and smirked, thinking, *Just wait 'til Mom hears what really happened!*

But before he had a chance, his mother lashed out, "How dare you beat your little brother! I don't ask for much. I just needed you to watch him for a few minutes while I get the house ready for the canasta group. You just march yourself up stairs and wait for your father to get home! Honestly, Jim Brown!"

"But Mom!" Jim Brown cried, as he pointed to the blood dripping down his leg.

"Not another word! Up to your room. Now! And clean yourself up." She walked away in a huff, still carrying Harold, who looked back at his brother and stuck out his tongue. He wasn't so happy when their mother called the trustee raking the petals from under the camellia bush and unceremoniously handed him off before returning to the house.

His mom was only 5'2" and Jim Brown towered over her, but her word was law around the house. He obediently trudged up to the back door, mumbling, "Whatever." As always, it summoned up all his feelings in that moment—*I'm right, and I don't give a darn what the world says!* He grabbed a piece of divinity from a silver tray as he passed through the kitchen and limped up to his room.

As he washed off his leg and watched the blood swirl down the drain, he thought about his mother. He knew she wanted this day to be perfect. She was what his dad called a social butterfly, someone who truly enjoyed people, and generally people enjoyed her. She had friends she'd met in kindergarten, and friends she'd made over the vegetable counter at Spires just last yesterday. She had prayer circles from church and social clubs from Starke. The canasta group was special. These weren't the ones she'd kick back with, laughing while smoking cigarettes, and sipping on homemade wine that everyone swore was, "Just a little grape juice, honey." No, this was the high society who wore their Sunday best and had their noses in the air. These were the ones his mother wanted to impress, to ingratiate herself to, to belong with. He understood all that, but she at least could have taken the time to listen!

That evening over dinner, his mother continued nonstop talking about her wonderful canasta party and the latest gossip she'd heard. Harold and Jim Brown eyed each other suspiciously, establishing a silent truce, as neither one knew how their father would react to the morning scuffle. It probably was best to let their mom go on talking—obviously she had already forgotten the altercation—and to let their dad go on eating, occasionally nodding and responding, "That's nice," implying he really was listening.

That night, even the house seemed to sleep in awkward silence. No boards creaked. The humming fans droned on inaudibly; even the familiar snoring from his parents' room was missing. Only Jim Brown could not sleep. His calf throbbed as he tossed and turned, and his head pounded, as thoughts flashed one after another. He was mad. He was mad at Harold; he was mad at his mother; he was mad that Bill was gone; and he was mad at all the injustices of the world. Suddenly, the oak branches gave a light tap against the house, and he could hear the leaves rustling in the gentle night breeze. A warm smile stretched across his face, and he subconsciously nodded his head, saying, "Yes. Yes, I'll climb your branches." And with that, he closed his eyes and went to sleep.

XX

OUT OF NOWHERE, A MOANING SOUND SWIRLED THROUGH HIS HEAD.
Slowly, he recognized the lonesome whistle of the CFC out of Flagler. Jim
Brown was still groggy as he lay in his bed. Through his barely opened eyes,
he could make out the horizon already streaked with pinks and gold, and
he knew the sun would soon follow. Quickly, he pulled on his jeans and
grabbed a clean T-shirt from his drawer. In the dark, it was difficult to make
out the color. He just hoped it wasn't the purple one his mother bought for
Bill last spring. Bill wouldn't be caught dead in purple, so he had tossed it
to Jim Brown, who, likewise, wouldn't wear it but had no one to toss it to
yet. It was usually scrunched up in the back of his drawer, but he'd have to
risk it since he wasn't going to turn on the light.

Then, like all Godwin men, he grabbed his pocketknife. It was auto-
matic. He'd heard it a thousand times, "If a man has his britches on, he'd
better have a knife in his pocket. And—it'd better be sharp." He'd never be
caught without his. Walking over to the window, he suddenly heard a *thump,
thump, thump*. He stopped in his tracks and listened again. He realized it
was the beating of his own heart.

The dew blanketed the ground, forming clouds of mist as it evaporated.
The thermometer he kept by his window already read sixty-five degrees; it
would be another scorcher. He climbed onto the windowsill and looked
something like a gargoyle as he crouched, wondering if this really was a
good idea. Then, with a divine leap of faith in his brother's words, he hurled
himself out.

At first, it felt as if he were flying in slow motion, then in a split second, everything changed, and he flailed like a sailor, grabbing for a lifeline in a stormy sea. He latched onto the first branch he saw. It bent almost to the breaking point, and Jim Brown knew he was going down. Then, miraculously, it snapped back with a whoosh. Jim Brown scrambled to a sturdier limb and then the next and the next. Startled, a murder of crows roosting in the upper branches began to flap their wings and cry, creating a cacophony. They were definitely not songbirds. Seconds later, they flew off, leaving him quite alone in the morning stillness—just as he wanted.

In the distance, lights flickered on and off as prison guards returned home from night shifts or prepared to start their day. Softly, the magic of the tree came alive. For the first time, he realized he had survived his brother's

crazy but awesome plan. He took a deep breath and settled into the fork in the tree, truly feeling alive and free. He was ready to tackle anything life threw his way. He imagined he was on the cliffs of Mt. Kilimanjaro, watching a herd of kudu, six hundred-pound antelopes with large curling horns, thundering over the plains. Then, he was standing watch in the Amelia Island lighthouse, looking for German U-boats. He'd overheard that the Japanese had already landed on the islands off the Alaskan coast and more German U-Boats were scouting the Eastern shores.

After a few minutes, his dreams faded as reality took hold. He enjoyed just sitting there, quietly watching his kingdom come to life. The open fields, the country roads, all the creatures who walked or swam or flew within its mystical boundaries—he knew every corner, every critter, and they knew him. He relaxed and took it all in.

Then, he noticed the sky was becoming a pale blue, and someone, probably his father, was in the kitchen banging pots and pans. Now or never, he climbed down from his invisible perch and set off on the dusty road before being discovered.

He jammed his hands into his pockets and kicked the nearest clod of dirt, watching it disintegrate as it bounced down the road. As he scanned the road, searching for the next clod to demolish, his eyes settled on a peculiar black rock sitting in the middle of the road. As he came closer, the rock rose up and moved forward. *Just a gopher tortoise*, he thought, and then became mesmerized as he watched it plod on. The tortoise seemed to march with purpose, and Jim Brown found himself envious. He wondered where he was off to with such conviction. He himself had no idea where he was going— today, tomorrow, the next minute—and yet, this simple turtle marched on.

His trance broke when he heard the rumbling of a car headed in their direction. He bent over and gingerly picked up the creature. The tortoise immediately pulled in his head and legs and arms, once again resuming his rock-like status. Jim Brown carefully turned him and looked in his eyes, saying, "Fellow, you may know where you're going, but if you stay on this path, you'll be roadkill in no time."

As if he understood, the tortoise defiantly shot out his head and legs and began clawing wildly in the air. Seeing the claws, Jim Brown put him down as quickly as possible. The tortoise picked up his pace and, in a few seconds, made a sharp right turn into the scrub brush. He was gone.

As he still pondered the life of a turtle dining on slugs, insects, and worms, he saw a new Ford come rattling down the road and recognized Doc Adams at the wheel. He must be returning from an early morning house call. Everyone knew he'd bought the car for the sticker price, never bargaining like everyone else. He just trusted everyone to be fair, and everyone trusted Doc with his life.

"Hi, John!" Doc waved. Jim Brown smiled and waved back. It was another of Doc's idiosyncrasies. He called all boys "John" and all girls "Mary"; that way he'd never be caught short trying to remember anyone's name—but he knew everyone and their secrets. Jim Brown smiled to himself, as he took a certain pride in knowing Doc really did know his proper name.

Jim Brown thought about cars as he walked along. In four years, when he got his license, he hoped he'd have enough money saved to buy one. Not a sticker price one like Doc Adams —there weren't many coming off the assembly line these days anyway, but a used, little blue coupe. His dad wasn't big on cars. Given a choice, he'd rather hitch up Old Dan to a wagon than climb into the state sedan. He often said that with a couple of buckets of feed, fresh water, four solid shoes, and a good rub-down, Old Dan would take him anywhere and bring him safely home. With a few clicks and a tug on the reins, Old Dan knew where Mr. Godwin wanted to go. It was either the dairy, the tannery, the fields, or his office.

On the rare occasion when he wanted to go to town or the depot, Dan would turn his head and twitch his ears, as if to say, "Are you sure?" and then he would break into his rhythmic clip-clop gait down the road. Mr. Godwin could settle in and close his eyes while he considered the day's headlines or the immediate demands at home or work. You couldn't do that with a car. A car needed water, oil, gas, your undivided attention, and, if you could find one, a good mechanic to keep the spark plugs firing, the fan belt turning, and the radiator from leaking. And on a long, dusty road in the middle of nowhere at high noon (or even better, a rain storm), you would need someone to change the inevitable flat tire. Jim Brown tried to argue the comforts and speed a car had—not to mention style—but his dad just shook his head, "What about ration stamps? You know the cost of gas is going up, if you can find some!" and that seemed to end the discussion.

Jim Brown had read that Joe McCarthy, the president of the New York Yankees, had given Babe Ruth a hand-built Lincoln Zephr Continental Cabriolet—now that was a car! Someday, maybe someday, he dreamed he would pull up next to Mr. Ruth and say, "Nice car, Mr. Ruth," or maybe, "Do you need directions?" or, even better, "Do you need someone to play ball?" Jim Brown was a real fan of the Babe. Everyone said that maybe a touch of the Bambino's magic had rubbed off on him when the Babe had hoisted him onto his shoulder during a barnstorming trip through Starke. It was years earlier; he was probably about Harold's size, but he could still remember the thrill. He couldn't quite get a left-handed pitch together like the Babe, but he could fire a right-handed pitch across the plate that few could see, let alone hit.

XXI

AS DOC ADAMS DISAPPEARED DOWN THE ROAD, JIM BROWN REALIZED
he was on his way to the duck farm—not so much by choice as just out of
habit. It wasn't a bad destination; he needed to check on them anyway. So,
like the tortoise, he picked up his step with conviction.

Money was tight, and the duck farm was one of his many schemes to
earn a few dollars—and it actually worked. Everyone for miles around knew
his ducks were plump and tasty, and for fifteen cents more, he'd pluck them
clean. They'd be ready for a special birthday or anniversary celebration.

One time, Mr. Wahtera selected a big, fat drake. Jim Brown had named him FDR after the president because he squawked the loudest and seemed to keep the others in line. FDR had been one of the first wild ducks Jim Brown had captured to start his enterprise. Whenever he arrived, FDR was there to greet him and alert the rest. He'd follow him as he cleaned the roost quacking his approval and tugging at his jeans for a special crust of bread. Jim Brown looked sadly at FDR as he scooped him up and realized that he couldn't wring his neck. Instead, he picked a fat duck; Mr. Wahtera would never know the difference. He actually received a larger bird. Jim Brown took FDR and tossed him outside the pen and vowed never to name another duck—it would be bad for business.

But a funny thing happened; FDR never left. He hung around and continued to greet Jim Brown and quack for his crust of bread. Finally, three months later, he just took off. Jim Brown told his dad that night at the dinner table. His dad looked up and, in his deep voice, asked, "Did you sell a duck recently?"

"Sure. Business has been really good," he proudly replied.

Returning to take a forkful of little acre peas, his father continued, "Ducks mate for life. You probably sold his mate."

The fork of fried fish just hung in mid-air as Jim Brown took in what his father just said. Had he actually wrung FDR's mate's neck? He could feel tears burning, welling in his eyes, but he refused to cry. He tightened his lips and swallowed hard. Then he asked to be excused.

"There's chocolate ice cream for dessert!" his mother cheerfully offered, unaware that his mind was reeling with thoughts of life and death.

"No, thanks," Jim Brown croaked as he got up from the table and took his plate to the kitchen sink. He sat on the porch and thought about FDR and wondered which duck... He sighed into the night, saying, "I'm sorry," and wondered if FDR heard or understood.

Suddenly, Peggy Tilley, the prettiest girl he'd ever seen, popped into his mind. She was Christmas and the Fourth of July all rolled into one. Though he'd never even tell his best friend, just thinking about her made his stomach do flip flops, his mouth go dry, and even his mind turn to mush! She also inspired him to run faster, jump the highest, and ace the Friday spelling tests. He sat back, closed his eyes, gave a sigh, and smiled. For a brief moment, the world seemed right again.

Back walking to the duck farm, while lost in thought, Jim Brown didn't realize that Marty Russell had joined him and was trying his hardest to keep step, a truly impossible task as Marty was a good foot, and then some, shorter than Jim Brown. He looked more like a companion dog trotting after his master. Jim Brown finally caught Marty out of the corner of his eye and slowed down.

"Hey, Jim Brown! Where ya going? Whatcha up to? Ya want some company? I don't have a thing to do. Well, there's always chores, and I promised I'd mow Miss Denton's lawn but..."

Jim Brown looked down at Marty, still trying to comprehend that he was no longer alone with his thoughts. Marty was a long-time friend going back to third grade. He came to Bradford Elementary School that year—shy, motherless, and short, an easy target for bullies and gossip.

XXII

MARTY KEPT TO HIMSELF AND WAS HAPPIEST WHEN HE FELT INVISIBLE.
The best time of day for most of the kids was going outside for recess, but for Marty, it was the worst. Their teacher, Mrs. Garrett, would inevitably select two captains, who took turns choosing classmates to form what she hoped would be balanced teams, though she never stuck around to see how the competitions—kickball, baseball, dodgeball, Red Rover—played out. Ben Wheeler, a school bully, was frequently chosen. He'd stand before the class, his eyes narrowing like a vulture contemplating roadkill. In a booming voice, he'd call for Peter... Maxie... Brian... And when they'd gone through the boys, he'd stare at the girls and point, "You...You... You..."

Finally, there would be Marty and a sweet, but totally uncoordinated, girl named Candy who was always, as they say, "out to lunch." Ben would roll his eyes and jerk his head at her before dashing out the door. Candy would bounce, smiling as she gleefully joined "her team." Marty would sigh. Without waiting for the perfunctory nod, he just walked out to the bench, alone.

But one day, Jim Brown was a team captain, and his first choice was Marty! Marty was totally startled and thought it was a mistake. He heard several classmates snicker, but Jim Brown repeated in a strong, confident tone, "Marty Russell!" Marty felt all his classmates' eyes turn toward him. He was stunned and couldn't understand what was happening. At one time, he dreamed of being picked, maybe third or fourth, but now his eyes burned with tears. *Was it a joke?* He just wanted to disappear. At first, he thought he might throw up, but then he found the courage to quietly walk over. His head held down, he quickly slipped behind Jim Brown.

As they walked to the playground, Jim Brown put his arm on Marty's shoulder and whispered, "Listen. I've been watching you. You're fast, and if you get on base, I know I can count on you for a run."

Count on me … did he say, "Count on you?" His eyes bulged, and he gulped. No one had ever counted on him before. He was terrified and didn't want to let Jim Brown down, but how could he get to first base? That was a big "if"; he'd never gotten to first base!

Jim Brown continued. He turned Marty to face him and stared him in the eye, man to man. "Just promise me you won't swing at the ball. It's not that I don't think you can hit, but Ben can't throw a ball in your strike zone. No offense, but you're just too short. So just promise me you won't swing," he paused, smiled, and added, "but it wouldn't hurt if you were to stare him down. You know, just shake him up a bit." Then, he gave him a conspiratorial wink and dashed over to the rest of the team. Marty couldn't help but grin back. This was a plan he could follow. So, with a renewed spirit, he sprinted to the field and reached the dugout before Jim Brown.

When Marty got up to bat, something took hold. He really wanted to hit a homerun for the team. Ben, as Jim Brown predicted, threw a high pitch. Marty swung, looping the bat, reaching high, and missing by a mile. The force sent him twirling in several revolutions. When he finally caught his balance, he saw Ben smiling and heard his teammates groan. The catcher casually tossed the ball back. Jim Brown coughed and dug his toe into the ground. He barely shook his head, but he gave the unmistakable message, "Don't do it!"

Marty paused and bit his lower lip. He remembered the plan; he remembered his promise. With confidence, he stepped up to the plate, raised the bat, and gave a cold, hard stare, locking Ben's eyes.

"What in the world?" Ben shook his head. Marty had caught him off guard with this clear act of defiance. He tried again to concentrate on pitching, but the next four balls went sailing over Marty's head, and he confidently trotted to first. With a nod from Jim Brown, he stole second. Then, Kelly Fitzgibbon connected with a line drive that squeaked by first base. Marty rounded third and slid home. Jim Brown was there to pat him on the back and say, "Well done!"

After that, Jim Brown helped him learn how to trap a ground ball and keep his eyes open when going for a fly. He didn't make the catch every time, but he was improving. As he got older and grew a few inches, Jim Brown helped him level out his swing and connect with the ball. He explained that Marty needed to think ahead. What was the play? If a new batter was up, the play was at first. If there was a runner at first, he had a choice to throw the ball to first or second. If the bases were loaded, the play was anywhere. He knew to call for the fly ball or back up his teammate. Jim Brown even tried to teach him the team signals, for example, a touch to the visor followed by a tug on the ear meant be prepared to steal. But most of the signs were for the in-field players, and Marty knew he would always be in left field. Most kids were disappointed when the coach assigned them to the outfield, but it couldn't get any better to Marty.

He never was the first pick, but he wasn't the last either, and he never forgot that moment when Jim Brown believed in him. That day, he learned to step out of his comfort zone, to trust someone, and to take the first step in becoming the person he was meant to be.

Jim Brown, on the other hand, never thought much about that time. He probably didn't remember that exact day. He just had a knack for seeing talent and for mentoring. As far as he was concerned, it was a win–win situation for all. Though it might be mentioned, he didn't suffer fools easily. Little did Marty realize, he was just two strikes away from remaining the last player chosen for the remainder of his school days, and worse, he would have just been a blip in Jim Brown's life.

Marty paused for a moment. Then, peeking through his hair that constantly fell over his eyes, he picked up again. "It's gonna be another hot day. Maybe we can grab some watermelon and go out to the swimming hole, or what about the movies? Do you know what's playing at the matinee?"

Jim Brown stopped in his tracks and saw Marty just grinning back up at him. He smiled and shook his head. Marty was right; it was hot, and the movies would be great. He hadn't been to the theater since it opened last October. The Carrier Corporation installed the latest in air conditioning, refrigerated air, with a capacity of thirty-five tons of ice. That sure would feel good. And the news reels were sending films from the German front. Greg Frese swore he saw his father in one; Jim Brown hoped he might see Bill one day. Now that would be worth paying for, to see his brother, a real hero in action instead of the Hollywood versions. But fifteen cents for the matinee was still steep, and Jim Brown was long past his days of sneaking in for free. Most of the movies he saw were at the prison. They were always a few months old, but the price was right.

"I think *The Maltese Falcon* is finally coming to the community center this weekend, but I don't know about the theater. Would be great if there were a John Wayne western," he sighed.

"Yeah," Marty agreed, and they both were quiet for a moment as they thought about the Duke. "Frank said *The Ghost of Frankenstein* came out in March; maybe it's made it to Starke. Did you know he saw *The Son of Frankenstein* ten times? I think he can recite the whole script!"

Jim Brown smiled. "He sure is a fan of Boris Karloff. I think he said they have the same birthday!"

"That would be the twenty-third of November."

Jim Brown shot Marty a quizzical glance and asked, "How did you know that?"

"Easy. Not many people around here eat lamb, and the Foleys have a standing order for a leg of lamb for his birthday. Frank says the lamb is good, but the leftovers are even better. His mother cuts the lamb into chunks, tosses in some green peppers and onions, heats it all up in the gravy—and here's the kicker—she then adds a jar of mint jelly! I can't imagine, but Dad says it probably would be good."

"Well, what's left for St. Patrick's?" Jim asked rhetorically.

But Marty piped up, "Corned beef and something called Colcannon. Curious what you can learn behind the meat counter... You know, Frank's an only child like me. You sure are lucky to have brothers."

"Really? A bratty brother who shoots you in the leg with an arrow?" and with that, he raised his jeans and showed him the hole, emphasized with a stain of iodine. "And what about Bill, who's who knows where, getting shot up without me?" Jim Brown went silent.

Marty grimaced at the sight of the wound and talk of Bill. Their conversation had just taken a turn that he had not anticipated. Trying to redeem himself and taking a moment to consider that there were ramifications about siblings he had never considered, Marty weakly suggested, "Hey, Jim Brown. Bill will be back before you know it." Then, more confidently, he added, "Or else we'll be at his side," followed by a sharp salute.

After a pause, Jim Brown smiled and, in a conspiratorial tone, offered, "Well, I'm headed to the duck pen. It won't take long to clean and spread the feed, but after that, since you mentioned the butcher shop, do you think your dad might need some help?"

XXIII

MARTY SCRUNCHED UP HIS FACE AND NERVOUSLY STAMMERED,
"Probably."

Marty's father was known to get into the moonshine. Rumor had it that his wife had died when Marty was born, and he'd never gotten over her loss. Women at the church tried to help, each with a casserole and her own brand of comfort, but over the years, he had slipped further away.

He was glad Marty made friends with Jim Brown because with his size and muscle, he could help hoist a side of beef onto a hook and after a few weeks, Jim Brown had learned to butcher a cow, a pig, or an occasional deer as well as Mr. Russell did. When they stopped by, Mr. Russell would retreat to the back room and leave everything else to Marty, who had to stand on an overturned crate to see over the meat counter. Marty was particularly diligent counting the red ration coupons, which were required for purchasing meat, fats, fish, and cheeses. His father was furious when they were introduced.

"You give me money, and I'll give you meat!" he declared. His customers were equally confused, and Marty got tickled as he watched them slowly tear out the appropriate points or barter a blue coupon, the coupon for sugar and other rationed foodstuffs, for a red to afford the family roast.

Like it or not, Marty knew once a month, Mr. Robert Stevens from the Office of Price Administration would appear to check the books and collect the coupons. Mr. Stevens was tall and lanky, always wearing a pin-striped suit and a black Fedora. His hawk-like nose jutted out from under the brim and twitched as he strutted like a rooster into the store. At the end of his long, dangling arms, he carried a dark briefcase, which he guarded like a dog with a bone.

"Fair is fair... We all must sacrifice... It's the American Way," Mr. Stevens would recite in a bureaucratic bass. In return, Mr. Russell would slam his books on the counter, followed by a shoebox filled with red and blue coupons, and storm off. Once, Mr. Stevens condescendingly asked if there wasn't an office for conducting business. Mr. Russell picked up a meat clever in one hand and a hook in the other and snarled, "This is a butcher shop. This," and he menacingly shook the hook and clever for emphasis, "is my business. You want a fancy, smancy office, go back where you came from." Mr. Stevens didn't say another word.

There had been a worn but comfortable wooden bench for customers to wait patiently for special orders, but on the days Mr. Stevens was scheduled to come, it was curiously missing. Mr. Stevens just stood by the counter and leaned awkwardly over the books, as he inspected the numbers and counted and recounted the coupons. They always matched, though Marty held his breath until the books were officially closed. The calculations were all his.

The first time he came, Mr. Stevens took an hour examining the records. But as the weeks went by, Mr. Russell became sloppy and splattered the pages with various animals' blood and occasionally dropped specks of chicken organs or pigs' innards on the cover. Mr. Stevens took to wearing gloves and cut his time to twelve minutes—which suited them both just fine.

As the town butcher, Mr. Russell's shop was also designated a fat collection depot. For every pound of lard, cooking oil, and fat, the donor received four cents. "Fill a tin and turn it in!" the radio jingle played morning, noon, and night to encourage everyone to participate. At first, Mr. Russell felt it was just another aggravation, but then he realized that his customers were happy to donate, and the fats were sent to factories to be recycled into soaps, which agreed with his sensibilities.

Jim Brown knew Marty was probably trying to escape unwanted directions for unwanted chores, dictated by unwanted scrutiny from unwanted adults, just as he had by jumping out the window that morning. But he also knew Marty understood that his dad would pay him well enough. Maybe later, they might hitch a ride to Starke and catch that movie.

With a sigh, Marty turned around and started walking down State Road 16 toward Raiford. They stopped at the duck pen and, in record time, cleaned and fed the ducks. Jim Brown made a mental note to bring a hammer and nails when he returned to make some minor repairs, and Marty sighed that all the ducks got stays of execution that day.

Next, they passed under the concrete arches marking the boundary for the Florida State Prison. It would be the last marker until the road intersected with another dusty track, CR 121, where signs of life would reappear at Spire's Grocery. Jim Brown picked up the pace and hoped it would be worth the effort.

XXIV

IT WAS A LONG, HOT, BLISTERING WALK TO RAIFORD. MARTY LOOKED
up to see if he could find any designs in the clouds, but it was a crystal clear,
blue sky. The clouds wouldn't roll in until the afternoon, so they were left at
the sun's mercy or, better put, misery. Jim Brown's shirt was already soaked
with perspiration, and Marty's shirt, which was missing three buttons, was
blowing out like wings as he jogged along beside Jim Brown.

Suddenly, as if out of nowhere, came three girls on bicycles. In the
lead was Peggy Tilley, her long brown curls bounced in the breeze and her
laughter filled the countryside: north, south, east, and west. They all wore

rolled-up dungarees with bobby socks and saddle shoes, but Peggy stood out like a sparkling diamond. Jim Brown stole a glance as she rode by. A shy smile involuntarily appeared and just as quickly faded away. She just had that effect on him. Peggy waved in return. Marty caught the whole scene and started to laugh. Jim Brown was jarred back to reality and rolled his eyes, pretending he had no idea what was so amusing, but Marty wouldn't stop.

"Oooo, Jim Brown's in love!" he teased, pointing his finger and making smooching sounds.

There wasn't anything he could say to shut him up, so Jim Brown just picked up the pace and walked on.

Suddenly, a cool breeze that made him shiver swirled from a winding dirt road, almost hidden by twisting vines, sharp palmettos, and tall pine trees. It led to a local "haunted" house even Jim Brown avoided; rumor had it that whoever went in never came out. Kids swore they felt their souls being sucked out as they passed by, so Jim Brown held his breath and sprinted over the driveway. As he breathed a sigh of relief, he turned to see Marty casually examining a smooth skipping stone he'd spied on the ground. He seemed hypnotized, as he felt the curves and tossed it in the air to test the weight.

Jim Brown yelled, "Marty!" His eyes popped, his mouth tensed, and his arms flung to the side as he jerked his head down the lane. He almost thought, at least in the moment, that Marty had become possessed!

"Huh?" questioned Marty, as he looked up and mirrored Jim Brown's arms and facial expression. "What?"

"Witch Hazel's!" he exclaimed and accented each syllable with a hand gesture. Though Jim Brown didn't actually believe all the tales concerning the mysterious cottage and its owner, he thought Marty did. If Marty were under a spell, he needed to jostle him back to reality to save him from being sucked down the path and disappearing forever!

The cottage was owned by Raiford's version of the Bayou Voodoo queen, Marie Laveau. She was at the heart of contemporary myths and was credited with creating potions and charms, conjuring visions, and talking with the dead!

"Oh, Miss McGonagall's," he calmly shrugged.

"Miss McGonagall's?" Jim Brown repeated while raising an eyebrow, "Miss McGonagall's?" he repeated and gave a tilt of his head. It was the first time he realized she had a name; she was a real person. He leaned in for an explanation.

"Oh, she's all right," murmured Marty.

Jim Brown silently waited for Marty to continue, as he knew the story had to be a whopper. Marty realized Jim Brown wasn't going to budge until he had an explanation. Where to begin—the truth seemed to be the best bet. He tossed the rock aside and launched into what he hoped would be a short account. Then he realized Miss McGonagall deserved better.

"Well," he drawled, "a couple of weeks ago, Dad had a delivery for her. I really didn't want to go—not that I was scared or anything, you know—but you've heard the stories. I tried to get out of it, but Dad was in one of his moods…"

"When is he not?" Jim Brown sarcastically interrupted. He didn't actually mean to say the thought out loud and immediately felt bad that he'd let the words slip. "Sorry," he confessed as his head dropped.

Marty paused and smiled. He knew Jim Brown was sincere and understood, and there was no need to defend his dad. He continued walking down the road and pulled his thoughts together.

"I made it to this very spot, and I just couldn't go any further. Then, I thought of Dad and the two fryers and slab of bacon I was carrying…"

Jim Brown nodded in sympathy.

"I didn't have a choice, so I stopped thinking and just charged on. I would make the delivery and be gone." He paused and looked up to Jim Brown for support. "I really was scared. When I got to the end of the lane, I was sweatin', and my heart was poundin', and I could swear that someone was watching me! I heard all these strange sounds, like snakes slithering or gators crouching, waiting to pounce. I even began to wonder—like the tales say, if anyone would ever find my body." He paused again for effect and studied Jim Brown's face to see if he was listening. He was.

"Then I saw her, all dressed in black, sitting in a rocking chair on the porch with a scrawny cat curled in her lap and another at her feet, its tail weaving in and out as the rocker swayed back and forth. My mouth was dry, and I just wanted to drop the package and run, but she called out, 'Get over here, you scallywag!' And just the way she said 'scallywag' made me laugh.

"I looked hard at her. You know, she really is pretty for an old lady—no warts or anything like that. Her hair is brown with streaks of grey and so curly; well, it just kinda looked like a bird nest sitting on top of her head. Then, she pulled out a plate of cookies from nowhere and a pitcher of fresh

lemonade, too ... and, well, I was hooked! You know, Jim Brown, she's a lot like me."

"Excuse me! What did you say?" Jim Brown was jolted back to reality and wondered again if perhaps he had been bewitched after all!

"No, really! She lost her mom and was passed around to all her relatives. Then, when she was sixteen, her father, who was a sea captain, came and took her on a trip around the world! She's seen the pyramids and live volcanoes. She even helped steer her dad's ship through the Panama Canal when it first opened! She said it's fifty miles long. You guide the ship into the first lock, and they close the gates behind you. The first time was pretty frightening, she said. Then they pump water in and the ship rises until you're almost even with the land. Then, they open the gates at the far end, and you float on through. You do that over and over, and eventually you float into a lake, which she said was 'breathtaking, a green jungle with beautiful birds all around.'" Marty mimicked her high, screechy voice.

"It was tricky to navigate the channel, so her dad took over and she just watched the shoreline as they drifted by. Then, they floated into the next series of locks, but this time after the doors closed, they pumped the water out, and the ship went down 'til they could open the gates and sail through to the next until finally you saw the ocean." Marty smiled, pleased with his lesson on the locks. "She always says, 'Off with you, scallywag, and don't come back!' Then, she gives me a quarter tip. I always smile and say, 'Thanks!' because I know she has a standing order with Dad, and I'll be back."

"I never would have guessed," whispered Jim Brown, shaking his head in disbelief. He actually was a little jealous of Marty eating cookies, listening to tales of worldwide adventures, and getting a full quarter tip. Though he was disappointed there were no boiling cauldrons, no bat tongues drying in the rafters, and no imprisoned children tied to stakes.

As if reading his mind, Marty added, "You know, she does have a strange laugh, like a cackle, and she has this unbelievable garden with all kinds of plants. She calls them medicinal, but they're all jumbled and viney. She even has a meat-eating plant; she let me feed it once. And she has one she calls a voodoo plant because it reappears every year out of nowhere! I don't think I'd want to eat anything she grows..." and he scrunched up his face at the mere thought of the awful, sour tastes. "But I think Doc Adams has," he added, trying to give her credence.

"What?" cried Jim Brown in horror and with concern.

"Well, I've seen him drop by..."

"Oh," replied Jim Brown, sighing with relief. "She could be a patient. You know Doc takes care of everyone."

Then, a sudden inspiration came to Marty. He stopped abruptly, turned around, and held his hands up like a policeman stopping traffic. Marty put down the pinky finger of his right hand and asked, "What do you see?"

Dumbfounded, as Jim Brown was still trying to get his thoughts around a man-eating, voodoo plant, he blurted out, "Ah, nine fingers."

"No, Jim Brown, look closely."

Jim Brown shrugged and shook his head.

"Look," and Marty explained, "one finger down, the first finger, one times nine is," then he wriggled the nine standing fingers. "Nine! Now watch." He raised his pinky finger and folded his ring finger down. "Two times nine, now watch." He wiggled his pinky finger while saying, "One," and then waved his left hand and the remaining three fingers standing on his right. "Eight." Then he repeated for good measure, "One, eight. Eighteen! Two times nine is eighteen. Now, three times nine." He lowered his third finger, the middle one, leaving two fingers on one side and seven fingers standing on the other. "Twenty-seven." He continued the process, lowering his pointer finger. Four times nine, and sure enough, Jim Brown counted three fingers standing, the pointer bent, and six fingers for thirty-six.

"Wait," cried Jim Brown, as the light bulb went on in his head. He held up his own hands. "Five times nine." He folded down his thumb and looked, "Four. Five. Forty-five." He continued folding his right thumb, his sixth finger, as he looked at the palms of his hands, and there it was, six times nine is fifty-four. His seventh finger left sixty-three; his eighth finger folded down divided his hands into seven and two standing fingers, seventy-two, and his ninth finger left—eighty-one. Finally, his tenth finger down left nine and zero.

"That's great! I could really use tricks like that. I hated multiplication!"

"Yeah. Miss McGonagall says that's why God made us this way, to help us find the secrets of the universe. You know, if the preacher told me that and then had an altar call, why, I would have been first in line to accept Christ as my Savior."

"I thought you were baptized last spring?"

"Well, I was, but this way I would have really meant it!"

"What else did she teach you?"

"It takes 340 squirts to the gallon," stated Marty rather pompously.

"What?"

"You know, if you're milking a cow, it takes 340 squirts to the gallon."

"You know, you say, 'You know,' a lot," smiled Jim Brown.

Marty frowned and was quiet a moment, as he wasn't sure if Jim Brown was serious or just being a smart aleck. He continued unfazed, "Well, she said she could teach me French."

"French? What would you do with French?"

"I don't know. If the world ever settles down, maybe I'll sail around it someday, and another language just might come in handy."

"I don't know," Jim Brown said considering the possibility. "I have enough trouble with English." He frowned. Everything went quiet. You could almost hear the grass grow or your brain tick.

Marty broke the silence. "You have to give her sympathy."

"Sympathy!" Jim Brown choked.

Marty looked up surprised. "Yeah, sympathy," he repeated. "You know. You have to feel sorry for her … all alone … misunderstood…"

"Exactly. She doesn't want your sympathy!" Jim Brown changed his tone and squeaked, "Gee, Miss McGonagall, I feel sooo sorry for you!" Then he waved his arms and bent in half, as if giving an exaggerated bow. He quickly popped back up and struck an authoritative pose with his hands on his hips. He stared directly into Marty's eyes and continued, "She wants understanding. She needs compassion."

"Huh? I don't get it. I mean, what's the difference? Compassion, sympathy?" Marty just shrugged.

"Do you know where sympathy is in the dictionary?" Jim Brown didn't wait for an answer. "It's between shit and syphilis."

"What's syphilis?" Marty interrupted.

It was Jim Brown's turn to say, "Huh?"

Marty just looked back sheepishly, as he trusted Jim Brown more than anyone, and he wasn't afraid to admit he didn't understand.

"Well," replied Jim Brown, taking a moment to collect his thoughts. He had just assumed Marty knew. "Well," he repeated and continued to look for inspiration. There was no one to pass this one off to, so he tried to find the words he thought his brother Bill would have used. In a quiet, deep voice, almost a whisper, he said, "You know, it's that disease you get from messing around with … certain women."

"Oh!" Marty's eyes popped, "Sure…" he replied, drawing it out, as he wasn't quite ready to be quizzed about sex. He wondered where the conversation was going, but he hoped they'd get back to sailing around the world soon. Little did he realize, so did Jim Brown.

Jim Brown raised his eyebrows and then confidently continued. "It doesn't really matter. The important thing is, you don't want either, and you don't want someone's sorry feelings either. Compassion's different. Frank says it comes from the Latin."

"He would know," chimed in Marty.

"Well, yeah, and he says it comes from 'com,' which means with, and 'passion,' to bear. So, if you had a bunch of firewood to carry, would you rather have someone heap their sorry feelings on you, or would you rather he bears it with you?"

Marty nodded and gave an understanding smile.

"And do you know where compassion is in the dictionary?"

Marty shook his head no.

"Between communication and competence—and when you're in trouble or hurting, you need both."

"Gee, that's brilliant. I'll remember that one." Marty continued. "You know, I did once ask her if she had something that would make girls like me."

"What's this?" interrupted Jim Brown. "Marty has a girlfriend?" he smiled, remembering how Marty had teased him earlier.

"Oh, n-n-no!" stuttered Marty, not wanting to get on THAT topic again. "I was just asking for future reference," he replied confidently and glanced sideways to check if Jim Brown accepted his excuse. "Anyway, she said that with all my natural charm, I'd be dangerous if she gave me anything." Then, he widely grinned.

Marty continued, thinking out loud. "Well, I think she likes to be alone anyway. I once asked her if she had any friends, and she told me that she enjoyed her own company. She trusted that anyone who needed her would find her, just like me. I think she would call me a friend and, Jim Brown, she is my friend." Then he gave Jim Brown a hard stare that said, "So don't mess with her!"

Recalling their previous discussion on being an only child, Jim Brown understood. He was glad they found each other. On a roll and wanting to change the subject, Jim Brown slyly smiled and asked, "Hey, Marty, what does G-H-O-T-I spell?"

"G-H-O-T-I," Marty repeated to see if he heard it correctly.

Jim Brown nodded,

"G-H-O-T-I," Marty repeated thoughtfully. "Ah, go-tee?"

"No," he smiled, shaking his head. Then, with an air of authority, Jim Brown stated, "Fish."

"Fish? Fish what?" challenged Marty, totally confused.

"Just fish. Let me show you." They stopped, and Jim Brown looked around to find a stick. Then, kneeling on one knee, he wrote in the dirt. "GH sounds like the 'F' in..." then he wrote "enouGH".

"The O is the sound O makes in the word wOmen."

Marty started to giggle.

"That's a short I. And the SH comes from the T-I in NaTIon," which Jim Brown wrote on the ground and circled. "See? G-H-O-T-I spells Fish. Mr. George B. Shaw, an English playwright, surely knows what he's talking about. He understands what we're facing. English is a tough language to learn!"

Marty shook his head and then grinned. "You sure there's a GH in enuff?" With that, he nudged Jim Brown, causing him to lose his balance and topple over. Without a second thought, he tore off down the road with Jim Brown in hot pursuit.

As they approached Raiford, a sandy-brown, wire-haired dog with pointed ears came trotting down the road. He broke into a full-speed run when he recognized Marty.

"Here comes Dog," smiled Jim Brown, noting the obvious.

Marty bent down to receive the full impact and playfully tussled the dog's head as he stood up.

"Why this here's Patrick O'Fleas," corrected Marty, as he struggled to stand up. The dog continued to nuzzle him, so Marty stroked his silky ears to the dog's delight. "Frank helped me name him. He says he's an Irish terrier."

"Naturally," chimed in Jim Brown.

"But he seems all-American to me." Panting, the dog appeared to smile in agreement as his tongue hung out and drooled over the ground; it was a natural condition. Patrick O'Fleas was always running, chasing rabbits, birds, dogs, or sticks or fleeing angry men, angry dogs, or hungry varmints. Panting was his way of cooling off and catching his breath.

For an instant, Jim Brown's mind wrapped around a buried memory of his dog, Boots, a mongrel pup left on the side of the road. It was a day when the stars were aligned, and his folks were preoccupied with his new brother. Boots was slipped in the back door and never left. He slept at the foot of his bed and followed him like a shadow everywhere he went, even school. His friends teased him, singing a parody to the familiar rhyme "Mary had a little lamb," but it went, "Jim Brown had a little dog whose boots were dark as coal … and everywhere that Jim Brown went, the dog was sure to go." That is, until that fateful afternoon when Boots disappeared.

At twilight, having spent all afternoon searching for him, Jim Brown found Boots whimpering under the oak tree. He called his dad who immediately comprehended the situation. Two red dots were near his neck, dots made by fangs—snake fangs, poisonous snake fangs. His dad knelt beside him and said the dog was in pain and the kindest thing to do would be to put him out of his misery. He then disappeared into the house, and Jim Brown knew he would return with his gun. Jim Brown was horrified and didn't know what to do. He knew his father was right, but it was Boots! He cradled the dog in his arms, as tears silently spilled down his face. When his dad returned, the gun wasn't necessary; Boots was gone. He and his dad buried him, not far from where he died. From that day on, he hated snakes with a passion. As quickly as the image appeared, it was gone. Jim Brown was happy for Marty, and he was happy for Patrick O'Fleas. They needed each other.

"You're full of surprises today," Jim Brown returned. He knew one of the benefits that came from being the butcher's son was that eventually all dogs—lost, strays, and neighborhood mutts—made their way to his back door. It was practical to call them "Dog," and it protected his feelings when they moved on or went back home. But it looked like Patrick O'Fleas might have found a home … and Marty a pet for keeps. Patrick stayed with them until a dove caught his eye. As if on cue, he charged off, disappearing between the rows of corn.

XXV

SPIRE'S GROCERY WAS NOW IN VIEW. WITHOUT WORDS, THEY DECIDED to get a drink of water before going on. Jim Brown's stomach grumbled, and he regretted not grabbing something to eat before he left home. Marty darted ahead and disappeared into the grocery store. As Jim Brown rounded the corner, he saw Mrs. Persin and Mrs. Clark standing under the grocery store awning. He whirled around, hoping to dodge back around the corner, but it was too late. They saw him.

Jim Brown liked Mrs. Persin. Her husband, Chuck, had gone off to World War I in 1917. He fought in the trenches but was struck down by a virus and died during the Influenza Epidemic of 1918. The virus turned out to be worse for the troops than the bullets and mustard gas combined. Mrs. Persin returned home to Starke just in time to fight the same virus that had killed her husband. Fortunately, she was under the care of Dr. Middleton, who worked twenty-two hours a day and was devoted to his patients, who included just about everyone in Bradford County. She survived, and she never left; she also never remarried but became everyone's favorite "aunt."

Her garden was filled with the most beautiful flowers, and her strawberries were the sweetest. She always had time for anyone, and she was a terrific listener. What was shared in confidence on her porch stayed on her porch, unless young love needed a push. She was an incurable romantic. She was always ready with a word of encouragement or just a silent hug, but if you looked closely, her eyes betrayed a touch of sadness. Her love for Chuck never died; it lived on in the love of those around her.

Mrs. Clark, on the other hand, was the busybody of Raiford. Her nose was long and pointed, probably from sticking it into other people's business where it didn't belong. Her voice dripped of honey, her smile concealed her secret intentions, and her arms reached like tentacles to grab people, making them commit to projects for which she would later take credit. She knew everything, and what she didn't know for sure, she filled in with her own imagination. Her gossip was a spider web, alluring and intricate. It drew people in, and they became addicted and entertained or stuck and devoured.

One day, she'd caught Jim Brown with his friends smoking behind the school, and before he got home, she was on the phone with his mother. It wasn't so much that his mother cared, but hearing it from Mrs. Clark made it dreadful. She knew it would be all over the county by dusk—and the truth would be embellished with, "And what kind of mother would ever … why that boy is headed for trouble … what would you expect…"

Jim Brown tried to convince his mother that it wasn't him. Why, everyone knew Mrs. Clark was near-sighted and vain, so she never wore her glasses. How could she be so sure? His mother wanted to believe him, but then she sniffed his shirt, sighed, and shook her head. As an afterthought, she shot back, "They weren't my cigarettes, were they?"

"No," he answered honestly.

Fortunately, there was also a natural fabric woven of kith and kin, neighbors and prayer partners, a counter-balance that protected all. With the Reddishes, Hicks, Alvarezes, and Griffises, one never was sure if he was talking to the second cousin on his father's side or the half-brother of someone's aunt three times removed. Everyone was related. Whatever was said about someone "in confidence" was sure to get back. This connection could be beneficial in many ways. If word got around that someone was sick, a crock of homemade chicken soup would magically appear. If there was a broken heart, a new beau would arrive on the doorstep with flowers. Or, if you did get into trouble, someone was there to straighten you out on the spot.

But to people like Mrs. Clark, information was power. As the chief spinner, Mrs. Clark could create a politician out of a ne'er-do-well or destroy an innocent child before he had a chance to finish high school. Unfortunately, her juicier pieces weren't always true, and if caught in a lie, she would just shrug and say, "Where there's smoke, there's fire." Once spoken, it was difficult to call the words back. People relish the notorious and scandalous. Everyone always tried to stay on her good side … or at least out of her conversations.

Mrs. Clark raised her hand and signaled for him to approach. Then, she caught Jim Brown by his neck and held him tight. He cringed, and a shiver ran down his back. He felt like a mouse in a mousetrap, and, suddenly, he had great empathy for the creatures he had thrown into the trash. He resigned himself to his plight and attempted to be polite by striking the attentive pose he'd learned from his father while waiting for Mrs. Clark to finish her latest bit of gossip.

"Have you tried those frozen vegetables?" Before Grace could reply, Mrs. Clark proceeded to answer her own question. "Well, I heard May Foley say they were hard and chewy, but then you know she's not much of a cook…"

Jim Brown almost laughed out loud as he pictured Frank gagging when he described the frozen peas his mother put on their dinner table the night before last.

Mrs. Clark continued, "Maybe they won't ration canned goods and these frozen vegetables will just be a faze we'll have to bear."

"But Betty, I heard…"

"Now, Grace, you know I go by Elizabeth," she purred. "It's so much more fitting for my social status."

Grace raised her handkerchief, as if to cover a cough and rolled her eyes. Suddenly, she realized that Jim Brown had caught her in this indiscretion. She lowered her eyes and coyly smiled. Jim Brown replied with a conspiratorial wink. "Of course, Elizabeth," she replied.

At that very moment, Jim Brown noticed Marty coming out the screen door. He casually reached up, as if stretching, joined his thumbs together and began flapping his hands like a bird in flight. It was a secret sign, signaling the approach of the principal, certain teachers, and all girls. It meant scram or duck out of sight before you're caught. But Marty was focusing on a nickel he'd found and was flipping it as he walked.

Jim Brown was beginning to feel desperate, as if watching an unavoidable train wreck when he looked down next to him and caught sight of Mrs. Persin who, by now, was flapping her arms like a snow hill crane and hopping from one foot to another, dislodging a few key hairpins and dangerously threatening to let her carefully coiffed bun come tumbling down!

"Grace!" Mrs. Clark's screeching voice broke Jim's trance. "What in God's name are you doing?"

Mrs. Persin stopped in mid-flap, arranged her hair, and smiled sweetly at Jim Brown, who, until that moment, had no idea what was happening! Then, it dawned on him that someone must have shared their secret sign with her but had forgotten to add the discretion part.

"Oh," she replied, glancing up to the street sign for time and inspiration. "Why, it's so hot," she smiled again. "I just thought I'd make a little breeze," and then looked directly into Mrs. Clark's eyes, daring her to suggest anything different. As if on cue, Marty bumped into the impromptu group.

"Oh, dang it!" he cried, as he dropped the nickel and then bent over to pick it up. "Nine consecutive flips," he grinned, looking up to Jim Brown.

Jim Brown rolled his eyes and directed Marty's attention to the two ladies standing beside him.

"Oh! 'Cuse me, Mrs. Persin, Mrs. Clark." He tried to continue smiling, but he felt like throwing up at the sight of Mrs. Clark (he and his father had been victims in her vicious web on several occasions). It faded to a grimace.

"Well, I never…" Mrs. Clark said, shaking her head in disgust. Then, she turned her attention to Jim Brown. "Stand up straight!" she commanded and slapped him on the back of his head for good measure.

Mrs. Persin winced. Had Jim Brown not been raised with discipline and love, he would have turned and walloped Mrs. Clark; instead, he took a deep breath and slowly let it out.

"I need you to mow my lawn on Monday right after lunch but before my bridge group arrives. Can't stand that racket interrupting everything," she added with a huff.

Of course not, thought Jim Brown, *and in the heat of the day, no lunch, no tip, I'll bet that suits you fine*. "I'm booked," he replied before she could go further.

Startled, but not missing a beat, she whirled around, pointing her boney finger at Marty, who was innocently standing there, barely paying attention, and demanded, "What about you?"

Caught off guard, he stuttered, "Yes, Ma'am, I guess I can."

Then she proceeded with a laundry list of trimming the hedges, pulling the weeds, and bagging all the clippings. "Immaculate" was the word she used; she wanted her yard looking "immaculate."

Whatever, thought Marty; a good word he'd picked up from Jim Brown. He would do his best, but he was stuck.

"Shouldn't we be going to the Women's Club?" Mrs. Persin interrupted. "They said they wanted to begin promptly at eleven."

"Oh my, yes! I'm leading the Pledge of Allegiance!" replied Mrs. Clark, as she turned sharply on her heels to leave. "Don't forget, Monday at noon!" she called to Marty.

"If you have time," Mrs. Persin whispered, "my garden needs a man's touch." She paused and added, "I'll have some cool lemonade, sandwiches, and chocolate chip cookies ready if you can make it around ten-thirty. That should give you plenty of time to get to Mrs. Clark's. That's if you can make it." She smiled hopefully.

"Sure," Marty grinned. Her yard wasn't much bigger than a postage stamp, and she couldn't afford to pay much, but her cookies alone would be worth the work. Besides, no one would ever turn Mrs. Persin down. With a sweet nod, she turned and toddled after Mrs. Clark.

"Didn't you see me signal?" cried Jim Brown after they were out of earshot.

"No, but I did catch Mrs. Persin!" They both slapped their sides and burst into fits of laughter.

Once they settled down, Jim Brown added, "When you see her Monday, you might want to explain 'the flap.' Maybe she can tone it down a little."

Marty nodded in agreement. Then he glanced at Jim Brown, cocked his head, and asked, "Are you really 'booked'?"

"Yeah," replied Jim Brown. "My every other Monday unless it rains, then it's Tuesday or Wednesday, at Big Mama's; and my mother promised Mrs. Walsh I'd do her lawn if I could squeeze it in."

"*Oh,*" sighed Marty, and then he began to make a metal note repeating, "'I'm booked.' I like that. It's crisp, no ifs, ands, or buts. 'I'm booked.' I'll have to remember that one next time Mrs. Clark catches me. But I'll be sure to recommend you to her." He smiled at Jim Brown, and they burst out laughing until they could hardly breathe.

XXVI

ACROSS THE ROAD, NEAR A SHADY COVE OF TREES, A STRANGER STOOD watching the ruckus. He was rather short by Raiford standards and had a stocky build with a thick neck, pug nose, and squinting eyes, though that might have been because he was looking into the sun. His thinning hair, which after being combed over in the morning and plastered with cream, still fell where it may. He was in desperate need of a haircut. His beady eyes leered up and down the road and came to rest on the boys. A wicked sneer spread across his face, as an evil plan popped into his head. Maybe there was some money to be made in this two-horse town after all. He hiked up his trousers and crossed the street.

Marty and Jim Brown stopped laughing and straightened up as they watched the stranger heading in their direction. The warm sensations they shared from the morning sun and friendly laughter turned distinctly chilly as the man's shadow fell across them.

"Name's Cecil A. Baxter. I'm looking for some men to do a job," he said, staring at Jim Brown.

Marty bent over and started giggling again, as his voice cracked when he repeated the one word, "Men?"

Jim Brown, on the other hand, straightened up and looked down on the man, making Cecil feel uncomfortable. This stranger didn't impress Jim Brown. His suit was rumpled and stained—his father would never leave the house like that—and there was something slimy about him that Jim Brown couldn't quite put his finger on. Still, the man had said a job, which meant money. It wouldn't hurt to ask. Imitating his father, Jim Brown tossed his head back, put his hands on his hips, raised his eyebrows, and asked, "What's the job?"

Cecil A. Baxter, feeling a bit intimidated, took two steps onto the porch to try and equalize their heights. Next, he pulled out an old stogie, which he clenched between his yellow teeth before striking a match against the holey sole of his shoe and lighting it. He took a long drag and then blew the blue plume of smoke into the boy's face, hoping to regain a bit of authority.

Jim Brown stifled an uncontrollable urge to cough, but he didn't budge. His dream of a decent job with big money was rapidly fading, but he was stuck and waited for his answer.

"Mr. ...?"

"Godwin."

"Godwin," Mr. Baxter replied and paused for a moment, trying to recall why the name sounded familiar. Nothing coming to mind, and he continued. "I work for the railroad, and currently we're backed up." He took another drag and then gestured with the cigar while saying, "Those cars over there carried a herd of cows for the prison, Florida State Prison," he repeated for emphasis.

Marty started giggling again, thinking, *This guy doesn't have a clue who your father is. "Florida State Prison"—duh, what a jerk!* Jim Brown quickly elbowed him in the side. Marty straightened up and tried to look attentive.

Mr. Baxter continued, completely ignoring Marty. "I need those cars cleaned out and back in service."

"How much?" Jim Brown replied.

"Fifty cents."

Fifty cents! Jim Brown took a breath. *When thirty cents an hour was the going rate, this insignificant man seemed made of money!* Returning to the moment, he thought to corroborate the terms. "Each?"

"Each car," Mr. Baxter agreed, nodding his head.

"No," Jim Brown said. "Each of us; we come as a team."

Mr. Baxter's head popped, and he almost choked on a puff of smoke as Marty shyly grinned back. "Hey, fellow, I'm not made of money. Seventy-five cents a car, and you pay for the help."

Jim Brown just stood there and casually looked up and down the empty street. The depot was a spur off the main railroad line, built specifically to bring supplies in and out of the prison. It was a whistle stop in the

middle of nowhere, and both of them knew that. Mr. Baxter had played his hand. While staring down at this clumsy, scam artist, Jim Brown confidently repeated, "Fifty cents, each car, each man."

Mr. Baxter paused for a moment and realized this kid was smart and had the upper hand—at least for the moment. He put out his hand in resignation and said, "A deal."

Marty stood in absolute awe while Jim Brown shook Mr. Baxter's hand and said, "A deal."

As Mr. Baxter walked away, a snake-like smile slithered across his face.

XXVII

"YOU DID IT, JIM BROWN! YOU DID IT!" CRIED MARTY. "FIFTY CENTS A car—for each of us! How many cars? There must be at least two, maybe three! This will be better than working for Dad. Anyway, I think he was butchering a hog." They looked at each other and said in unison, "Use every part but the squeal!"

"Yeah," agreed Jim Brown, "but now we've got to do it. Come on, let's see what I've gotten ourselves into."

They crossed the road as a small breeze sent clouds of dirt devils spinning through the air and walked over to two livestock cars that sat off to the side. A barn cat was contently curled up in a ball in the shadow of a train engine, trying to escape the noonday heat and flies. The tip of her nose twitched, and her tail flicked at the no-see-ums, but to the casual observer she was as still as a rock and oblivious to the comedy about to unfold.

As they walked closer, Marty felt his stomach tighten and swallowed hard to keep from throwing up. The stench was almost unbearable, and they both noticed an ominous cloud of steam escaping between the rails. They looked at each other and shrugged, then burst into laughter. "Oh my gosh! These cars are full of SHIT!" they exclaimed.

Marty couldn't hold back any longer and threw up, which didn't help the air quality. "Sorry," he murmured, "low gag reflex."

Jim Brown didn't blame him and felt dangerously close to throwing up as well, but there wasn't anything in his stomach. They held their breath and slid open the cargo door. As expected, the heat, the odor, and the flies hit them full force. Jim Brown closed his eyes and raised his arms to ward off the onslaught of flying debris. Seconds later, the air settled down and he surveyed the scene. He dropped his hands and cocked his head as a brilliant plan popped into his mind. A smile broke across his face.

Marty, who was on the verge of tossing his cookies again, noticed Jim Brown and exclaimed, "Are you crazy?"

"No, Marty, no! Look and see! Look!" Jim Brown coughed, as the air was beginning to choke him again.

"What? I don't have to open my eyes! I know what's there! We could smell it across the yard!"

"Yeah, but Marty, it's soup. Really, look at it. It's SOUP!"

"So…" replied Marty, shaking his head as he stepped up next to Jim Brown. Nothing changed.

"Marty, it'll be a piece of cake! All we have to do is hook up a couple of hoses and spray the cars down. We'll be done in no time!"

"Done in no time, maybe," Marty grinned after a moment. "But 'piece of cake'? How 'bout 'moose shit pie'?" he countered. Jim Brown went to give Marty a playful shove, but Marty saw it coming and leaned out of the way.

Together they sped off to collect as many hoses as they could find. They screwed them together, making two giant hoses and connected them to the double faucet outside the depot. Saying a prayer, they turned the water on full force. The hoses came to life like a nest of snakes uncoiling as the water pulsed through, first just a trickle followed by a continuous stream. The hoses held. They each took an end and, with a silent nod reassuring they were in it together, they began to march toward the first car like soldiers going into battle.

Jim Brown climbed into the car and turned to give Marty a hand. To his surprise, Marty was already beside him raring to go. They put their thumbs over the ends of their hoses to increase the pressure and began to work in unison, spraying the straw and manure toward the door. It was slow at first as they sprayed back and forth, but then, unexpectedly, the slimy concoction began to move in a single mass. The water pellets sounded like machine gun bullets, as they hit the bare floor, inspiring the boys to fight imaginary enemy soldiers invading the Florida beaches.

"Circle to the left! I've got the right flank covered!" yelled Jim Brown over the mayhem.

"Trust me! I've got them in sight!" returned Marty, as he maneuvered to the opposite side. On and on, the enemy retreated and spilled out the door. The first car was cleaned, and they were on to the next.

"Second verse, same as the first!" called Marty as he climbed aboard. Again, the slimy soup began gushing out the door, spilling on to the ground; however, after a while, the war returned to a tedious, backbreaking job.

Without even thinking, Marty knew exactly where to aim his hose. In hindsight, Jim Brown knew he should have seen it coming, but he didn't, and when the pressurized water hit him right behind the knees, it swept him off his feet and slammed him into the disgusting river of manure and straw. Well, he wouldn't take that sitting down! Slipping and sliding, he worked his way back to his feet. The whole time, Marty continued spraying him while doubling over in fits of laughter, but when he realized Jim Brown was back on his feet, he knew it really was war!

The water hoses fired relentlessly back and forth. As there was no place to run for cover and no trashcan tops

to use as shields, the boys took the water full force and, inevitably, one or the other was on the floor, sliding like a hockey puck over the thin layers of scum and muck. They didn't even notice the straw and manure sloshing in retreat. Without even trying, Jim Brown and Marty had cleaned the second car, and they both dropped in exhaustion. It was Jim Brown who first noticed the stranger standing on the depot platform. He nodded to Marty, who was already scrambling to the door. Quickly, they ran over and turned off the water faucet, wound the hoses into two neat coils, straightened their clothes as best they could, and walked over to meet the railroad agent. Both boys were curious to see if they would get their money. Jim Brown was certain he would see to it that they were paid in full. The work wasn't difficult, but it was work, and the agent had agreed to the terms. Now the work was done, would he come through?

XXVIII

CECIL A. BAXTER ALREADY HAD HIS WALLET OUT. "GUESS YOU'RE READY to be paid," he said as the boys approached.

"Two clean cars as ordered, ready for service," replied Jim Brown. His green eyes stared defiantly at the man as he waited to see what would happen next. To his surprise, the man handed him a one-dollar bill, and turned without a word and gave a dollar bill to Marty. Marty accepted the bill. His mouth fell silently open as his eyes focused on the crisp dollar he now possessed in his hand.

"One dollar each, as we agreed," said Mr. Baxter. "I don't suppose you men would be interested in more work tomorrow?"

Marty regained his voice first and said, "What do you have in mind?"

Baxter grinned and thought to himself, *I've got them now.* "Well, I have ten more cars coming in tomorrow morning at six," he paused and looked

Jim Brown in the eyes. "It's a quick turn-around; they have to be ready by sundown, so I have a contract if you want the job."

Where he pulled it from, Jim Brown had no idea, but there in one hand was a rather official-looking document and in the other hand, a pen.

"Come on, Jim Brown, we can do it," Marty whispered anxiously. Turning, so the railroad agent couldn't hear, he continued. "We finished these cars in less than two hours, and we weren't even trying hard! We can do ten cars in four hours, five tops."

Jim Brown was still stunned as to how the events were unfolding. This strange man appeared out of nowhere, hired them to do a job at a generous rate, had paid them in full, and was now offering them another job! There must be a catch! But there the money was in his hand. It was easy money, and it seemed on the up-and-up. *Ten cars,* he thought, *heck, we could do twenty!* And his eyes began to sparkle.

"Only ten," Jim Brown replied, with a slight croak in his voice. "You sure you can't double that?" he asked with more resolve.

"Just ten," Baxter said with a smile. "You might notice," he continued, turning to Jim Brown, "that since time is of the essence, I've doubled the pay, but there is a non-completion clause."

Jim Brown's eyes popped again, and his mouth dropped open. *What did he say? Did he double the salary?* His mind swirled with dollar signs. Marty, afraid that Jim Brown might actually say no, or that the agent would come to his senses and change his mind, nudged him and silently mouthed, "Sign it!"

Jim Brown shook his head to clear away the dollar signs and wondered if this fellow just had money to burn—from his appearance that wasn't likely—or maybe he was just plain dumb! He straightened his back and tried to look as adult as a twelve-year old, dripping wet and smelling like an outhouse, could. He took the contract, casually attempted to decipher the legalese, and noticed something about a penalty if the cars weren't ready for service by sunset, but there it was: ten cars in ten hours, a dollar per car, and he was authorized to hire another worker at the same rate. He couldn't imagine what could go wrong. The stranger seemed good for the money. And if he wanted to pay that much, gee, he couldn't pocket that much mowing lawns every day for a week! *Why not?* his mind kept repeating.

"Sure," said Jim Brown, and he took the pen and signed.

"You witnessed that, right?" he said, turning to Marty.

"Sure, why not? I'll sign," replied Marty as he reached for the pen.

"That won't be necessary," Cecil replied, snatching up the papers and pen. "I'll see you tomorrow morning, early." Then, he turned and walked away whistling.

Something felt fishy about the exchange, but Jim Brown couldn't help smiling ear to ear, dreaming about the easy money he would pocket this time tomorrow.

"Come on, Jim Brown! Let's go to Spire's and grab a Nehi and some moon pies. Aren't you starving?"

"As a matter of fact, I am. Sounds like a great idea," Jim Brown said and put his arm on Marty's shoulder.

"Hey, Jim Brown, it'll be my treat!"

"Even better." And off they marched.

"Jim Brown, what do you think—maybe we should incorporate! You know, form a company, Russell and Godwin, Manure Movers, Inc.?"

"Uh, that would be 'Godwin and Russell,' but we can work out the details later."

"Where have you boys been?" cried Mrs. King, as she crinkled her nose when they walked through the door.

Since they'd been drenched in manure all afternoon, they'd become immune to the odor. "Why, we've been working hard," replied Marty, with an air of disappointment. "We're starved! We need your two coldest Nehis and some moon pies. And I'm buying!" he continued proudly.

"Coming right up," said Mrs. King, smiling. "But wherever you were working, it smells like you were rolling in manure!"

Jim Brown turned to Marty, and they both broke into laughter. Mrs. King had no idea how close she was to the truth. "No, ma'am," they replied in unison. Marty added stoically, "It was just honest labor."

They both finished their Nehis in a single gulp and debated buying a second. Jim Brown offered to treat, but then they thought it might be better if they started hiking home. Tomorrow would be a long day, and they'd need their rest. They turned their bottles back for the two-penny refund and ate their moon pies as they headed home.

"Don't you think that guy was strange?" asked Jim Brown.

"Sure," replied Marty, "but his money spends as well as anybody else's. And though I have to admit, I wouldn't want to do it all the time, it really wasn't that bad." Jim Brown had to agree.

"Think there will be more trains next week? We'd have a thousand dollars by the end of summer if this keeps up! What would you do with a thousand dollars, Jim Brown?" asked Marty.

Forgetting his suspicions for the moment and turning to dreams, Jim Brown paused and replied, "Well, I'd save most to buy a car when I turn sixteen, but if there was any money left over, well, maybe I'd buy some golf clubs."

"Golf clubs? I didn't know you played golf!"

"Well, I don't. But I just thought I might like to try," Jim Brown replied, nodding his head for emphasis.

"Golf clubs! Heck, I'd get a speed boat and rule Kingsley Lake!" And with that, Marty got a second wind and took off speeding in circles around Jim Brown, humming like a motorboat.

They said good-bye where the road split. Marty headed for his dad's butcher store; it was closer than home, and he hoped to catch a ride. Jim Brown started down State Road 16. The afternoon clouds circled above, and he was sure he was in for a soaking. Just as he was beginning to think—or at least was trying to convince himself—that it might even feel good, Mr. Hopper, one of the officers who worked for his dad, was driving back from

Lawtey. He recognized Jim Brown and stopped to give him a lift. Jim Brown was thankful, but then he wondered if Mr. Hopper didn't regret his offer, as the car immediately filled with smell of manure.

"Been tangling with a skunk?" he asked.

"No, sir… I was just working at the railroad depot." Nothing more was said between them. They kept their windows rolled down and their heads as far out as they could reach, even as the rain began to pour.

After what seemed like an hour, but was only fifteen minutes, Mr. Hopper pulled off road near a driveway. Jim Brown said his thanks, as he hopped out and closed the door in one fluid motion. Mr. Hopper didn't reply; he just put his foot to the gas pedal and roared off. Jim Brown ran to the house and dashed up the stairs before his mother got a whiff of him.

"Where you been, Jim Brown?" called Harold, as he raced up the stairs after him.

"Working," he replied, as he slammed the door to his room in Harold's face.

"I want to work," cried Harold, pounding on his door. "Let me in!"

"Go away, Harold! I'm going to take a bath!" Jim Brown called through the door.

"Oh," he heard Harold say, as he beat a hasty retreat and scurried as fast as he could back down the stairs.

Jim Brown gently pulled his cigar box from beneath the mattress and put the dollar bill with the rest of his hard-earned money. Three aggies, which he won shooting marbles after school, rolled around in the box, and two silver dollars from his grandmother clinked together at the bottom. He smiled at a folded piece of notebook paper; it was a note Peggy Tilley had slipped him after school. Then he carefully closed the lid and returned the box to its hiding place for safekeeping. He grabbed a towel and slipped across the hall to the bathroom. Even though the water was barely tepid, the shower felt good as the grime and the stink swirled down the drain. Before he left, he splashed on a few drops of Bill's cologne for good measure.

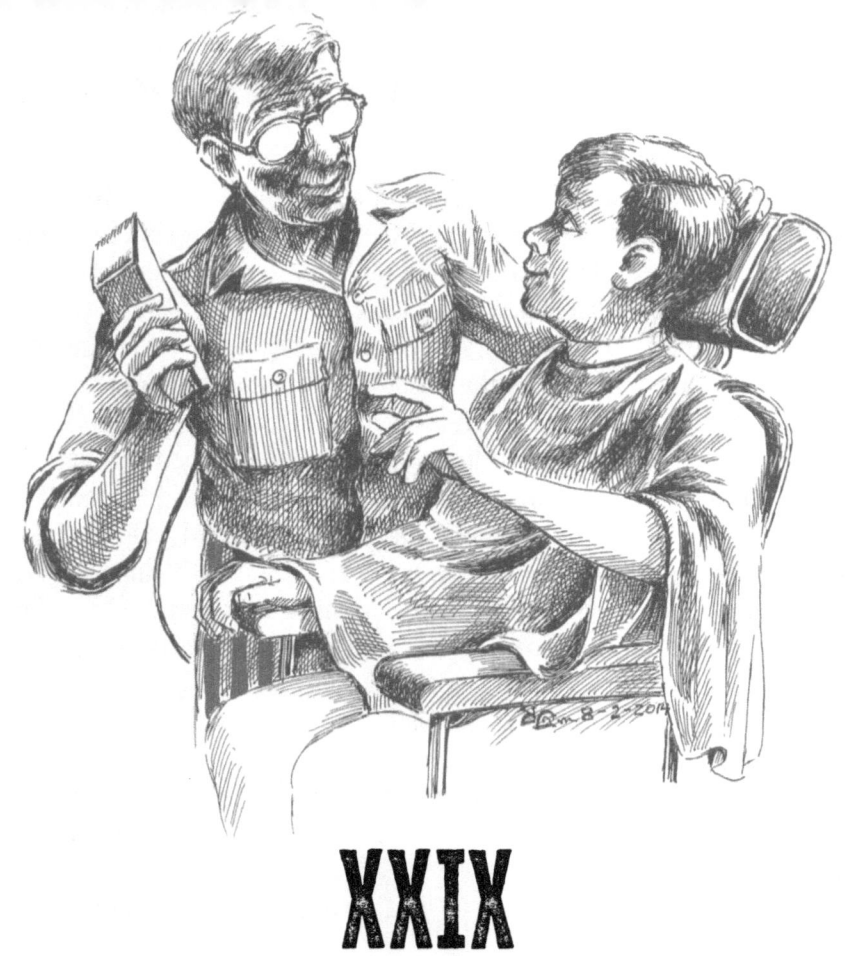

XXIX

THAT NIGHT, IT WAS QUIET AROUND THE HOUSE. HIS FATHER HAD GONE
to Tallahassee for a meeting, so everyone was a bit more relaxed. Jim Brown
tuned the radio to *Suspense,* a new show all the kids were talking about.
Normally, his mother would change the channel because she said it gave
her goosebumps, but tonight she was curled up on the couch, absorbed in
a woman's magazine. Even Harold seemed content stacking blocks in the
corner and knocking them down with squeals of delight. After the mystery
ended, his mother suggested Jim Brown might want to take Harold up and
get him ready for bed.

Jim Brown nodded and tucked a squirming Harold under his arm. As
he headed for the stairs, he turned and said, "Oh, by the way, I have a job
tomorrow … down at the depot." His mother remained quiet and didn't

even bother to look up, so he continued. "I'll have to get up early to get to Raiford by six…"

"Isn't it the second Saturday?" she interrupted, looking up from her magazine. "Aren't you and Harold due for haircuts?" It was a routine that Jim Brown tried to avoid. The second Saturday of the month, all the State Farm boys lined up at the prison for haircuts. The "barber shop" was a twenty-by-twenty-foot square room with beige linoleum, now yellowing with age—though no one cared as the floor was perpetually dusted with hair trimmings of various colors and paint chips from the prison green walls the condemned boys would sometimes flake off as they waited their turns. There were three barred windows in the back and three chairs manned by three convicts in striped uniforms. The directions were always the same: "Short on top and tight on the sides." Old Joe would nod his head, shake the sheet, and wait for the next miserable creature to climb onto the seat.

Jim Brown always gave a pleading look and mouthed while holding his thumb and pointer finger apart. "A little longer on top … please!" Old Joe would grin his toothless grin and give a quick wink. Jim Brown returned with a sigh of relief as he dutifully took his seat. He actually didn't mind getting his haircut. Yes, there was the tweak when the scissors were dull and the occasional nip on an ear lobe when the boys absentmindedly turned their heads at the wrong moment. It was more the wait, sitting erect and still for forever, and the inevitable itchy neck from the tiny, clipped hairs that stuck to your sweaty neck.

Harold, who usually threw a fit, hadn't learned how to behave, and there was a price to be paid. Old Joe never said a word but would take the shortest blade he could find and go to work. It was a win-win situation. For the boys like Harold, they'd get a shorter cut, which would make the parents happy, and they might even skip a week or two until the next trim. For Joe, word got around that if they behaved, he might give them the cut they wanted instead of the prison regular.

Old Joe was a sad fellow Mr. Godwin looked after. He was a lifer by choice. Somehow, he'd never gotten the love a family gives, and he'd never met a good woman to feed his dreams and keep him in line. He began drinking booze instead. When he got old enough to hold a job, he drank his paycheck away, lost his job, and turned to robbing liquor stores. Thus, he found himself behind prison bars. The first time he served his sentence, Mr. Godwin said, "Now Joe, stay straight. We don't want to see you back!"

"Yes, Boss," Joe replied.

The second time, Mr. Godwin said, "Take care of yourself, Joe. Good luck!"

"Thanks, Boss."

By the third time, Mr. Godwin shook his head and said, "See you in six months?"

Joe gave his toothless grin, as the alcohol and poor hygiene plus a fight or two had claimed them all. "You know it, Boss!" The prison gave Joe a home. It gave him discipline, three square meals a day, a bed, and a job. It kept him out of trouble, which the real world couldn't seem to offer.

"But, Mom," cried Jim Brown in shock, "this is for real money!"

Shocked by his tone, she glanced up again and then replied, "Well, if it's that important, I guess you can skip tomorrow. I'm sure they will fit you in next Saturday." Then, she got up and changed the radio station.

Jim Brown smiled as he carried Harold up the stairs. He wrestled him into his pajamas and stood by the bathroom door as Harold begrudgingly bit on his toothbrush. Then he slammed the door on Jim Brown as he called, "Privacy! I have to pee." If Harold only knew, he thought, he'd had enough shit that day. After a minute, Harold came charging out the door. Jim Brown scooped him up and tossed him into bed.

"You gonna tell me a story, Jim Brown?" Harold asked as his eyes started to close.

"Not tonight, Harold, maybe tomorrow." He quietly closed the door and walked down to his room.

There, he changed into his pajamas, knelt beside his bed, and said a prayer for peace and asked God's blessings on everyone and anything else he could think of. Exhausted, he soon was fast asleep.

XXX

MORNING CAME QUICKLY. JIM BROWN WAS UP, DRESSED, AND IN THE kitchen, wolfing down a bowl of cereal and a piece of toast. He got out four slices of bread to make two peanut butter and jelly sandwiches and, as an afterthought, threw out four more slices to make sandwiches for Marty. Since Marty didn't have a mother, his lunches, if he remembered to bring any, were always strange: a stick of pepperoni, a chunk of salami, or some strange meat—whatever he could grab from the butcher shop. The meat was always good, but just not what you'd call a proper lunch. He tossed in a couple of pears from the prison's farm and patted his pocket to make sure he had a dollar to cover the cost of two cold Nehis, with some change left over for candy bars or maybe ice cream sandwiches. The Nehis sure hit the spot yesterday.

Then, Jim Brown rustled through the catchall drawer in the pantry to see if he could find a jar of Vicks VapoRub. He hoped if they put a little under their noses, it might subdue the stench. But after what they experienced yesterday, it probably was like trying to stop a raging bull; it was coming whether he wanted it or not. Then, he was out the door before anyone in the family had opened their eyes and gotten out of bed.

The sky was still dark as he turned on to SR 16. A wagon pulled over, and Jim Brown recognized Mr. Griffis, called Uncle Nathan by everyone, at the reins. His face was deeply lined from hours spent in the sun, and his eyes were in a permanent squint, which, if you didn't know better, you'd think he was sitting up straight, sound asleep. But very little got by him, and he didn't tolerate foolishness nor stupidity.

"Where you off to at this hour, Jim Brown? Do you have some time to plant a few more palm trees?" he asked.

Jim Brown smiled back and said, "Not today, Uncle Nathan. I'm going to the depot in Raiford. I have a job waiting for me."

"Well, I'm headed that way. Hop on board, and I'll give you a lift."

Jim Brown thought a moment, considering how slow they'd go, but then a ride's a ride, and he'd need his energy once he got there. "Thanks," he called, as he jumped on the back and stretched out.

Jim Brown had been on this road countless times. He knew every bump, and Mr. Griffis hit each one. Even in sunlight, the countryside was unchanging. You just drove on and on—past the cornfields and scrub brush—until you saw Spire's Grocery Store at the T-intersection. Jim Brown was thankful that Mr. Griffis wasn't a talker. He could tell you everything about Florida agriculture, but he didn't waste his time on idle chatter. Jim Brown just closed his eyes and let the miles slip by.

Eventually, he felt Mr. Griffis pull up on the reins and realized they must be in Raiford. He sat up, thanked him again, and rapidly jumped off the wagon. To his surprise, as the wagon pulled away, he saw Marty sitting on the porch outside Spire's.

"What took you so long? I've been here for hours!" he called.

"Right," said Jim Brown. "Have you seen Mr. Baxter?"

"I think he's down at the diner having a cup of coffee. He should be here soon."

The boys started to cross the road, and as if on cue, Cecil A. Baxter exited the diner and headed their way.

Mr. Baxter didn't say a word; he merely pointed to the ten cars lined up on the sidetrack, turned, and walked away.

Jim Brown and Marty looked at each other and shrugged. They didn't need any instruction, but a word of encouragement might have been nice. Jim Brown turned to Marty and pulled out the Vicks VapoRub.

"What's that for?" he asked.

"To keep you from throwing up," he replied with a grin. After a generous application, they walked to the hoses they had neatly coiled the day before. They each took an end, and Jim Brown turn on the water, full force. Together they walked to the first car, but already something seemed wrong. There was no steam; there was no odor. Jim Brown opened the door. As his eyes adjusted to the darkness, his mouth dropped open.

XXXI

RIGHT ABOUT NOW, THOUGHT CECIL A. BAXTER WITH A WICKED GRIN.
The contract he'd made with the boys was generous by the day's standards.
He could have easily gotten colored men for a third the price, but then he
never intended to pay the boys a dime. As a matter of fact, if he played his
cards right, they, or at least Jim Brown, whoever he was, would be paying
him. There was no way these boys could clean the cars by sundown. He
pulled open the door to the diner and strolled back to his seat at the counter.

The diner's full name, as painted on the storefront plate glass, was "The
Baker Street Diner," which led to some confusion, as the establishment
obviously sat on Main Street. Ralph's wife, Maddy, thought it was a nod
to her and her legendary tender muffins and mile-high cakes, which, while
disappointing regular customers, were temporarily replaced with flakey, sin-
gle-crust pies due to wartime restrictions. But the truth be known, it was
a quiet salute to Ralph's role model, Sherlock Holmes. Ralph loved solving
puzzles, including crimes. If life had offered him other options, he would
have chosen heading a detective agency. Not to say he wasn't content with
Maddy and the diner; he was, but there were always dreams, books, and the
occasional mystery life offered.

The name, however, did not escape a few—very few—locals, and once
a month, the "Irregulars" met at the same time, same table to discuss local
crime and entertain thoughts that just perhaps there was a conspiracy, a
Moriarty, behind the current world situation. The Irregulars were indeed
irregular by local standards: the Catholic priest, Father Vince Germano

from St. Edwards; Elder Manley from the First Methodist Church; Most Reverend Rayford Simpson from the AME Church in Reno; and, of course, Ralph. Who would have thought?

Ralph gave Father Germano credit for bringing the group together. It began when Father Germano wandered into the diner and remarked on the name. Ralph sat down and, two hours later, said he had a friend who loved solving mysteries as much as he did. It was only when Elder Manley arrived and recognized Father Germano that he realized he'd made a connection with a Catholic priest! But the deed was done. Reverend Simpson's initiation was a bit more complicated.

When Father Vince Germano arrived in Starke, he was informed that a car came with the position. Catholics were few and far between, and he needed transportation to respond to all the bishop's demands, which were considerable. The car was a necessity.

His attitude toward cars was similar to Jim Brown's father's. Growing up in New York City, he viewed cars as expensive status symbols; and his family had neither the money nor the need for status. Everyone already knew who you were. Vince's father was a grocer, highly respected for his honesty and generosity—he gave what he had, though there wasn't much. He didn't need ostentatious bling to define his place in the neighborhood. Besides, there were no parking places and no free time to drive nowhere in particular.

Vince marveled at the machines as they drove by, but, like his father, he didn't need one. He could walk anywhere—to friends, school, the grocery store, and, of course, church—in less than thirty minutes. And on the occasions his gang wanted to explore the city or go to the Bronx Zoo, they would jump on the back of street cars and hold on for dear life. That was an adventure in itself! Of course, his mother highly disapproved, if she heard about it, which wasn't often. The guys always walked to the edge of their territory before hopping rides.

The bishop just tossed him the keys at their first meeting. With fear and trembling, Father Germano accepted them. Nothing was said about a driver's license; the bishop must have assumed everything was in order. Fortunately, one of his parishioners, a police officer, quietly stepped in when he learned of the dilemma. After a few circles around the parking lot, Father Germano understood the gears and the brakes. Then a few passes at angular parking, and he accomplished the task. Parallel parking was another trial.

He asked if he promised to always find an angular parking spot, could he be exempt from that test, but the officer rolled his eyes and shook his head no.

Somehow, he did manage to get his license. The officer who administered the test was generous, but made the priest promise to find some back roads and practice. The first few weeks, his brains, his body, and even his faith were rattled. But one morning, he got up early, hoping for less traffic, with the goal to see the sunrise over the Atlantic. The beach would encourage him to face his fear while the trip itself would give him the practice he needed. He arrived safely. Seeing a deserted beach for the first time was an awesome experience, a worthy reward. Time passed, and Father Germano realized he had to face the drive home. He rolled the windows down. The air blowing in his face made him feel relaxed, and he felt true freedom, true peace, and knew God was in his co-pilot seat. If Joe Green could only see him now!

But the peace was not to last, and the car chose to present its own problems. One day, he drove to the grocery store and got caught in a sudden thunderstorm. He frantically pulled over and searched for the car manual to learn how to turn on the windshield wipers. And then there was today, as he sat on the dusty roadside in total silence. He had no idea what was wrong. It was as if the car had taken one last breath, as a cloud of steam escaped from the engine and then shuttered to a stop. It refused to budge. *There had not even been time for last rites,* he mused. He had no idea what to do next.

Suddenly, a sleek, black Dodge appeared out of nowhere and came to a stop. A smartly dressed man wearing a Derby set at a jaunty angle stepped out and walked over.

"Car problems?" he asked.

"Yes, sir," Vince replied.

Rayford Simpson's head snapped. No white man had ever called him "Sir." He cocked has head like a sparrow to get a better look at this helpless soul and stifled a smile. He continued, "Did you cuss at the car?"

Vince looked up and said, "We had words."

"Did you kick the tires?"

"I sure did," Father Germano replied, standing up and feeling a pinch of confidence, as if the man seemed to have a true understanding of the situation.

"Did you bang on the hood?"

Father Germano opened his eyes wide as he realized he'd done every-thing the man said! *Maybe, I'm not stupid*, he hoped. "The very next thing," he replied confidently.

Then, Rayford dropped the bomb. "Did that do any good?"

Vince's shoulders drooped as he sighed, "No."

Rayford chuckled as he popped the hood and peered in. He diagnosed the problem immediately. "You need water," he announced.

"I sure do," agreed Vince.

"Not you!" Rayford cried, shaking his head incredulously. "The car!"

"The car?" replied Vince in awe, as he counted on his fingers the three things the mechanic had told him: gas for the tank, air in the tires, and oil, but the mechanic would do that. Now, he mentally added water to the list, but where? He came and looked over Rayford's shoulder. Both men topped out near 5'9"—that was with shoes and socks and standing tall. Now their faces were just inches apart.

"Phew! You're a bit strong, my friend," said Rayford with a smile as he stepped back.

Father Germano realized he had overstepped his boundary, as it was plain to see this man took pride in his appearance. He knew he was in no position to put his best foot forward as he stood, dripping sweat and dust. "Oh, sorry," he whispered as he took a step back. "I just wondered where to put the water."

Again, Rayford shook his head. *How had this stranger made it this far in life?* He patiently explained the radiator *and* the battery needed water regularly, particularly in warm weather, which was just about all the time in Florida. It was obvious the stranger was not from around there, even if his license plate, which he had noted earlier, was made in Raiford. It wasn't hard, he continued, and he happened to have a few gallons in his car. As an afterthought, he added, "Water's a good thing to carry, particularly if you drove"—and here he paused to think how to refer to the jalopy without being rude—"an older model." He continued noting that it was not good to add water to an over-heated engine; the block could crack, but since his car had sat there for a while, it was probably safe.

Rayford went to his car and returned with a heavy container filled with water. He looked at Father Germano and offered him a swig.

Father Germano declined, feeling it was his penance to pay, but Rayford insisted, recognizing Vince was also on the border of dehydration. Rayford shook his head in disbelief. Father Germano gratefully accepted.

Rayford expertly filled the radiator and, for good measure, topped off the battery. Father Germano marveled that he didn't spill a drop on his suit, though he noticed beads of sweat collecting over his brow. He wished he could offer him a handkerchief; his was already soaked. In one motion, Rayford heaved the container back into his car and smoothly retrieved a handkerchief from his pocket to mop his brow. He returned, slammed the hood down, and gave Father Germano a thumbs up to give the motor a try.

Father Germano said a quick prayer and turned the key. The motor choked, then fired up, and soon began purring sweetly. He left the motor running—afraid to turn it off—jumped out of the car, and, without thinking, gave Rayford a bear hug. Rayford was caught off guard. He regained his balance, tipped his hat, and turned to walk away, leaving an awestruck priest standing in the road still at a loss of how to return this remarkable act of kindness.

Father Germano yelled, "If you're in Starke on Sunday, drop into St. Edward's."

Rayford stopped cold in his step and whirled around. "What did you say?"

"You know, come to church," Father Germano replied, still grinning like a kid.

Rayford grinned back and returned to where Father Germano stood. "Can't do," he simply replied.

"Sure, you can," Father Germano insisted. Taking a step closer and grasping his arm, he continued. "All people are welcomed in God's house."

"Oh, I know that," replied Rayford. "But I'll be preaching to my congregation!"

They simultaneously broke into laughter.

"You sure don't look like any priest I've ever seen!" Rayford remarked shaking his head.

"Pax Domini sit semper vobis cum. In nomine Patri et Filii et Spiritus Sancti," Father Germano replied, while making an exaggerated sign of the cross.

Rayford smiled and extended his hand. "The Most Reverend Rayford Simpson."

Father Germano shook his hand and replied, "Father Vincent Germano."

Rayford paused and then offered, "If you're free during the week, stop by, and I'll teach you a few things about Auto Mechanics 101. That's how I put myself through the seminary; well, that and Myrtle's help." He gestured toward a pretty, but obviously over-heated, woman fanning herself in the front seat of his car.

It was the first time Father Germano saw her. Feeling apologetic, he gave a friendly wave, which she returned. "I'd like that," he said. And thus began their friendship. Reverend Simpson taught Father Germano how to change his oil and recognize trouble signs. He introduced him to spark plugs, pistons, and fan belts. Father Germano shared his knowledge of world history with Reverend Simpson, which included kings and queens of Africa, and his love of mysteries, non-fiction and fiction, which included Sherlock Holmes.

XXXII

THERE CAME THE INEVITABLE DAY WHEN FATHER GERMANO LITERALLY
dragged Reverend Simpson to the Baker Street Diner. Reverend Simpson felt
uncomfortable at first and always wore his Roman collar to remind himself,
as well as others, that he was a man of God. The customers at the diner
likewise felt a wave of discomfort and nudged each other, directing their
attention to the black man sitting on their seats, eating off their plates. But,
as he became a monthly regular, only passersby looked twice. The locals, recognizing Father Germano and the preacher, felt they must be meeting here
to solve local problems and discuss plans to care for the poor and support
the prison ministries. After all, that's what men of God did, right?

But Reverend Simpson earned his place at the booth and in the group. Ralph liked his contagious laugh and keen mind, and nobody relished Maddy's pies more than Reverend Simpson. With each bite, Ralph thought for sure the reverend was having a religious experience. The Most Reverend Simpson's only regret was that his wife, Myrtle, never found peace in the kitchen. It was a real drawback for a minister's wife, who was expected to fill baskets for the less fortunate and shine at potluck dinners. But she had a sweet voice that would calm an angry alcoholic or soothe a colicky baby, though they had never been so blessed. She could organize the women, teach the children, and make heaven on earth for Rayford and all who knew her.

The "Experience," as the Baker Street Irregulars and the regular diners dubbed the communion of Reverend Simpson and the pie, was watched with awe. It actually began long before the reverend took his first bite. The moment he entered the diner, he took a deep sniff and let out an audible sigh. After he took his seat, he carefully reviewed the daily selection of desserts. His mouth watered, as if he could actually taste the words. After several false starts, he confidently made his selection and sat back, anticipating its arrival. When their waitress, Carel, approached, her tray heavy with their orders, Rayford's eyes twinkled as he examined each selection and patiently waited for his to be served. As Carel was also aware of his addiction to the diner's sweets, she coyly teased him and served him last. Before she could take her hand away, the reverend's fork was poised and ready to dig in.

As a warm knife slips through butter, Rayford's fork cut the tip of the pie into a perfect bite. He slid the fork under the morsel and raised it to his lips. In a single moment, as the pie touched his tongue, his eyes closed, and his mouth filled with an explosion of flavor. Unconsciously, he sighed, "Ummm, Ummm, Ummm," and he continued to eat bite after bite until the plate was clean. Then, he would reach for his glass of ice-cold milk—not coffee, not tea, not soda, as they would be insults to Maddy's pies—and take a long gulp or two or three and then—and only then—would he lean back in complete satisfaction.

Ralph was the first to notice the ritual and nudged the preacher while silently nodding at the Reverend Simpson. The preacher then kicked Father Germano under the table. He wasn't pleased being interrupted, as being a single man, he enjoyed the desserts as much as the reverend, but then he followed the preacher's eyes to Reverend Simpson. The three became enraptured with the performance. Only as Rayford licked his fingers to pick up imaginary crumbs did he realize that their eyes were trained upon him. He cocked his head and looked back, unable to comprehend what was happening. The three men burst into laughter!

"You make that pie look better than sex!" Ralph cried out. Then, totally embarrassed, as he remembered the company he was keeping, he immediately apologized. Father Germano gave a forgiving smile and returned to eating his pie, as the reverend and the preacher just chuckled at Ralph's uncomfortable situation. No matter how much Reverend Simpson tried to contain his delight, each time they met, he savored each bite more than the last … and the diners wouldn't have it any other way.

The Irregulars actually solved a local robbery, but by the time they marched into the sheriff's office to share their findings, the culprit was already behind bars. Sheriff Rod Walsh immediately sat the four down and explained that cases rarely wrap up so easy, and that even though one man may be brought in, he might have confederates that could put them—and their families—in danger. The men nodded in agreement; solving crimes was a serious business, not a hobby. Please, the sheriff begged, leave locking criminals up to him, and he would leave saving their souls to them.

The men agreed there were enough concerns to occupy their minds and talents, but, secretly, they each longed to pull out a pipe and tackle a real-life mystery again. Little did they realize, Sheriff Walsh was impressed with their "elementary observations" and thought one day, if he really were stumped, he just might call on them.

XXXIII

"A COFFEE, MISS CAREL," CECIL A. BAXTER CALLED TO THE WAITRESS.
"And I think I'll have a piece of pie."

Miss Carel, the darling of Raiford, looked up from wrapping the silver-ware in paper napkins, surprised to see a customer so early. She sweetly replied, "I'll be glad to get you coffee, but the pie doesn't arrive until ten. Why, it's not even a quarter past six."

Cecil A. Baxter scowled and said, "I'll take the coffee. Double cream and lots of sugar."

Miss Carel paused and, looking at the unimpressive stranger, commented, "These are tough times, you know, rationing and all. It'll cost you extra."

Taking the cue, he grumbled, "Just bring the coffee. Black."

Meanwhile, back at the railroad station, the boys had thrown open the door of each car, only to confirm that the inside of each one was identical. On the bright side, there wasn't much to smell. The slush of manure and straw they had so easily washed away the day before had dried and turned as hard as brick. These cars weren't fresh; they were weeks old, and the floors were covered a foot deep with immovable crap, Mother Nature's concrete. They weren't sure what to do, but they did know they had to get started. They returned to the first car with hoses in hand and gave it their best shot. The water splashed and puddled and streamed out the cracks on the side, but the manure and straw repelled the water and remained as hard as rock.

Jim Brown told Marty to keep on spraying. Maybe, by some miracle, the brick would soften. He left and returned shortly with a pickaxe he'd found lying against the depot wall. Marty stopped and looked at Jim Brown, who gave a shrug. He lifted the axe over his head, and with all his strength, he brought the axe down.

D-OI-N-N-G-G-G! There was a crash, but the manure didn't budge. As a matter of fact, as if in retaliation, the manure held tight to the axe point, and it happened. Slowly the handle began to vibrate. The vibrations traveled up Jim Brown's arms and through his body until his brain began to rattle. Like a jolt of electricity, he automatically released the pickaxe and fell back onto the wet cattle car floor. Twice more, he swung with all his might, and each time, his hair stood on end and the manure won the battle. Marty wanted to laugh, but he knew this was not the time. There was nothing funny about their predicament.

"We're in trouble," Jim Brown said when he caught his breath.

Always the optimist, Marty replied, "No, we ain't! Come on, Jim Brown. We've only just begun. It's just some old straw and manure. The water's going to work … eventually. We'll get a better pickaxe and a shovel!" He forced a smile and added a touch of confidence by slapping Jim Brown on the back. "Come on, let's see what we can find."

"Sure," agreed Jim Brown with a weak smile, but he'd already felt the sting of the dried manure and straw, and he knew a jack hammer—if he could find one—wouldn't budge this stuff. He swallowed a bit of his pride, as he felt his dream of easy money slip away. Without further talk, they left the hoses running in the car and jump out in search of more tools. Jim

Brown returned with two shovels, a sledgehammer, and a chisel; Marty had a second pickaxe and a saw.

"What's the saw for?" asked Jim Brown. Marty just shrugged and tossed it to the side. They both checked the first car. Jim Brown boldly led the way; Marty held back. He closed his eyes tight and said a quick prayer, followed by the sign of the cross, before looking inside. Water covered the floor an inch deep and was streaming out every door, every crack, and every crevice, but the manure was still as hard as cement. They picked up their gear and went to the next car.

As Jim Brown climbed aboard, the first thing he noticed were the patterns of light as the rays pierced through the car slats. It reminded him of prison bars, one after the other after the other, and he felt crestfallen as the stifling heat and confinement overwhelmed him. He didn't say a word but went straight to work. The noise that filled the countryside was unrecognizable, but it was loud and continuous.

XXXIV

THREE HOURS LATER, THE MID-MORNING SUN SHONE BRIGHTLY AS THE two boys slumped against one of the railroad cars, totally exhausted and covered with dirt and sweat. Bits of hay swirled in the water puddling at their feet, while two tumble turds fought over a piece of reconstituted manure. The only sound for miles around was the water sloshing out of the hoses. Marty turned to Jim Brown with a look of total defeat. Jim Brown stared blankly ahead and seethed in anger. They'd been hoodwinked, but they'd not been beaten, not yet. And, if he were still breathing, he would never turn over even one penny to the railroad agent. He got up without a word and began to walk away.

"You're not leaving, are you?" yelled Marty, his eyebrows raised with concern and confusion.

"No," replied Jim Brown. "I'm going to get us a drink."

"Sounds great," Marty called, relieved but still puzzled. Actually, walking away might be an answer. Marty sure wouldn't argue, but he knew Jim Brown wouldn't. He couldn't.

Jim Brown walked over to the grocery store. He pushed the screen door open and bells jingled, announcing the arrival of a customer. The electric fan swirled back and forth, offering little relief from the heat. He walked automatically to the back where the soda bottles were kept in the cooler and brought two grape Nehis to the counter.

"Working hard again?" smiled Mrs. King.

"Yes, ma'am," he replied, as he pulled the crumpled, wet dollar bill from his pocket. After he got the change, he walked to the pay phone on the side of the store, trying to rehearse what he might say. His pace slowed, as the right words never came. He stared at the phone, put the pop bottles on the ground, and clenched and unclenched his fist. Finally, he removed the receiver and dropped a nickel into the slot. He heard it clink, and then a dial tone sounded. His fingers automatically dialed the number that went directly to his father's office. He listened to the tick, tick, tick as each number registered and heard a click as his father picked up the phone before the second ring. He felt his presence before he even said, "Florida State Prison, Assistant Superintendent Godwin speaking."

"Dad," Jim Brown said, "I'm in trouble." There, he said it, straightforward, direct. There was a silent pause, and Jim Brown knew his father was waiting for details, so he dove in. "Yesterday, I met Mr. Baxter at the railroad depot, and I signed a contract to clean ten cattle cars." He took a breath and continued. "It really was a great deal," he said in his defense. "And Marty and I thought we could do it. Heck, we thought we could do twenty, easily." *Too much information*, he thought. *Get back to facts!* "But Dad, I can't do it. And there's this fine print that if we don't finish by sundown, I'll owe the railroad money."

The silence continued. Then he heard three words: "I'll be there." With that, he heard his father hang up the phone. The money automatically dropped down, jingling as it went. He hung up the receiver, took a deep breath, and slumped against the building. His heart rate returned to normal, so he picked up the bottles and started back to Marty.

Jim Brown wasn't sure if he was in worse shape or not, but there was a small, almost indistinguishable sigh of relief as he walked back to the railroad cars. Marty's face lit up when he saw Jim Brown approach carrying the drinks. They weren't as frosty cold as yesterday's, but they'd still taste good. Jim Brown told Marty about the phone call.

"You mentioned my name?" Marty asked.

Jim Brown shook his head up and down confirming Marty's worst nightmare.

"What did he say?"

"'I'll be there.'"

"That's it?"

"'I'll be there.'"

They sat in silence as they finished their drinks. Though it wasn't even ten o'clock, Jim Brown pulled out the sandwiches and offered one to Marty. He gladly accepted and tossed Jim Brown a chunk of meat. "What's in this stuff?" Jim Brown asked after taking a bite.

"Oh, you don't want to know. Dad calls it blutwurst," Marty said.

"It's not bad. Where'd your dad learn to make this?" asked Jim Brown.

"Well," considered Marty between bites, "he said my granddad lived in this town in Germany called Wertheim—it sounded pretty swell. It had a castle with a huge wall around it. And there was a clock tower with two faces, one for the town workers and one for the royals. The workers' clock had two hands, so they would know the exact time because time is money while the royal face had only one hand because they lived on ish-time." To explain, Marty dropped his voice and said, "I'll leave for the hunting camp eightish." Then he raised his voice an octave and threw out his pinky finger before continuing, "But be sure to be back fourish for crumpets and tea!" He grinned at Jim Brown rather pleased with his performance. Jim Brown cocked his head and smiled as he considered the concept.

"Granddad said Wertheim is between two rivers—the Tauber and the Main—and just about every year, they would flood. They even had a house they'd mark to show how high the water came, going back hundreds of years. His father was a butcher, and my granddad and his brothers worked for him. But between the floods and all his brothers, Opa, that's Granddad, hopped on a barge and went down the river. He eventually jumped a ship and came to Jacksonville. He didn't much care for the ocean, but he loved the beach—so, he just kinda stayed and began working as a butcher. One day, he took a bunch of sausage to the judge's house and said he wanted to be an American citizen. And the judge said if a man could make sausage this good, there had to be a place for him in the United States. So, he helped him become a citizen, and he had a standing order for sausage every week—and that's how he met my grandmother; she worked for the judge.

"Nana said the Big Depression was much worse in Germany. Even their postage stamps became worthless. The government had to recall all the stamps and over-print them with new values, like one-mark stamps went to one million!"

"Really? That much?" replied Jim Brown in disbelief as he considered the consequences.

"I'm not kidding! I saw some on old letters Opa put in the Bible! Nana said that was why he lost touch with his family. They just couldn't afford to write. Anyway, one summer, my dad came to work for Opa, and he met my mom, their only child. When they married, he got Mom and all the recipes. But after I was born and Mom died, Dad got tired of Opa's growling and Nana's tears, so we moved here and set up shop. But don't tell anyone they're German recipes! Please! Jim Brown, you can't tell anyone! You know how people feel about the Germans these days!"

Jim Brown saw true terror in Marty's eyes, and he knew Marty had every reason to be concerned. He hadn't given it much thought until then, but only yesterday on the playground, kids had chased Ernst Protzmann from the swings, yelling, "Hotsi, Totsi! You're a little Nazi!" And the adults avoided Schultz's Department Store in Jacksonville because he was a "Kraut."

He'd even heard on the radio that the government rounded up all the Japanese Americans on the West Coast and put them into internment camps, even if their parents, grandparents, and great-grandparents were born here and were true Americans. Jim Brown didn't know any Japanese Americans personally, and he knew even less about their culture. Hollywood showed bold samurai warriors and beautiful Geisha girls who painted their faces white and wore embroidered silk. In the newspapers, their ambassadors wore top hats and even smiled the day before Pearl Harbor was bombed. They always seemed to bow a lot, had slanted eyes, and straight, dark hair, but that was all he knew.

He remembered seeing a picture of Mount Fujiyama in *National Geographic*; it was so serene and symmetrical. But here we were at war, and his brother was in the thick of it. He loved history and really paid attention during class, but his teachers never taught him how to interpret these events. He wasn't sure what to think, but he still understood when someone was being treated unfairly. Putting American families behind bars wasn't right, Japanese or not. He considered news reports and how everyone felt. They were suspicious; they were frightened. He kept returning to the one thought—we were at war. Maybe they might be spies, or maybe they might be safer being guarded for the time being, even if they were patriotic ... but deep down, he felt there had to be a better way.

Marty burst out in desperation, "I'm no spy! I don't even speak German, and the only secrets I know are the signals you taught me in baseball—and they don't even play baseball in Germany!" Reaching for "the end of the rope," he added, "Dad's English!" followed by a groan, "but don't tell Frank."

"Hold on, sport!" Jim Brown could feel how Marty was truly suffering. "First of all, if it makes you feel any better, Frank has already told me that with 'Godwin' and 'Reddish,' I probably have a good dose of English heritage. And other than his Irish glare every so often, our friendship survives. Secondly, you've sat through enough of Miss Lester's lectures. We're all Americans! That's what makes us great ... a little of this, a little of that—stone soup, American stew, tossed salad. But, jeepers! I promise I'll keep 'Opa' just between us. I won't tell a soul! Cross my heart."

Marty's mind and heart were still spinning; and as tears began to stream down his face, he blurted out, "But I do love them."

It was Jim Brown's turn to be caught off guard. He didn't know what to say. He thought how grateful he was to have a family—with all their quirks! Finally, he turned to Marty, and, in a sincere voice, he began, "Marty?" He waited until Marty looked up and continued, "We all have families. Some are luckier than others. But friends are the family you choose, and you know we are friends—and I feel damn lucky to call you a friend."

Slowly, a smile returned to Marty's face. He realized, once again, Jim Brown was there for him. Then, his old self returning, he grinned back and replied, "And a friend in need is a friend indeed. You are lucky I'm here."

Jim Brown laughed and replied, "That I am."

Marty knew Jim Brown was right, but he still wondered if he'd said too much, even if it was to best his friend. Hoping to change the subject, he asked, "Hey, Jim Brown, how did your folks meet?"

"Don't really know." He paused, as he had never given it much thought. "I guess they just grew up in Lawtey together." Then his mind began to think about his father, and so did Marty. Without a word, they stood up, grabbed their shovels, walked to the nearest car, and climbed in. The rest and sandwiches had given them new strength physically. Mentally, they became doubly motivated because the one thing they knew for sure, they'd better be working hard when his dad arrived. They weren't working on royal ish-time. Every second counted.

When Jim Brown climbed into the box car, he saw Marty in a curious position, head bent down, hands together in prayer, and he heard a tiny whisper, "Now I lay me down to sleep. Pray the Lord my soul to keep…"

"Hey, Marty! What are you doing?" cried Jim Brown.

"Well, I thought it might be a good time to say a prayer, and this is the only one I know." He looked up, dejected. Then, with an expression between woeful and righteous, he challenged, "What would you pray?"

Jim Brown thought a moment and wished, like the prayer suggested, he was sleeping because then he could wake up from this nightmare. Not happening, he knew, so in resignation, he lifted his eyes to the heavens, brought his hands together, and said, "And if I die before I wake, I pray the Lord my soul to take…" He hoped it would be quickly, for surely this job would kill him.

Then Marty gave a resounding "Amen!" and smiled.

Jim Brown repeated, "Amen."

XXXV

HIS FATHER HAD BEEN PREOCCUPIED WITH THE DEMANDS OF HIS JOB.
It was a challenge to run the State Prison, keep the men in line, and feed
them on nine cents a day, but the tone in his son's voice caught his attention.
He stepped out of the office and told his secretary that he'd be gone for an
hour. If time had permitted, he would have climbed into the wagon and let
Old Dan do the work, but time was crucial. He walked directly to the sedan.
He nodded at one of the guards he passed, opened the car door, and slid in.
He stepped onto the clutch and turned the key in the ignition. The motor
rumbled to life. *Good start*, he thought; next, he stepped onto the gas pedal
and eased the shift into first, then slowly released the clutch. The motor
growled, and the car leaped forward. Quickly, he reengaged the clutch and
ground the gears into second, and finally, after shifting to third, the motor
hummed as he hit the open road. He relaxed his hold on the steering wheel
and settled in; he was off to Early Taylor's cracker shack.

Mr. Godwin was a man of few words. He could instantly size up a situation and methodically tackle any problem, but this was different. He found
it difficult to keep his mind on the road. He heard his son's voice over and
over in his head, "I'm in trouble." He raised an eyebrow as he smiled and
nodded. *Yes*, he thought, *this was a sign of a real man when a boy recog-
nizes that he needs help and has the courage to ask. Oh, there were lessons
to be learned, but his boy had called, and he wouldn't let him down.* His
boys were everything to him.

The reality was the railroad agent had taken advantage of his son, and no one, especially this huckster, would do that. He knew the contract was not worth the paper it was written on. Heck, the boys were minors. But there it was his son's signature on a contract, and he knew—and he agreed—that his son's word meant something. This conniving contractor was not going to drag his son's name through the dirt and, like his son, he would be damned if he would pay him a penny. He grit his teeth and narrowed his eyes, and the veins at his temples popped. Quietly, he regained control. He had a plan, a good, honest plan, and he returned his focus to the road.

Early got his name the old-fashioned way. He earned it. He was in the fields early to gleam the most corn and pick the sweetest strawberries still covered with dew. The farmers would all say, "Hey, you're early, aren't you?" and he would reply, "Why, yes. Yes, sir, I am Early," and the name just stuck. He sometimes was unjustly called lazy because, in the heat of the day, he could be found snoozing under an oak, but the fact was he'd gotten there early and had already worked more than any man would. He always carried his load and even helped others make their quotas. He believed the early bird catches the worm, literally—he was up at the crack of dawn to catch fat night crawlers and go fishing.

At seventeen, he had whisked Minnie McAlester across the Georgia state line "to jump the broom." They had stopped at the first AME he could find because he was a man of God. Minnie was a perfect fit for Early, though unlike Early and his name, there was nothing "Minnie" about her. Her heart was the size of Texas, and when she sang in the AME Church, her voice could be heard throughout Bradford, Clay, and Union Counties, and parts of Alachua and Putnam, too. Her voice came in handy once the children began to arrive.

Early was proud of his house, even if every board creaked; he called it his alarm system. No one was coming in, and with all those kids, no one was sneaking out without Early's knowledge. The roof was tight—he saw to that—and the floor was swept clean—Minnie was particular—and between the creaks and hollers, love grew. Early had one hiccup in his life—he stayed late at a bar one night and got into a fight over Minnie; after all, she was the only one in Early's eyes worth fighting for. Early wasn't muscle-bound. He was tall and lanky, but he was wily and deceptively strong. He knew the man had a glass jaw and struck him with everything he had at just the right moment, so they say. What he couldn't foresee was Moose—who also came by his name naturally—falling and hitting his head on the bar corner.

That's how he came to meet Mr. Godwin at the State Prison. Minnie and the kids visited Early every week. Like Early, they were always first in line. Early was released early on good behavior, and Mr. Godwin knew he would not be back. Early had found his piece of heaven on earth, and with hard work and help from the Good Lord, he would keep it. He never touched liquor again, unless it was for medicinal use, for communion, or for a very special celebration, and he never went back to the bar. If the truth be told about that night, however, the blow that sent Moose to the floor could just as well have come from Minnie, who was standing quietly in the shadows behind him, but no one ever spoke about that night again ever.

When Mr. Godwin drove up, Early was sitting on the porch with old Gator Bait. Early jumped to his feet, partly out of habit from his prison days, but mostly out of respect.

His friend, Gator Bait, was beyond his jumping years, but he nodded his head out of respect for Mr. Godwin, and Mr. Godwin returned the gesture. Like Early, he was tall and lanky; the name did not fit unless you knew his history.

As a kid, Gator Bait would hang around the Pure gas station, hoping to pick up any odd jobs. During alligator season, the trappers always stopped to pick up some cold drinks and crackers to take with them, and if they were lucky, some poor soul to carry the stinking chicken carcasses they used as bait; and that's where Gator Bait came in.

"I'm your man!" he'd call.

"Sure, kid," they'd laugh, as they tossed the canvas bag his way.

Once near the creek, the lead man would call, "Gator bait!"

"Here I is!" he promptly called, appearing out of nowhere, canvas bag in hand.

At the end of the day, they handed him two dollars—a real man's wage—which he promptly gave to his mother. He never forgot the surprise and smile on her face. It was worth every cringe-filled moment he'd spent with the trappers.

But after the first two trips, Samuel, that was his real name, broke down and cried to his mother that he just couldn't take the stench anymore. He threw up all the time, and the men just laughed.

His mother cradled him in her arms and rocked him until the tears dried up and the sobbing stopped. Then, she whispered that she had an old family trick that would cure the vomiting and make those men stand up in awe. He never shared the secret potion, but, boy, did it work. He made more money each season as he learned to spot the gators, and the trappers tipped him handsomely for every gator they caught.

His friends teased him, calling him Gator Bait, but he was proud of what he did, and the money he made was good. He earned their respect, and the trappers even asked for him by name, Gator Bait.

Sometimes, the trappers asked him to join them on a night hunt; he always refused. He had a healthy respect for the critters. He'd seen them stalk prey and turn in death rolls until the victim struggle no more. One evening, walking home from a church meeting with his father, he slipped and started to skid towards the creek. He froze as he saw more glittering eyes than he could count silently floating over the water, straight toward him! He wondered if they knew he was Gator Bait, but he didn't want to find out! He didn't even feel his father's strong grip as he snatched him from the bank. Holding tightly to his father's neck, his father calmly said, "Dem gators are always out at night. Don't you ever come down here in the dark." Gator Bait shook his head in agreement and didn't let go of his father until they arrived home.

Everyone in Starke knew old Gator Bait and his goat cart. He went around town and encouraged all the colored boys to sign up for soldiering. He always had the Good Book on his knee and though he had trouble reading, he could quote the Bible, book, chapter, and verse, as well as any scholar.

"Mr. Taylor," Mr. Godwin called, as respect is a two-way street, "I have a problem that I hope you might help me solve."

Early cocked his head. Curious, he walked down to see what Mr. Godwin had to say. Gator Bait, meanwhile, leaned over so far he almost lost his balance, but, darn, he didn't want to be left out of something this significant.

Mr. Godwin gave Early the facts: ten stockcars encrusted with manure had to be cleaned by sundown. Early understood and quickly determined the number of men needed to complete the job. In no time, he rounded up four friends. Each brought his own shovel and pickaxe ready to work.

"That should do it," nodded Mr. Godwin in approval. They tossed their tools into the trunk, and the men squeezed into the car—the four men with broad shoulders were packed like a can of sardines in the back while Early sat in the front. Silently, they drove to the Raiford Depot.

The men Early brought were hard workers. If it was tedious work, he would have called on his sons, but Early knew they'd need muscle, and lots of it. The men came because they were Early's friends, and they needed the money. They also trusted Mr. Godwin, as nothing had been said of pay, but they knew he would be fair, and they were even more curious how a white boy got himself in such a mess.

XXXVI

WHEN THEY ARRIVED AT THE DEPOT, THERE WAS NO ONE IN SIGHT. BUT a telltale stream of water glistened in the noonday sun around a cattle car and strange sounds, separated with gut wrenching grunts, erupted from the car next to it.

"I'll be back at five-thirty," Mr. Godwin told Early.

"That'll be fine, Boss," he replied.

Early didn't have to give directions. The men had already sized up the situation for themselves and separated into teams to tackle the remaining cars. Laughing and shaking their heads, they realized what a mess they'd gotten themselves into, but they also understood a boy with dreams trying to earn money and an evil man who destroys dreams and robs a man of an honest wage. They'd get the job done. They were all on board, body and soul.

Jim Brown and Marty were absorbed in their work. Their backs were already breaking, their hands blistered, and their legs trembled as they lifted chunks of manure that begrudgingly released from the floor boards. They didn't notice Early climbing on board, but when they paused to take a breath, they felt the car shake. Jim Brown jerked his head around and saw Early give a mighty swing and a chunk of manure come flying. As he stood up, Early gave Jim Brown a shy grin, and Jim Brown returned with a confused, half-wave. It slowly dawned on him that his father was responsible. Then, he heard a chorus singing, "Come to the water…" And Early joined in, "Come to the water, my children! Come to the water…"

"Rock of Ages" might be more appropriate, Jim Brown thought, but he picked up his axe and began to swing again, this time with conviction. For the first time since he arrived that morning, he actually felt there was a chance the job would be completed, and completed on time.

Marty, meanwhile, slipped to the door and with a sad smile waved good-bye. Jim Brown understood. Marty had stuck by him longer than anyone else would have and had given one hundred percent, but now he was worn out and would only be in the way. Jim Brown returned an understanding smile and waved good-bye.

The spirituals that filled the cattle cars gave rhythm to their strokes and diverted their attention from the work and pain involved. Before he knew it, the second car was cleaned, and they silently moved to the next.

By five-fifteen, the men had gathered by the road. The cars were clean—not sparkling clean like the cars yesterday, but clean enough to meet the contractual agreement. To his utter amazement, he looked up and saw Marty crossing the road, his arms filled with cold Nehis. He passed them out to the grateful men and then handed Jim Brown the last. "It's the least I could do," he said. "Miss McGonagall said to 'give 'em hell!'"

Jim Brown noticed his hands all bandaged and realized she was probably responsible for the Nehis, too. She really did care for Marty. He looked at Marty, saluted him with the empty bottle, and said, "Thanks, Marty. Really, I mean it, thanks. Next time you see Miss McGonagall," here he paused, acknowledging there would be a next time, "you tell her we did."

About that time, Mr. Godwin pulled up in the wagon harnessed to Ole Dan. There was no need to rush this time. He took out his wallet and paid the men. Each man gratefully accepted the money and added, "Thanks, Boss!"

Then, he turned to Jim Brown and said, "We'll settle up when you get home." The men climbed on board with a little regret. They truly wanted to see how the scene would play out. But they were bone-tired and, in their hearts, they knew that the flim-flam man had been bamboozled; and that was good enough for them. As Mr. Godwin snapped the reins and Ole Dan began to trudge back toward Starke, the men smiled and gave Jim Brown and Marty a wave. Jim Brown returned with a casual salute as the wagon disappeared, trailing a cloud of dust.

"Guess there goes our profit," said Jim Brown, as he sat down next to Marty, "And probably my duck money, too."

"Ah, come on, Jim Brown, we'll make a bunch more. Next time we'll check the cars first!"

"Next time! You little goofball!" And with what little strength he had left, Jim Brown wrestled Marty to the ground.

XXXVII

THE FOREMAN HAD BEEN LAUGHING ALL DAY, SHARING HIS STORY OF the two gullible boys and how he managed to get them to sign a contract that would have his cattle cars cleaned for free with anyone who would listen or the poor souls who happened to sit down next to him. He didn't include that he would pocket the money allotted for the job, and if he was lucky, he might even double the sum as Jim Brown would have to cough up a few extra bucks. In truth, the railroad wasn't concerned about a day or two more. Then he began to think of a real dinner at Miss Morhard's Boarding House.

"Hey, Miss Carel," he called, leering her way, "you busy tonight?"

She smiled and rolled her eyes while silently mouthing, "No way!" to Big Bertha, the counter waitress.

Cecil A. Baxter was arrogant enough to take her silence as an agreeable, "Why, no, sugar. I'd love to spend an evening with you!" He began to plan a night of cheap romance.

The Baker Street Irregulars were seated in their booth and looked at each other, wondering the same thing, "Is this man a member or your church?" Each shrugged and turned to Ralph. Ralph, likewise, shrugged and, in conspiratorial tones, whispered he recognized the man as a railroad employee who passed through every few months, but had not much else to offer. As offended as they were, they felt there were not enough clues to get involved and turned their attentions back to the generous slices of strawberry pie topped with extra whipped cream that had magically appeared.

"Well, it's time to go collect," he said as he stood up, scraping the chair across the floor. The railroad chief who had joined him an hour earlier stood up, shrugged to the few remaining customers, and followed him out the door.

Smugly puffing on his stogie, Baxter and the chief slowly sauntered down the road to the rail yard. "There's no reason to rush," Baxter said, with his best effort to show sincerity. "I really want to give them every chance I can." In his mind, he pictured their meeting, his feigned surprise and disappointment. "Why, boys, you mean you're not finished? I thought you could do twenty!" Then he caught himself unintentionally laughing out loud. He quickly pulled a dirty handkerchief from his pocket and covered his mouth. The chief just shook his head and continued on.

They quickened their step as they rounded the corner and saw the exhausted boys sitting outside the first car. Baxter smirked and nudged the chief in the side. "Taking a break?" he coyly asked.

Jim Brown slowly raised his head and stood up. "The job's done," he quietly said.

"Well, you boys can come back tomorrow," continued Baxter, giving an understanding nod, totally ignoring what Jim Brown had said. "You know you need to finish…"

"The job's done," repeated Jim Brown in a voice that rang as cold as steel.

Baxter stopped talking, cocked his head, and looked directly into Jim Brown's eyes. The smile began to fade as he realized Jim Brown was staring back, unflinchingly.

"What-t-t-t did you say?" he stuttered. The stogie dropped from his mouth, and he raced from car to car, not waiting to hear an answer. He threw the doors open and barely took the time to look in. When he reached the last car, his step had slowed, and he was wheezing. His humor had vanished, and he desperately tried to scheme a way to deny paying the boys. But the job was done. The jig was up, and the sun was setting. Jim Brown held out his hand to be paid.

Baxter began to pull out his checkbook.

"In cash," Jim Brown said.

"In cash?" repeated Baxter. Jim Brown didn't flinch.

Baxter grimaced and pulled out his wallet. He carefully counted ten dollar bills and started to hand the money over when he stopped and grinned, "You boys wouldn't be interested in…?"

"No," Jim Brown cut him off.

Defeated, he thrust the money into Jim Brown's hand and turned to pay Marty. Marty just nodded to Jim Brown, so Mr. Baxter turned back and begrudgingly counted out ten dollars more. Then he spun around and walked away.

"Hey!" the chief called, as he winked at Jim Brown. "No tip?"

Throwing up his hands in disgust, Mr. Baxter grumbled, "A contract pays what a contract states! He gets what he gets!"

Jim Brown smiled and shrugged his shoulders. The chief smiled and shook his hand while he slipped him two dollars more.

"Good job, Mr. Godwin, good job." Then he turned and walked away, whistling a happy tune.

Jim Brown was lost in that euphoric moment. He had forgotten that Marty was there until he tugged at his sleeve,

"That was great!" he said grinning ear to ear, "And tell your dad thanks for me when you get home."

Jim Brown reached down and shook his hand. "Great job, Mr. Russell, great job."

With that, Marty gave a wave and dashed off for home. Jim Brown pocketed the money and then began the long trek home.

Luckily, he had only walked a quarter mile when Mr. Griffis offered him a ride the rest of the way. "Hard day?" he asked as Jim Brown climbed on board.

"Hard day," replied Jim Brown.

XXXVIII

WHEN HE FINALLY GOT HOME, HIS FATHER WAS ALREADY SITTING IN
his easy chair, listening to the radio and reading *The Bradford Telegraph*.
It was a good sign. Jim Brown walked over and handed him the twenty-two dollars.

"I've got my duck money upstairs." He paused for a moment. "And
next week…"

"This will do," his father said, taking the money. "Go and get cleaned
up. Your mother has a special supper planned."

Jim Brown smiled, and his shoulders relaxed. "Thanks, Dad. And Marty
said to say, 'Thanks,' too," then he turned to go upstairs.

That night, Early's mother, his wife, and their five children gathered
around the table. It almost looked like Thanksgiving. There was a platter
piled high with golden fried chicken, bowls filled with fresh collard greens
from the garden, and tender, flakey biscuits. Summer corn on the cob,
drenched in butter and seasoned with salt and pepper, was stacked like
Lincoln logs, while a sweet potato pie was cooling on the windowsill for
dessert. Early's wife gave him a squeeze, and he hugged her in return. The
rest of the family impatiently waited for grace before digging in.

The other men's tables were similarly set, the fixings bought with the
money they'd earned that day. Laughter rang from the households, as the
men told the story of the boys and their dreams, the manure as hard as concrete, and the slick-talking railroad agent who got his comeuppance.

True to his father's word, his mother took out a thick steak from the icebox, which he grilled to perfection. Bowls of green beans seasoned with a slab of salt pork and heavenly hash stood next to a platter, with mounds of mashed potatoes smothered with rivers of brown gravy streaming down the sides. For dessert, there was the last of the fresh strawberries sliced over sponge cake, topped with generous dollops of sweetened whipped cream—a true feast in these times of troubles.

Jim Brown barely made it to the table. He'd never felt this exhausted in his entire life! Every muscle in his body ached; his hands were both bandaged, and he could hardly keep his eyes open. Before the steaks made it to the table, Jim Brown was out like a light. But his last thoughts were of Marty, a true friend; the men who helped him win the day; and his dad, a real hero.

"What's wrong with Jim Brown? What's his face doing in his taters? Can I have his dessert?" cried Harold.

Meanwhile, somewhere in the Pacific, Bill sat down with his army buddies to another meal of K-Rations: mystery meat, beans, and applesauce. As the grumblings grew louder, Cookie, the mess sergeant, yelled to no one in particular, "Someday, when you get back home to your sweet brides, and they serve you tough biscuits and burnt meatloaf, you'll remember me and this gourmet meal!"

Spontaneously, they all broke into laughter, and just as unexpectedly, they became silent. They were all thinking of their homes, their sweethearts, and mouth-watering apple pie.

All the families, near and far, were alike in many ways. They all gave thanks for their food and families. They praised the Lord for His mercy and many blessings. And they all prayed for peace and better times.

Back at the boarding house, Cecil A. Baxter removed his last, almost clean, wrinkled shirt from his suitcase. He dressed quickly and smoothed his hair with his hand before walking down the street toward the diner. His step was light, and he hummed a merry song as he purposefully disregarded the way the afternoon had played out. A minor, well, perhaps a major setback, but then maybe Miss Carel might take pity on him and pick up the tab and offer comforts into the night. To his surprise, stepping out the door of the diner, arm in arm, came Miss Carel with handsome Ed Brenner. She didn't even notice Cecil when she passed, her head resting on Ed's shoulder and his green eyes gazing into hers. Cecil's mouth gaped open, and he automatically turned to watch them get into Ed's car and drive away. His head drooped. Would nothing go his way?

Cecil turned back to the diner and watched as Big Bertha changed the daily special. His spirits rose a little as he hoped for pot roast or maybe thick fried pork chops. His mouth watered. It wouldn't be the boarding house fare he'd been dreaming of, but it would fit his budget and his belly—and he wouldn't have to feed the traitorous waitress! Big Bertha only wrote one word; then she turned and waddled back inside the diner.

Like a kaleidoscope, his face changed with every turn of emotions, from rosy to smug anticipation to shocking confusion, from open surprise to crestfallen disappointment. His face turned green as the menu registered. The billboard read:

TODAY'S SPECIAL

Yesterday's

Fried Liver and Onions

Spinach

Boiled Potatoes

Tapioca Pudding

$1.15

"Oh, my God!" he exhaled in a less-than-prayerful tone. Thunder rumbled in reply as the clouds rolled in. Instantly, the sky let loose a torrential downpour. Baxter's head dropped. His shoulders slumped forward, and he trudged across the already muddy road. The rainwater washed away his footprints.

Outside the diner, he struggled to pull open the door as gusts of wind pushed the door closed. Once inside, the lights blinked off and on as another clap of thunder announced his arrival. He looked around, hoping to find someone to impress or fleece, but the room was empty. He shook his arms and head like a dog drying himself after a bath and slowly slid into the nearest booth. He shuttered as a chill swept through this body. The rain, beating against the glass window, concealed the heavy footsteps of Bertha as she stomped over in her orthopedic shoes. She took her pencil from behind her ear and patiently held it poised over her pad, ready to take his order.

Baxter jumped when he finally felt her presence. She just smirked and raised her eyebrow. "The special?" she asked, already scrawling down the order.

"Yeah," he grumbled and, with a snarl, added, "And throw on some extra onions."

"Supplies didn't come today," she smiled sweetly. "We're short on everything, including onions."

With a huff, he smiled while growling. "In that case, hold the onions, hold the liver, and while you're at it, hold the spinach. Just bring me a hamburger."

Bertha smiled an equally disarming smile, placed her hands firmly on the table, and leaned into Baxter's space, establishing an assertive stance. In a low, but discernible whisper, she replied, "I told you the supplies didn't come. So, you can have liver." And with that, she stood up putting her right hand out to one side for emphasis, "Or you can have liver." She paused again, putting her left hand out in mirrored fashion, "Or, you can have the special. And, oh," she leaned in again, this time her nose almost touching his, "why, that's liver." Without waiting for a response, she stood up and turned on her heel. Sashaying over to the counter, she purred to the cook, "One special, Porge."

Porge nodded and went to work. The raw liver hit the griddle with a loud sizzle and the greasy smoke drifted through the diner.

Baxter's mouth dropped open, and his eyes popped. Then, unwilled, uncontrolled, he banged his head on the table again and again and again.

EPILOGUE

THIS STORY FALLS INTO THE CATEGORY OF HISTORICAL FICTION; THERE-
fore, I included many historical events that I hope you will research further.
If you are interested in the account of the German Intelligence Operation
which occurred in June of 1942, you might google "Operation Pastorius"
or take the old fashion approach and read the book *Operation Pastorius:
Eight Spies Against America* by George J. Dasch. I also drew upon opportunities my life gave me. I was a docent in the Frontier Army Museum
in Fort Leavenworth, Kansas, as well as the Hershey Museum in Hershey,
Pennsylvania. As an Army Wife, our family was fortunate to spend five years
in Wertheim, Germany. I am thrilled to share some of the sights we enjoyed
there. As a lifelong student of history, I have enjoyed many books on the
subject. In preparation for writing this book, I read copies of the *Bradford
County Telegraph* for 1942, which offered a historical outline as well as
details of lifestyles at that time. Accepting the responsibility to not mislead
my readers, I double checked details on Wikipedia.

Finally, to be complete, I would like to share "the rest of the story" of
several characters whose lives may not have made it into the pages of history books but whose lives mattered very much to those who knew them as
well as to this story.

Bill Godwin came back from the war and married his sweetheart, Wanda. They eventually moved to Ohio where Bill owned an engineering company. They had a son and a daughter, and they lived happily ever after.

On October 24, 1944, the USS Princeton was attacked by a Japanese bomber off the coast of the Philippines. One bomb hit the center of the aircraft carrier, igniting fires from oil and ammunitions on board. Because the flight deck was made of wood, the fires rapidly spread. Owen Tilley gave his life that day.

On April 4, 1955, a woman smuggled a gun to a prisoner incarcerated in the Florida State Prison. In his escape attempt, being unfamiliar with the administration building, he accidentally found himself in a conference room where Mr. Godwin was conducting a meeting. Desperate, he shot Mr. Godwin, who was unarmed, twice. Hours later, he died. Eve Godwin moved to Starke, where she lived next door to Harold until she died in 1982.

Jim Brown Godwin followed his father's footsteps and worked as a correctional officer, beginning his career at Belle Glade Correctional Institution. He was transferred to Florida State Prison as manager of the cattle industry before being promoted to chief correctional officer. Six years later, he was promoted to assistant superintendent, the same job his father held. He earned the respect of his peers, his superiors, and the inmates. He was a modest man, never seeking unearned praise, but on a quiet evening, after a bourbon or two, he would share stories of his time in service and insights into some of the worse criminals who passed through the penitentiary gates. In 1970, he was promoted to superintendent of Desoto Correctional Institution in Arcadia, and in 1973, he transferred to the Reception and Medical Center at Lake Butler as superintendent. At his retirement ceremony in 1985, many took the opportunity to acknowledge his accomplishments. He built his home in Starke, on the land he loved. He married his sweetheart Peggy Tilley in 1949. They also had a son and a daughter. Theirs was truly a match made in heaven. In 2004, he died of a massive heart attack.

Harold, lovingly called Weird, never left Starke, and Jim Brown was always there for him. He worked for the Florida Department of Transportation, but his true loves were working on his farm, hunting, fishing, and playing the guitar in the bar off SR 301 just across the county line. He proudly raised his family in Starke and died of cancer a few months after his older brother, Jim Brown, passed away.

Frank Foley is also a real-life character, but he grew up in New York. He graduated from Fordham University and NYU Medical School and joined the Army, serving with the Army of Occupation in Japan. He became a flight surgeon in the air force, where he rose to the rank of colonel, commanding several military hospitals around the world. His career afforded him many opportunities, including a secret mission to Saudi Arabia in 1951 and assisting on the autopsies of the Apollo astronauts Command Pilot Gus Grissom, Senior Pilot Ed White and Pilot Roger Chaffee. His blood type was O-negative, the universal donor, and when necessary, following surgery, he was known to give direct transfusions to his patients when they had a rare blood type or when blood was in short supply. He received numerous awards and acclamations for his service, but I think he would have traded them in to have called Jim Brown Godwin a friend. They did meet once, June 9, 1971.

CAMEOS

Dr. Adams and Dr. Middleton were both doctors who devoted their lives to the citizens of Bradford, Union, and Raiford Counties.

"Uncle Nathan" Griffis and Barney Sission were true characters in Starke.

And of course, you recognized several historical figures including Babe Ruth, Franklin D. Roosevelt, George B. Shaw, Jimmy Doolittle, Sam Rayburn, Jeanette Rankin, and others.

Daudi Okelo and Jildo Irwa are the first Ugandan martyrs recognized by Pope John XXIII.

The Bishop from Uganda presented the Catholic Church in Oviedo relics from the martyrs.

Cecil A. Baxter, Grinner, Early and his family, Gator Bait, as well as many other characters were fashioned after real people, though their names and some details are fictional.

On February 19, 1942, President Franklin D. Roosevelt signed the Executive Order 9066, directing persons of Japanese descent to move voluntarily from their West Coast homesteads to the interior states by March 23.

Ten concentration camps were built between California and Arkansas to house the families. Some Asian Americans were given a forty-eight-hour extension to sell their homes, furniture, farms, and stores. If arrangements could not be made, they were still forcibly rounded into the internment camps for an undetermined period of time for "the safety of the country." Japanese families complied with patriotic spirit and tried to make the best out of less-than-desirable living conditions on the remote federal tracts, surrounded by barbed wire, sentries, and searchlights. They continued to raise the American flag every morning, to say the Pledge of Allegiance every day in school, and every Saturday evening, sing "America the Beautiful." They believed in their hearts that one day their contributions and heritage would be woven into the definition of being American. There would be "liberty and justice for all."

In January 1943, twelve hundred men volunteered to serve in the 442nd Regimental Combat Team to fight the Germans. It became the most decorated fighting unit in World War II receiving: 1 Congressional Medal of Honor, 52 Distinguished Service Crosses, 342 Silver Stars, 810 Bronze Stars, and 3,000 Purple Hearts with 500 Oak Leaf clusters. After the war, the families were allowed to return to their communities, but most had lost their businesses and homes. Still, they worked to build America stronger.

In 1990, the government finally apologized for the violations of their civil rights and authorized 60,000 survivors to receive a reparation of $20,000 each.

The performance of the Black soldiers in World War II must also be recognized. Prior to the war, Black men had fought to protect the United States throughout our nation's history. They even served in both the Union Army and the Confederate Army. Men of color generally served in volunteer units, as there were no provisions for Black men in the regular army on either side. In 1869, the 9th and 10th Calvary and the 24th and 25th Infantry were formed. They were an integral part of the frontier army and proudly earned the name "Buffalo Soldiers" from the Native Americans. These units were segregated and led by white officers. From 1866 to 1898, only eight Black officers were commissioned, five chaplains and three Calvary lieutenants.

Radical changes were needed, and the contributions of the Black soldiers in World War II brought opportunities and provided the key to opening the door to civil rights. In 1948, President Harry S. Truman officially ended segregation in the military. Black men have since risen to the highest ranks in the military, serving as a four-star general, General Colin Powell, and the Commander-in-Chief, President Barak Obama.

APPENDIX

Lord, bless this food to our use and us to thy service, and may we ever be mindful of the needs of others.

NAPOLEON BONAPARTE NOTED THAT AN ARMY MARCHES ON ITS stomach, and, true to form, the soldiers of World War II settled into K-Rations and C-Rations and whatever they could barter for in the foreign lands they found themselves. The government even approached Mr. Milton Hershey to produce a chocolate bar that would meet military specifications, including a high melting point and a calorie count to sustain a man in combat when food could not be distributed. The Quartermaster General himself awarded Mr. Hershey the Army-Navy E Flag to fly over his factory for the development and production of the "Field Ration D," a 4-ounce bar with over 600 calories.

Back home, there also were challenges to putting food on tables. As mentioned, victory gardens helped replace the empty vegetable stocks in the grocery stores, and mothers became inventive as they stretched their budgets and rations to feed their families. Oleo/margarine or lard replaced sweet butter. Honey, fruit, syrup, or reduced measurements substituted for sugar. New products, including spam and frozen vegetables, also hit the market shelves. Flour was enriched and margarine, fortified to help maintain nutrition. Even powdered eggs, which the soldiers adjusted to, eventually made their way onto the grocery store shelves in the form of cake mixes.

In 1943, Florence Brobeck published her book, *Cook It in a Casserole*. She included a letter written by Hendrik Willem van Loon of Nieuw Veere, Old Greenwich, Connecticut:

> People sometimes ask me whether there are absolutely no mitigating circumstances for Adolf Hitler and I invariably answer, "No, not a single one!" and every day there is new proof of my contention that for absolute inhumanity, the little Corporal stands alone and is a very bad edition of the unspeakable Genghis Khan.
>
> But now I am beginning to have my doubts. The Nazi leader, without in the least knowing what he was doing, is bestowing one blessing upon the people of the United States. He is forcing us to return to the oldest and most satisfactory mode of cooking. He has brought us back to revere and respect the casserole—that earthen jar which from now on is to be the mainstay of the American family's intention to live well and feed itself in an interesting and amusing fashion until the scourge of Hitlerism shall once more have been removed from the face of a rejoicing globe.

It is an interesting introduction to a cookbook, but then war invaded every sphere of life. The humble, nutritious casserole could incorporate any available foodstuff, including leftovers. Rice, noodles, and breadcrumbs could supplement rationed proteins. Casseroles also extended portions and were timesavers. They could be made in advance and frozen. Even clean-up was easier with one dish for prep and serving, important for women who were entering the workforce in support of the war effort. It also encouraged the cook to use earthen or glass pans, another important consideration as all metals were directed to support the war effort.

THE FOLLOWING RECIPES ARE EXAMPLES OF HOMEMADE WWII FARE:

Meatless Meatloaf

2 Cups Cold Baked Beans

2 Cups Breadcrumbs

1 Cup Nut Meats

2 Eggs

2 Tablespoons Melted Butter

1 Chopped Green Pepper

1 Chopped Onion

Mix well and shape as a meatloaf. Pour over this 1 can tomato pulp or 1 cup catsup with a little water. Baste frequently and bake about 30 minutes in a moderate oven.

Flourless Chocolate Cake

5 Ounces Chocolate

1 Pound Oleo

8 Eggs

2 Cups Chopped Nuts

Melt chocolate and oleo together in a double boiler. Cool to room temperature. Separate eggs. Beat egg yolks and blend into chocolate mixture. Whip whites to stiff peaks and fold into mixture. Gently stir in nuts. Pour into a spring form pan. Bake for 45 minutes at 375.

Hold Your Sugar Icing

1 Teaspoon Gelatin

Cup Cold Water

$\frac{1}{3}$ Cup Sugar

2 Egg Whites

½ Teaspoon Vanilla

Soften the gelatin over cold water; then place it over a double boiler and slowly add the sugar as the mixture gets hot. When the sugar is dissolved, carefully beat in the egg whites. Add the vanilla and continue to beat to the proper consistency.

Sugarless Chocolate Cookies

1 Cup Oleo

$^3/_4$ Cup Strained Honey

$^3/_4$ Cup Maple Syrup

2 Eggs

2 ½ Cups Flour

1 Teaspoon Salt

1 Teaspoon Baking Soda

1 Teaspoon Vanilla

1 Cup Chopped Nuts

Semi-Sweet Chocolate cut into pieces

Cream oleo, honey, and maple syrup. Beat in two eggs. Sift together flour, salt, and soda, and add gradually to the mixture. Stir in vanilla. Mix well. Fold in nuts and chocolate. Drop by ½ teaspoon on a greased cookie sheet. Bake 350 degrees for 10–15 minutes.

With pumpkin pie and carrot cake, Pea Mint or Chocolate Beet Ice Cream (Mr. Hershey introduced quite a variety of vegetable ice cream flavors at his park in Hershey, Pennsylvania), the zucchini stands tall in the dessert column. Here are two recipes mentioned in Chapter XI.

Zucchini Cake I

2 Cups Sugar

1 ½ Cups Oil

4 Eggs

1 Teaspoon Vanilla

2 Cups Flour

2 Teaspoon Baking Soda

1 Teaspoon Salt

1 ½ Teaspoon Cinnamon

3 Cups Grated Zucchini

(Raisins and/or pecans optional)

Grease and flour a tube pan (you might even fit it with aluminum foil). Pre-heat the oven to 325 degrees. Mix the first four ingredients and beat until smooth. Sift together the next four dry ingredients and stir gently to blend. Take one cup of the dry mixture and toss it with the grated zucchini to cover the grated pieces. Take the remaining dry mixture and stir it into the wet mixture. Gently fold in the zucchini mixture and stir until well-blended. Pour into the prepared tube pan and bake for one hour. Test with a toothpick for doneness. The cake, when cooled, may be iced with a cream cheese frosting, or dusted with powdered sugar.

Chocolate Zucchini Cake

1 Cup Brown Sugar

½ Cup White Sugar

½ Cup Butter

½ Cup Oil

3 Eggs

1 Teaspoon Vanilla

½ Cup Buttermilk

2 ½ Cups Flour

2 Teaspoon Baking Soda

½ Teaspoon Salt

4 Tablespoon Cocoa

3 – 4 Zucchinis, grated (two healthy cups)

1 Cup Chocolate Chips

Grease and flour a tube pan. (I suggest lining it with aluminum foil for added protection.) Pre-heat the oven to 325 degrees. Cream the first seven ingredients until smooth. Sift the remaining dry ingredients, stir gently to mix well, and then, in small batches, gently toss in the grated zucchini. Fold the zucchini mixture into the wet mixture and stir until well combined. Pour the batter into the prepared pan and sprinkle the chocolate chips evenly over the top. Bake for 45 minutes and test with a toothpick for doneness.

FINALLY, A RECIPE FROM OUR MILITARY MESS HALLS:

SOS

1 4.5 Oz Jar Sliced Dried Beef

2 Tablespoons Butter

2 Tablespoons Flour

1 Cup Milk

2 Hard Boiled Eggs, roughly chopped

Salt and Pepper to taste

Buttered Toast

Fill the dried beef jar with hot water and let it sit. Melt the butter in a fry pan and add the flour. Stir until the mixture is bubbly. Pour in the milk and stir until the mixture is smooth and creamy. Lower the heat. Drain the dried beef and chop. Add the beef and chopped egg to the mixture. Check for seasoning. If necessary, add a splash of milk to get the right consistency. Serve over buttered toast.

PRAYERS FOR OUR SOLDIER—FOR YESTERDAY, TODAY, AND, SADLY, PERHAPS FOR TOMORROW

Dear Lord, guard and guide our soldiers. Protect and defend them. Keep them safe from harm. Walk with them daily, and give them the strength, the courage, and the wisdom to do Your will. Comfort them in times of darkness and bless their daily efforts until You bring them safely home. We humbly pray.

Amen.

USMA Cadet Prayer

Oh God, Our Father, Searcher of men's hearts, help us to draw nearer to Thee in sincerity and truth. May our religion be filled with gladness and may our worship of Thee be natural. Strengthen and increase our admiration for honest dealing and clean thinking, and suffer not our hatred of hypocrisy and pretense ever to diminish. Encourage us in our endeavor to live above the common level of life. Make us choose the harder right instead of the easier wrong and never to be content with a half-truth when the whole can be won. Endow us with courage that is born of loyalty to all that is noble and worthy, that scorns to compromise with vice and injustice and knows no fear when truth and right are in jeopardy. Guard us against flippancy and irreverence in the sacred things of life. Grant us new ties of friendship and new opportunities of service. Kindle our hearts with fellowship with those of a cheerful countenance and soften our hearts with sympathy for those who sorrow and suffer. Help us to maintain the honor of the Corps untarnished and unsullied and to show forth in our lives the ideals of West Point in doing our duty to Thee and to our Country. All of this we ask in the name of the Great Friend and Master of Men.

Amen.

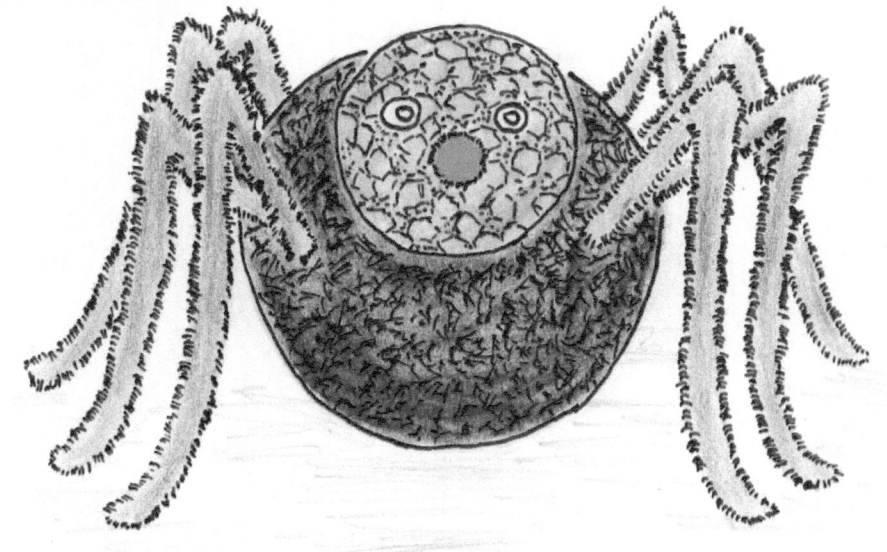

HOW TO MAKE A CHRISTMAS SPIDER

Supplies

Styrofoam balls in two sizes, 5-inch and 3-inch circumferences

Glitter, in various colors

Plastic sandwich bags

Chenille Pipe Cleaners in various colors

Small red pom-poms

Small beads (gold or pearl work well)

Number 8 small pins

Toothpicks

White craft glue

Plastic bags

Wax paper

This craft is ideal for all ages, requiring minimum skills and minimum supervision.

On a sheet of wax paper, place a spot of glue, roughly the size of a quarter. Roll one large and one small Styrofoam ball in the glue to coat each ball.

Place the balls inside a plastic bag, which has been filled with enough glitter to cover the balls. Gently toss the balls in the glitter. Remove them from the bag and roll on the wax paper to secure the glitter. Let dry for a minute or two.

As the balls are drying, select matching colored chenille pipe cleaners and cut into three-inch pieces. When the balls are dry enough to handle, dip an end of the chenille segment into the glue and gently press into the large ball, four on one side, four on the other, creating the body and legs. Gently take a leg and bend it up, then down, and a tiny end out. Repeat on each leg, forming legs and feet to stand on.

Next, take the smaller ball and insert a ½-inch piece of toothpick that is covered in glue. Then, carefully insert the remaining end into the spider body between the two sets of legs.

Almost done! Place a small dab of glue on the front of the head and gently push a small pom-pom on for a nose.

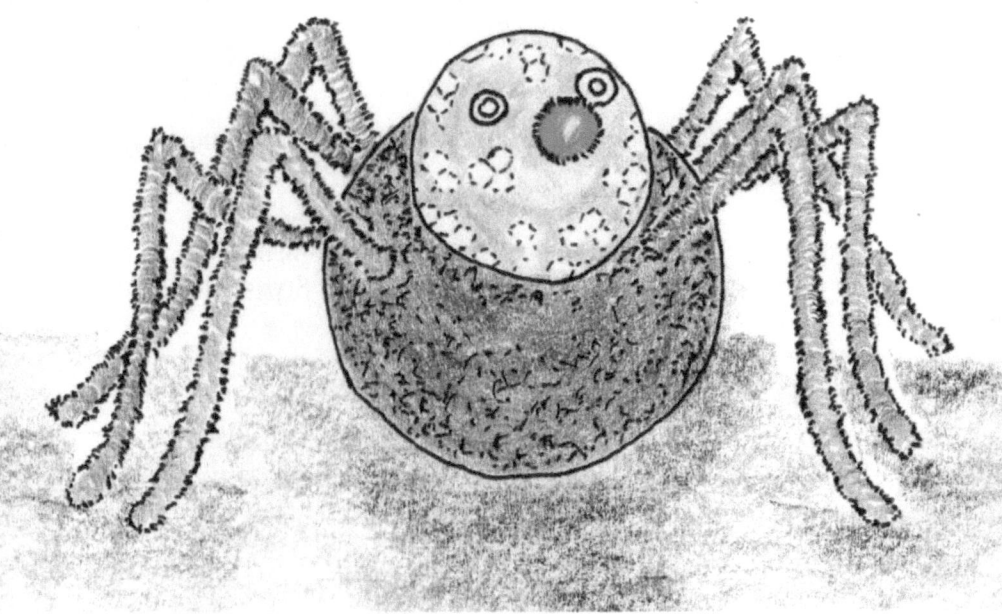

Finally, slip a small bead onto a small pin and insert it into the head just above the nose to the right; then repeat and insert the pin above the nose to the left to create two twinkling eyes.

You now have a perfect Christmas Spider!

FOOD FOR THOUGHT: QUESTIONS TO HELP YOU DIGEST THE THEMES IN MANURE

JIM BROWN LEARNED SO MANY LESSONS IN THE SUMMER OF 1942. HE loved sharing this story with friends and family. As you read this story, here are some questions to keep in mind:

1. Nations do not just choose to go to war randomly. The United States of America actually adheres to Principles of Just Wars. They include:

    a. Last Resort: War is waged only after all efforts of diplomacy and non-violent options have failed.

    b. Just Cause: War is waged in self-defense or to re-dress an injury, which is clearly stated. The people support the cause.

    c. Legitimacy: War is waged by an authority, Congress, who legally represents and is supported by those injured and those engaging in retaliatory actions.

    d. Right Intentions: Civilized nations try to limit the violence to that which is necessary to achieve a just end.

    e. Potentiality: War is waged only if there is a reasonable chance of success.

f.   Just Goal: The goals are clearly identified and include a lasting peace.

How did World War II meet those principles? How did WWII affect the lives of Jim Brown and his friends? How are we alike and how are we different today?

2.   People frequently ask, "Where were you when you first learned..." a world-changing event. History is made every day. What happened today? What happened the day you were born?

3. If something tragic happened in your life, how would you feel? What would you do? How could others reach out to you? Consider Hannah in this story. Consider Jim Brown's mom.

4. Can you be right and wrong at the same time? Can you do something wrong, but with good intentions, or something right with bad intentions? What are the consequences?

5. MANURE introduces us to several fathers. How are they alike? How are they different? What makes a good father?

6. What makes a good friend? Is age a factor? Is race a factor? Is religion a factor?

7. What is the difference between a mentor and a bully? Is there someone who is a mentor in your life? Have you ever mentored someone? How can you stand up to a bully?

8. What is gossip, and how can it hurt?

9. What is a "good name," and how did Jim Brown build his?

10. What or who influences the characters' opinions? What or who influences your opinions?

11. Adults can be imperfect. Describe Cecil A. Baxter's flaws.

12. How did Jim Brown earn money? What can you do to earn money?

13. What was it like to live on the prison grounds? Have you ever gone to work with a relative?

14. In 1942, there were no televisions, no cell phones, no computers. How has technology changed your lives? How might the story have changed if Jim Brown had those tools?

15. George Bernard Shaw wrote that GHOTI is pronounced fish. Consider: the baker coughs as he ploughs through the bread dough. English can be challenging. Can you think of other words that are difficult to spell or to read?

16. What lessons did Jim Brown learn that summer?

17. Everyone handles stress differently. How did some of the characters handle stress? How do you handle stress?

18. Is it fair to profile groups? A Chinese Proverb says:

Tell me, I forget. Show me, I remember. Involve me, I understand.

If I understand, I respect. If I respect, I treasure.

It is important to know your family history and to share cultures differences as we assimilate to create the American, an ideal who continues to evolve. What does it mean to you to be an American?

19. Can you turn ordinary experiences into extraordinary opportunities?

20, Who is Father Germano, and what is his role?

21. Traditions are important as they help mark historical dates, family events, religious celebrations, and other significant cultural events.

What traditions does your family recognize? How do you celebrate these moments: dress, food, tests, fireworks, performances?

22. Body language—facial expressions, how you sit, stand, or move—speaks volumes. What messages did the characters send? What messages do you send?

23. What was your favorite scene?

24. Who was your favorite character? If you could spend a day with this character, what would you do?

25. Who was your least favorite character? What would you say to that character?

26. Food is used to nourish, to celebrate, and to comfort. What was the role of food in this story? What is your favorite treat?

27. Wayne spoke up when Deke's story disturbed him. Have you had a story whose ending makes you sad or uncomfortable? Have you ever had a dream that turned into a nightmare? Take control and re-write your ending.

28. In 1942, much of the United States was segregated. How did this help the growth of our country? How did it hinder? What are your dreams for the future?

29. Hide and Seek: when writing a story, the author is trying to share his vision with the reader. Figures of speech are handy tools to help writers achieve this challenge. Two figures of speech commonly used are metaphors—comparing directly (e.g., "mashed potatoes could make such heavenly pillows"), and similes—comparisons using like or as (e.g., "he... looked something like a gargoyle as he crouched on the window sill"). How many can you find? Do they help?

30. Richard Lovelace (poet, 1618–1658) wrote, "Stonewalls do not a prison make, Nor iron bars a cage." In 1942, Asian Americans were

placed in concentration camps, while German Americans were isolated by prejudices and false assumptions. How did their spirits soar above these unjust limitations? Have you made false assumptions of others? Have others made false assumptions about you? How can you break through these bars?

I truly enjoyed bringing to life people who were very dear to me and creating a few characters I would have enjoyed meeting. I hope you will love them as much as I do.

SOLY (Story Over, Live Yours)!

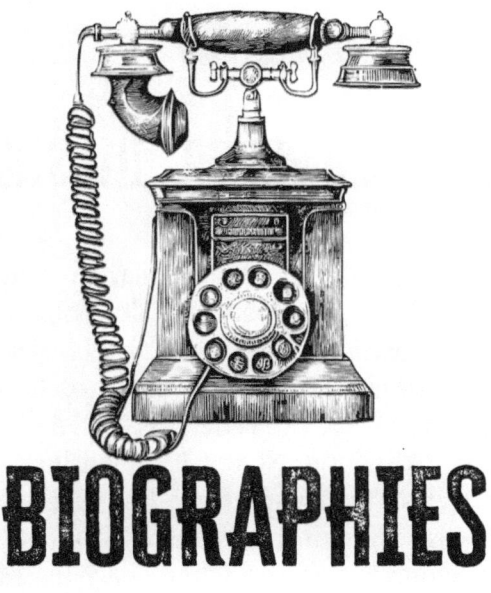

BIOGRAPHIES

ROGER MANLEY, ILLUSTRATOR

Roger grew up on a farm in Andrew County, Missouri, and attended elementary and high school in King City, Missouri. He received his BA in sociology in 1974 from Park College in Parkville, Missouri, and his master of divinity in 1979 from Midwestern Baptist Theological Seminary in Gladstone, Missouri. Roger is a retired minister of the Presbyterian Church (USA), a retired army chaplain, and a retired steel worker. He and Pam, his wife, currently reside in her hometown of Leavenworth, Kansas. He is the father of two grown children and proud grandfather to three grandsons.

Art has always been primarily a hobby for his own enjoyment, though he has sold various drawings and paintings over the years. Most of his work has been given either as personal gifts or as donations for fundraising projects of nonprofit organizations. In 2019, he completed a series of biblical panels done in oil for the Pilgrim Church in Leavenworth, Kansas. In many of Roger's illustrations, he places a tiny snail made of his initials, RGM. Look to see if you can find them in this book.

JAMES B. GODWIN, JR., ILLUSTRATOR

Jim was born and raised in Starke, Florida. His fondest memory was being the co-captain of his high school football team, the Tornadoes, composed of the toughest, determined twenty-one players led by the toughest and determined coaches: Head Coach David Hurse, Coach Tony Griffith, and Coach Mike Sexton. Following two perfect seasons, the Tornados achieved back-to-back Class "A" Florida State Championships. After graduating from the United States Military Academy, Jim served thirty years in the army and ten years as a government contractor. Currently, he enjoys being with family   including five grandchildren   playing golf, woodworking, keeping up with friends   old and new   and visiting Starke where his mother, Peggy, and sister, Cheryl, and her husband, George Canova, still live.

PEGGY GODWIN, AUTHOR

A military brat and an army wife, Peggy is the mother of three and grand-mother of five. She and her husband, James Brown Godwin, Jr., currently live in Central Florida on an old orange grove. She earned her undergraduate degree in Russian area studies from Fordham College MC, and her Master of Science in counseling and psychology from Troy State University.

More books from
Accomplishing Innovation Press

Workbooks

4HP Writer's Resources
The Author's Accountability Planner

The General Worldbuilding Guide
The Science Fiction Worldbuilding Guide
The Paranormal Worldbuilding Guide
The Romance Worldbuilding Guide
The Fantasy Worldbuilding Guide

Jörgen Jensen with Peter Lundgren
Mind Over Tennis: Mastering the Mental Game

Josh Stehle
I Am A Suphero Expert: Growing Up with my Autistic Brother

Kiyomi Holland
HeARTwork

Lael Giebel
Sustainability is for Everyone: Beginning Steps to Creating a Sustainability Program for Your Business

Letitia Washington
The Psychology of Character Building for Authors

Megan Mackie
Advanced Con Quest

N.B. Johnson
Wonders and Miracles

Valerie Willis
Writer's Bane: Research
Writer's Bane: Formatting 101
Writer's Bane: Plot & Foreshadowing
Writer's Bane: Revisions & Edition (w/ JM Paquette)
Writer's Bane: Character Development

Academia & Textbooks

Dr. Jenifer Paquette
Sentence Diagramming 101: Fun with Linguistics (and Movies)

Textbooks
Composition and Grammar: For HCC by HCC

Discover more at
ACCOMPLISHINGINNOVATIONPRESS.COM